DEMOCRACY
BY DEFAULT

DEMOCRACY BY DEFAULT

Dependency and Clientelism in Jamaica ─────────────

───────────── Carlene J. Edie

Lynne Rienner Publishers ▪ Boulder & London
Ian Randle Publishers ▪ Kingston

Published in the United States of America in 1991 by
Lynne Rienner Publishers, Inc.
1800 30th Street, Boulder, Colorado 80301

and in the United Kingdom by
Lynne Rienner Publishers, Inc.
3 Henrietta Street, Covent Garden, London WC2E 8LU

Published in Jamaica in 1991 by
Ian Randle Publishers Ltd
206 Old Hope Road
Kingston 6

Library of Congress Cataloging-in-Publication Data
Edie, Carlene J.
  Democracy by default : dependency and clientelism in Jamaica /
Carlene J. Edie.
      p. cm.
  Includes bibliographical references and index.
  ISBN 1-55587-225-5 (alk. paper)
    1. Jamaica—Dependency on foreign countries. 2. Jamaica—Economic
policy. 3. Jamaica—Commerce. 4. Jamaica—Politics and government.
5. Democracy. I. Title.
  HC154.E34 1990
  338.97292—dc20   90-47119
                                                                  CIP

National Library of Jamaica Cataloguing in Publication Data
Edie, Carlene J.
  Democracy by Default: Dependency and Clientelism in Jamaica
  Bibliography: p. Includes index
1. Jamaica—Politics and government
2. Jamaica—Social conditions
I. Title
32097292
ISBN 976-8100-00-1

British Cataloguing in Publication Data
A Cataloguing in Publication record for this book
is available from the British Library.

Printed and bound in the United States of America

*To the memory of
my maternal grandmother,
Vida Keane-Dawes*

*and to my daughter,
Khadija*

Contents

Tables and Figures

Abbreviations

ACB	Agricultural Credit Bank
ALCAN	Aluminium Company of Canada
ALCOA	Aluminum Company of America
AMC	Agricultural Marketing Corporation
BITU	Bustamante Industrial Trade Union
BLP	British Labour Party
CARICOM	Caribbean Common Market
CBI	Caribbean Basin Initiative
CDB	Caribbean Development Bank
CDWA	Colonial Development and Welfare Act
CEOs	Community Enterprise Organizations
CIA	Central Intelligence Agency
CIDA	Canadian International Development Agency
EDB	Export Development Bank
EDF	Export Development Fund
EMOs	External Marketing Organizations
ESF	Economic Support Funds
EXIMBANK	Export-Import Bank
GDP	Gross Domestic Product
GNP	Gross National Product
HEART	Human Employment and Resource Training
IADB	Inter-American Development Bank
IBA	International Bauxite Association
IBRD	International Bank for Reconstruction and Development
IMF	International Monetary Fund
ISER	Institute of Social and Economic Research
JAMAL	Jamaica Movement for Advancement of Literacy
JBC	Jamaica Broadcasting Corporation
JBI	Jamaica Bauxite Institute
JCTC	Jamaica Commodity Trading Corporation
JDF	Jamaica Defense Force
JDP	Jamaica Democratic Party
JIDC	Jamaica Industrial Development Corporation
JLP	Jamaica Labour Party

JMA	Jamaica Manufacturers Association
JNIP	Jamaica National Investment Promotion Ltd
JP	Justice of the Peace
JPS	Jamaica Public Service
MP	Member of Parliament
NEC	National Executive Council
NIEO	New International Economic Order
NSC	National Sugar Company
NWU	National Workers Union
OPEC	Organization of Petroleum Exporting Countries
OPIC	Overseas Private Investment Corporation
PL480	Public Law 480
PLO	Palestine Liberation Organization
PNP	Peoples National Party
PPP	Peoples Progressive Party
PSOJ	Private Sector Organization of Jamaica
QRs	Quantitative Restrictions
REC	Regional Executive Councils
SIA	Sugar Industry Authority
STC	State Trading Corporation
TNC	Transnational Corporation
TUC	Trade Union Congress
UN	United Nations
UNIA	Universal Negro Improvement Association
USAID	United States Agency for International Development
WMLA	Working Man and Labourers Association
WPJ	Workers Party of Jamaica

Acknowledgments ──────────────

This book began during my graduate studies at the University of California at Los Angeles. I would like to thank Professors Richard Sklar, Michael Lofchie, and Pierre-Michel Fontaine, whose encouragement is responsible for my being in the field of political science. Their support meant much to me as a graduate student at UCLA. The works of the New World Group of scholars at the University of the West Indies kindled my interest in Caribbean political economy. They developed an excellent tradition of West Indian scholarship to which junior scholars like myself are indebted. Professors Percy Hintzen and Carl Stone have read and criticized my work and have provided a model for me in their own fine work on Guyana, Trinidad and Tobago, and Jamaica.

I am indebted to several other colleagues for fruitful discussions during the work on this book. I would like to mention Valerie Bunce, Jane Mansbridge, Ladipo Adamolekun, Mazisi Kunene, and Femi Badejo. René Lemarchand, Keith Legg, and Pansy Robinson, scholars with a deep understanding of clientelism, appreciated what I was trying to say and offered valuable critiques of earlier drafts. Richard Hart and Wendell Bell (although they do not share my perspective) took time away from their work to read my manuscript and offer valuable suggestions.

I have benefited greatly from institutional support. The UCLA Department of Political Science provided a travel grant for a field trip in 1983, as well as a valuable teaching assistantship in the spring of 1984, my final quarter of graduate study. The University of Michigan provided a postdoctoral fellowship during the 1988–1989 academic year, which enabled me to revise my dissertation into this book. Purdue University provided a fellowship during the summer of 1989, which allowed me to complete the revisions suggested by reviewers. Secretarial assistance at the University of Michigan and at Purdue, especially from Mary Brejak and Claire Windler, helped ensure the completion of the book. Linda Chatfield and Donna Dove of the University of Massachusetts typed the final copy; they both handled the manuscript in a highly professional manner. Aidan Harrigan, my research assistant, also helped to edit the final draft. I must thank the editors at Lynne Rienner Publishers for their assistance, patience, and commitment to the project.

Numerous politicians, professionals, and ordinary Jamaicans have assisted me. I am indebted to the residents of Spanish Town, Western Kingston, and May Pen, who invited me into their homes and shared their personal experiences with me.

My friends have contributed in more ways than they will ever know. My extended family in the United States—Arie Udeze, Corine Williams, Winnie Harding, Charles Harding, Ruth Brown, Sukari Saloné, Joao Da Costa, Debbie Madison, Pauline Hill, Angela Jackson, Laverne Gist, Arveal Turner, Cecile and Wallace Martin, Linda Robinson-Edwin, Marie Kellier, Festus Brotherson, Jr., the Asfall family, and Kenneth Dawes (my cousin and close friend)—has been my rock as I moved around the country.

I would like to thank my father, Herbert (Guy) Edie, for the assistance he gave me during my years as a student at UCLA. He may be the only person who is more excited about this book than I am. Even before its completion, he often asked in a serious tone, "Den, how you gwen promote it?" I am glad I was able to complete it to give him the chance to promote it.

The book is dedicated to the memory of my grandmother, and to my daughter. My grandmother would have been proud to see it. My husband, Mohamed, and my daughter, Khadija, shared me with the book. I thank them for their patience and love. I particularly appreciated Khadija's good humor each time we relocated to another state in search of research funds. "Mommy, after Evanston, Ann Arbor, Michigan, after Indiana, Massachusetts . . . after Massachusetts, where, Mommy?"

—Carlene J. Edie

Introduction ———————————————————

This book, written by an Afro-Caribbean female political scientist, is intended to be of some service to the majority classes in Jamaica in helping them to better understand their situation. As a child and an adolescent growing up in Jamaica, I was introduced to issues of social and political development through my interactions with the Rastafarian community in my home town of Spanish Town, as well as from the late-night stories about Marcus Garvey of my grandmother. Those experiences helped to sensitize me to the issues of race and class in Caribbean society. From these perspectives, I developed a profound commitment to the search for answers to the questions that troubled us then and continue to trouble us now.

It is common knowledge to those of us from Jamaica that patron-clientelism has become a way of life in the postindependence period. However, with the exception of Carl Stone, political scientists have scarcely touched the subject. When I try to explain the extent and the consequences of this phenomenon to outsiders, I am often faced with a loss of words to convey this human tragedy. It was a very personal experience with this Jamaican patronage mentality that motivated me to write this book. I wish to share this experience with my readers in the hope that they too may be able to better understand the nature of the problem.

In January 1981, Jamaican Prime Minister Edward Seaga announced that the fifty-two U.S. ex-hostages held in Iran for more than one year would be given free vacations (all expenses paid) by the Jamaican government. He made this announcement in Washington, during his visit as the first foreign leader received by Ronald Reagan, the newly elected U.S. president, and it was carried on all major networks. I wrote a letter to the editor of the *Jamaica Daily Gleaner* (Jamaica's largest daily newspaper) condemning this proposal and suggesting that there were needy Jamaicans who could use this money. The letter made no mention of Michael Manley or the opposition Peoples National Party.

Within a week after the letter was published (in both the local as well as the North American edition of the newspaper), I received more than two

1

dozen letters addressed to my post office box in Los Angeles—half in support of my position, and half condemning it in vituperative terms. All the letters were from strangers. I wish to share the following unedited excerpts:

Hello Carlene,
    Good day to you. This is my first letter to you. I am totally agreed with you. Mr. Seaga have no right to use poor payer tax money to welcome his big friends when our country is short of foreign exchange. I do share your views. Miss Carlene, my problems is this. I am a young boy, 18 years old, 5' 6" tall, black complexion. My mother has 7 of us. Our father stop supporting us because he say we are from the opposition party while he is from the ruling party. Miss, I am unable to go to school. Most of the night we have to go to bed hungry. I would like to go back to school but I need some books and a pair of shoes. Can you help me. I would be only too glad. . . . Regardless of how small, it will be greatly appreciated. Please don't send cheque, it's too hard to change. . . .

Your unknown friend,
Signed

Carlene Edie,
    You are an *ungrateful bastard*! After all the United States of America has done for Jamaica and Jamaicans like yourself, by having you here in this country, getting you out of the slums you ran away from, a simple gesture like that of the Jamaican Prime Minister should be applauded. One week holiday for 52 brave Americans is a simple token of "Thank you America."

Goodbye ungrateful,
Unsigned

Hi Carlene,
    Here's hoping you are doing fine. I read your article and felt quite relieved to know that there are still Jamaicans abroad who still love Michael Manley. In the past election campaign the Seaga followers burnt out everything we own and shot my husband. I will be having another baby soon. As a good sister, I am actually begging you to send something for my children for me. Please ask your friends to see what they have. Many nights we are hungry (no job) and what daddy hustle is just for the little girl. There are still patriots here and I can assure you that even though they have burnt us out we are still standing firm and we know that our youth will survive.

Signed

Dear Carlene Edie,
    I read your letter to Mr. Seaga. I must say that not all Jamaicans will agree with you because many are here half-starved and have crowned Mr. Seaga for what they say, "making a master stroke," by inviting the 52 American hostages to Jamaica, all expense paid. I like you am in total disapproval with such a move, and I want to let you know that myself and members of my party (the WE Party) hail you a sensible Jamaican.

Signed

These letters convey four striking facts. First, they suggest that the Jamaican people have accepted the limits imposed by the scarcity of economic resources. Permeating the society is the belief that the U.S. government and those who live in the United States possess the resources that are needed to improve their lives. Second, there is a sense of gratitude on their part to the overseas patron. Third, the poor seem to become willing clients to people like myself (the middle classes), who appear to be ready to lead their cause, in order to improve their own position. They do not hesitate to ask for material resources, as they desperately need them. Fourth, the letters capture the well-publicized fact that party competition during election campaigns is often characterized by violence, murder, and fraud. This phenomenon has divided and destroyed families.

In my view, the Jamaican political order since 1944 exhibits two crucial features: first, external dependency, and second, a party system based on clientelist patronage. The resource base of this patronage lies overseas and the political dynamics are always centered around the state-controlling elite's capacity to secure resources from external patrons in order to maintain its domestic support base.

This book deals with political changes and economic developments that took place during Jamaica's transition to independence and beyond, and assesses their significance for Jamaica today. My focus is on the interrelated topics of *clientelism* and *dependency*. The significance of clientelism is that it constitutes the single most important mode of politics in Jamaica. This was true during the transition to independence, and it remained true in the early postindependence period. It remains true today, after the country experienced both socialist-reformist and capitalist-reformist governments; the majority of the population still seeks patron-client relations with political leaders in an attempt to gain access to resources needed for their livelihood in exchange for their political support. A study of clientelism involves looking at what constitutes the very basis of Jamaica's political economy.

The related focus on dependency involves a study of Jamaica's external relations with international capitalist governments and institutions. It does not, though, involve a recitation of all the numerous issues covered by Caribbean dependency scholars. Rather, the focus is on the *interrelatedness* of dependency and clientelism. For me, the significance of the dependency concept is that it accurately locates the source of patronage required to maintain the Jamaican state system. A study of dependency and clientelism emphasizes the connections between external and internal domination and dependency and the impact of that interrelatedness on Jamaica's political economy.

There is already an abundance of Marxist and non-Marxist scholarship on Jamaican political economy. This book may draw heavily on the dependency scholarship prevalent in the region, but it also calls attention to its major shortcoming: the lack of a class analysis of state and politics in the periphery. At the same time, my focus on patrons and clients may annoy dependency scholars because it does not, among other things, pose the problem in terms of class conflict between the bourgeoisie and the proletariat.

There is a need for new and refreshing insights on Jamaican political economy. My main concern is to flesh out a careful analysis of Jamaican society and politics. This book may lead to a reconstruction of dependency perspectives on Jamaica, but that is not my primary objective. My aim is to suggest a new framework that can give us a concrete understanding of the problems that characterize developing nations. The current literature has been very abstract, dealing in highfalutin theories, with little mention of the day-to-day realities of the existence of the average Jamaican. My framework (by linking macro- and microanalysis) has the potential of presenting a clearer picture of Jamaica's political problems and the options available for addressing them.

The first chapter of the book outlines the theoretical and analytical framework, defines the important concepts used throughout the text, and briefly discusses how these concepts are manifested in Jamaica. It begins with a discussion outlining the background and setting of the book, in which I argue that dependency and clientelism are manifested in Jamaica through the plantation structure, party political organization, and Jamaica's international relations. It then introduces the theoretical framework of the book—dual clientelism—explaining my use of the concept of clientelism and its dual facets. Two major points are emphasized. The first is that the general literature on clientelism, and Carl Stone's specific work on clientelism in Jamaica, is limited in that the point is not made that in developing nations patronage relationships are formulated within the context of external dependency relationships and that the revenue base of patronage is overseas. The second point is that the dependency literature on Jamaica is extremely valid in its identification of the international economic order as a central variable in underdevelopment, but suffers a major shortcoming in that it does not state that dependency relationships are maintained through a structure of internal clientelist political control.

Chapter 2 addresses the political decolonization period, 1944–1962, and the emergence of the clientelistic postcolonial state. It is argued that Jamaica's postemancipation legacy created the conditions for the emergence of political clientelism in the modern period. Economic impoverishment and political and social deprivation led to riots in the 1930s and the subsequent transfer of power from Britain to indigenous political leaders. Although I concur with most other assessments of the 1944–1962 period as one characterized by a smooth and orderly transition, I explain that cohesion and consensus were maintained through an emphasis on external economic dependency and clientelist patronage as agents of stability. Jamaican political scientist Trevor Munroe's (1972) pioneering study, *The Politics of*

Constitutional Decolonization: Jamaica, 1944–62, awakened us to some of the techniques of middle-class domination of the constitutional process, but his study reduces the political changes of the period to a phenomenon determined by the capitalist and middle classes. There ought to be a fuller examination of the circumstances that led to a multiple class convergence of interests in the creation of a democratic political system. The important question raised in Chapter 2 is: How and under what circumstances did divergent class interests converge? In answering this question, the focus includes phenomena such as the existing socioeconomic conditions in Jamaica, international resource transfers from Britain and North America, and mobilizing strategies that emphasized, above all, clientelism.

Chapter 3 is a critical chapter in the book. It explains that party politics works in the Jamaican milieu through the mechanism of clientelism. The party system has been consolidated in the postindependence period as a network of patronage-based factions of the Jamaica Labour Party (JLP) and the Peoples National Party (PNP). Party officials, labor leaders, state bureaucrats, government ministers, members of the private sector, intellectuals, and others are all engaged in patron-client relationships with high-ranking party and state officials. Clientelistic networks are also extended downward into the local electoral constituencies in both the urban and rural areas. Rank-and-file supporters are tied into these party organizations through bureaucratic favors. Lower-class brokers are used to mediate the flow of government resources from the capital city of Kingston, and these brokers are expected to deliver the votes at election time. Resources trickle down through patron-client channels as the state-controlling elite attempts to prevent lower-class anti-government mobilization. Jobs, housing, food, birth certificates for travel, furniture, household appliances, and other assets are distributed to the clients and constituents of party elites. This process weds clients to the state and the party system.

Chapter 4 elucidates the nexus of clientelism and control at the domestic level and international dependency. The main argument of the chapter is that the state's capacity for patronage is determined by external resource transfers from actors within the international capitalist system. Thus, although the state is the most powerful local institution, state-controlling political leaders are involved in a subordinate client relationship with international actors in an effort to obtain continuous patronage to maintain their dominance and control in the domestic arena.

Economic growth based on the massive intrusions of foreign capital during the 1950–1964 years enhanced the distributive capacity of the state, and the resources under the direct control of the government agencies increased. The middle classes, who controlled the state, were willing to promote economic policies favorable to the dominance of their groups as well as a coalition of capitalist interests within Jamaica. The local capitalist class, sponsored by the state, was not allowed to get involved in competition with foreign investors. State power was used to restrict their ability to become dominant. Within this structure of "dependent development," political clientelism became an excellent strategy because the state was able to contain all social groups through patronage networks. External dependency enabled the state to achieve its internal political ends, as it gave it the economic base that offered a significant degree of autonomy from all social groups. Dependency and clientelism clearly erode the state's capacity to both implement development policies geared toward accumulation of domestic surpluses as well as its ability to organize the economic system to meet the collective needs of the population. Economic arrangements continue to be neocolonial, but, using a clientelist strategy, the state is able to block mobilization of the majority classes against the status quo.

Chapters 5 and 6 are case studies of the politics of the Manley and Seaga periods of government. The discussion in both chapters is aimed at demonstrating the analytical value of the dual clientelism framework. Dual clientelism determined the politics of both administrations, as ideological differences, governing styles, and class alliances were overridden by the embedded character of domestic clientelism and changes in international political and economic support for the two administrations.

Chapter 5 analyzes the Manley period using a novel approach. Existing explanations of the "democratic socialist" policies of the Manley government are inadequate in some important respects, most notably in their failure to link the populist domestic policies to the dynamic, nationalist, and Third World–centered foreign policies. Democratic socialism is not to be taken at face value. I argue, instead, that the ideology of democratic socialism emerged in Jamaica in order to justify both a certain pattern of resource allocation favoring the middle classes and a pattern of international alliances to counter U.S. hegemony. Democratic socialism, although pitched to the interests of the poor and the lower middle classes, did not result in significant expansion of benefits of health, education, and welfare. Instead, state expansionism justified programs that were directly beneficial to the middle classes of the state. I argue that the defeat of the Manley government was in fact due to international capital being withdrawn from the government as a result of U.S. pressure and the subsequent breakdown of patronage relationships between the political leaders and the middle and lower classes and the elites.

Chapter 6 demonstrates the persistence of clientelism and dependency in the Seaga period. Seaga immediately distinguished himself as a leader capable of attracting resources from abroad, and established a patron-client relationship between himself and Ronald Reagan whereby U.S. officials often referred to him as "our man in the Caribbean." Although the Seaga government received massive amounts of aid from abroad, it was still unable to meet the patronage demands of its poor clients. The government advocated orthodox liberal economic policies and privatization while the state sector continued to play a leading role in the economy. Trapped by its desire to maintain democratic party politics and sociopolitical order, the Seaga government was forced to continue clientelist policies to appease the poor while it continued its commitment to the private sector. The government placed itself in a double bind, eliminating through its commitment to privatization the state monies it required for clientelist patronage. After a political tenure of eight and a half years, most political observers were able to predict the JLP's demise at the polls. That was indeed the outcome.

Chapter 7 assesses the implications of a new PNP victory and the future of the state-centered patronage system. I argue that if the clientelist system is unable to cope with the threats posed to its existence by both the volatility of the electoral process and the shrinking of its resource base, and it can no longer accommodate its poor clients, then the state may be forced to move toward authoritarianism in order to maintain its dominance. In such a case, the state would shift to a system of coercion and control that is best exercised in a one-party system or a system of one-party dominance. This relieves the state from the need to secure the vast resources necessary to support an extensive system of patronage. Under these circumstances, political opponents and their mass supporters are demobilized and neutralized whereas the population is regimented. Democratic party politics in Jamaica has been undermined by the past JLP and PNP governments' inability to make significant changes in the lives of the population. The political economy of Jamaica is unlikely to be transformed by orthodox liberal or socialist economic policies unless the system of international and domestic relations are dismantled. Chapter 7 ends with a discussion of the lessons that the Jamaican experience may have for developing nations.

The title of this book, *Democracy by Default*, is meant to underline the ambiguity in the meaning of democracy in the Jamaican milieu. Democracy takes on a vast number of meanings in the literature, but what does it mean in underdeveloped economies? The point that is being underscored in the book is that democracy in Jamaica rests not on a political culture committed to liberal democratic values and behavior, but rather on what might be called "democracy by default." Dual clientelism, which seems inherently authoritarian, and is linked with such in most developing nations, has the opposite effect on Jamaica. In the Jamaican case, dual clientelism prevents authoritarianism by dispersing resources; democracy, as a result, survives by default.

1

The Nexus of Clientelism and Dependency: Toward a New Paradigm

Perhaps the most neglected fact about existing democracies in developing nations is that, although the form of their political institutions may resemble those in Western democracies, the substance is significantly different and is often antidemocratic. The substance tends to be undermined by a host of internal and external socioeconomic and political factors. Nonetheless, the presence of a small number of "successful" democratic political systems in developing nations remains a striking fact suggesting perhaps that these nations do have the capacity to use dysfunctional characteristics to maintain a democratic political order, despite the counterproductive consequences that may result from it.

In many developing nations, politicians representing middle-class interests have gained control of the state[1] in the postindependence era. The concentration of resources in the state, and the control of the middle class over these resources, constituted the basis of bureaucratic control over the majority classes. The introduction of representative institutions, in this context, has served to galvanize lower-class support for competing party factions, as middle-class leaders preferentially deliver extremely scarce resources in exchange for support. Institutions intended for interest-group mobilization (such as labor and party organizations) have been controlled by those representing middle class interests and have become instruments of control of the lower classes. Clientelism emerged under conditions of scarcity and impoverishment and became one of the means of providing resources to party supporters at critical junctures of their lives. The political leaders needed votes in order to guarantee control of the state and access to state resources. The poor desired goods and services for their daily necessities. A reciprocal relationship has been established where the vote is exchanged for strategic resources such as food, furniture, clothing, a job, or a home.

Clientelism has been sustained and complemented by the structure of international disparities of power and wealth. The political leaders of many developing nations have become dependent on the resources of powerful international actors for domestic programs and for the survival of their regimes. International resource transfers have been employed by the middle class for translating its class power into control of the state. As a consequence, the ruling middle class has often accommodated international actors in order to obtain the transfer of strategic resources required to make domestic clientelism possible. The critical issue has become one of national self-determination and autonomy (in the interests of the domestic middle class) versus powerful international actors with strategic resources. These arguments provide the main thrust of the analysis that is developed in this book.

EXPLAINING CLASS AND RACE CATEGORIES

"Class" is generally considered to belong to the framework of Marxist economic and social thought. My use of the term in reference to social forces within Jamaica can be distinguished from the way it is used by writers such as Trevor Munroe, George Beckford, Michael Witter, Don Robotham, Fitzroy Ambursley, and Mark Figueroa.[2] I have adopted Guyanese political sociologist Percy Hintzen's definition of class as an "aggregated socioeconomic category with common objective interest which, when acted upon, can produce unified political action of one form or another" (Hintzen 1989:20).

Carl Stone identified the following aggregated socioeconomic categories in the contemporary Jamaican social structure:

1. An upper class of capitalists (large-scale business owners and large planters);
2. An upper middle class of professionals, owners of medium-sized businesses, college-level educators, corporate managers, senior bureaucrats in the public sector, and leaders of voluntary associations;
3. A lower middle class of small-scale business owners, primary and secondary schoolteachers, white-collar workers (in private business, in civil administration, and in the parastatals), skilled workers, and owners of medium-sized farms; and
4. A lower class of small peasants, agricultural workers, unskilled and semiskilled laborers, and the substantial number of rural and urban unemployed.

These class categories will be used throughout the book. (For a fuller discussion of classes and their development and evolution in Jamaica, see Stone 1987.)

The Upper Class

A new upper class has emerged in the postindependence period, consisting mainly of whites, Syrians, Lebanese, Chinese, East Indians, and Jews. (Blacks are absent from this group.) It is estimated to be about one-tenth of the population. This tiny elite is exclusively in business and represents twenty-one powerful capitalist families in the country. Their names appear again and again in leadership positions in economic organizations, churches, lodges, and more select voluntary organizations. The formerly exclusive upper class of English planters no longer exists, as the expansion of the commercial, manufacturing, and service sectors has allowed significant participation in business by new immigrant groups arriving from Asia and the Middle East in the late nineteenth and early twentieth centuries (Wilmot 1984). East Indians and Chinese were brought into Jamaica and other British colonies as indentured laborers to replace blacks on the sugar plantations after emancipation in 1838. The descendants of both groups have been upwardly mobile, becoming part of the upper and upper middle classes as business owners and professionals. By 1963, there were 70,000 Chinese in Jamaica, controlling 90 percent of the provision trade and 95 percent of the supermarkets, along with laundries and betting shops (Reid 1977).

The Upper Middle Class

British welfare policies implemented in the aftermath of the 1938 labor riots led to expansion of the state as its bureaucracies assumed new functions related to political and social reforms in the society. The postcolonial welfare state that emerged after the Colonial Development and Welfare Act (CDWA) of 1940 gave a significant number of educated blacks the opportunity to join the ranks of the upper middle-class brown professionals employed by state agencies. The expansion of secondary educational opportunities also led to the recruitment of blacks as civil servants and teachers. The black middle class became confined (for the most part) to state employment. Although the black middle class remained outside of the capitalist sector (controlled by whites, Lebanese, Syrians, Chinese, East Indians, and Jewish business owners), it has evolved into the most dominant and powerful class in the politics of the postindependence period in Jamaica.

The Lower Middle Class

Members of the lower middle class are generally black. It represents the lower level of the middle class, having occupations such as primary and secondary schoolteachers, civil servants, security personnel, white-collar jobholders in the private and public sector, small business owners, and own-account small farmers. The lower middle class tends to be highly organized in trade unions and represents the most highly active party cadres in both the JLP and PNP.

The Lower Classes

The majority of blacks are located within the lowest socioeconomic categories. A small proportion of the black population continues to work as small farmers in the rural areas, but blacks have now largely become a part of the urban work force. Most of the people in this category are semiliterate or illiterate. Most small farmers have their roots in the small farming traditions of land ownership. A substantial percentage has strong roots in the petty commodity sector of small farmers and traders (Stone 1980:51–69). The urban lower class is the most deprived group in the society in terms of income, employment security, education and ownership of property. In addition, the urban lower class generally lacks access to water supplies, electricity, private toilet facilities, and adequate housing. The rural lower class has extremely limited access to domestic water supplies and electricity, but a majority enjoy private toilet facilities and homeownership. The greatest resource of the lower class is its large numbers. However, it has not been able to organize and unite its members in pursuit of its own political interests because of its clientelistic relationships with the dominant parties.

BACKGROUND AND SETTING

Jamaica is a former British colony in the Caribbean. It has a population of approximately 2.5 million on an island covering 44,000 square miles. Approximately 78 percent of the people are black or African; 15 percent brown or light-skinned colored; 3 percent East Indian; 2.4 percent Lebanese, Syrian, and Jewish; 1 percent Chinese; and less than 1 percent European and other races.[3] The society is stratified along racial and class lines stemming from plantation slavery. The class structure is characterized by a high degree of maldistribution of wealth, as well as a high, although declining, correlation between wealth and whiteness, near-whiteness, and minority ethnic characteristics. European, Lebanese, Syrian, Jewish, East Indian, Chinese, and brown groups belong to the upper class of capitalists. Blacks are noticeably absent from this group. The middle class consists of some members of the East Indian, Chinese, and European groups as well as significant numbers of blacks and browns. Blacks represent the largest racial group in this class. However, the majority of blacks are located within the lower classes. A small number of East Indians are poor agricultural laborers and are among the poorest of the lower classes. The lower class is disadvantaged relative to the upper class in terms of literacy, education, employment, security, and ownership of property (Stone 1973).

Throughout the British West Indies, the 1930s was marked by working-class uprisings against the colonial state in protest against low wages, poor working conditions, and oppressive social conditions in general. Labor riots broke out in Jamaica in 1938, when an alliance of dispossessed black workers and peasants initiated militant political action against the colonial state. Although the initiatve against the colonial ruling class came from the black lower classes, the leadership of the labor movement that subsequently emerged was quickly passed into the hands of the colored middle class. A former overseer and businessman, Alexander Bustamante, and an attorney, Norman Manley, stepped into the uprising, formed a union and a party, and became self-proclaimed leaders of the dispossessed workers and peasants. Manley represented Bustamante against the legal challenges of the colonial system in terms of rights, and to organize workers and engage in industrial action. Out of this involvement, Manley subsequently formed the PNP in 1938, with the Bustamante Industrial Trade Union (BITU) as its worker-based institution. After the BITU-PNP split, Bustamante formed the Jamaica Labour party in 1943, and the PNP organized allied trade unions such as the Trade Union Congress (TUC), and later the National Workers Union (NWU). The JLP-BITU/PNP-NWU party-union nexus emerged as the dominant political force in postwar Jamaican political history.

Britain granted Jamaica its independence in 1962. Since then, the Jamaican government has been based on a system of parliamentary democracy patterned after the British model. Labor and party organizations dominated by the middle class continued to monopolize electoral loyalties four decades after their formation. During this period, third-party movements have failed to intrude upon that monopoly. Middle-class domination of labor and party organizations provided the framework for the development of clientelism later on.

The Jamaican economy modernized rapidly in the post–World War II period. Monies from the British Colonial Development and Welfare Act of 1940 provided the infrastructure for subsequent inflows of foreign capital. Jamaica attracted an abundance of North American capital through the government's "industrialization by invitation" program, which offered a wide range of tax concessions and other incentives to foreign capitalists. As a result of the discovery of bauxite, the economy was transformed from one dominated by agriculture to one more diversified, with new sources of revenue from bauxite and the expanding tourist and manufacturing industries.

Industrialization increased the demand for heavy equipment from the United States and Canada. At the same time, the United States imported Jamaican bauxite, an increasing quantity of sugar, and light manufactures. Traditionally, the island had been a British market, but by 1969 it had shifted its trade to the United States. Between 1960 and 1964, exports from Jamaica to England increased by 22 percent, from £18 million to £22 million, whereas those to the United States increased by 66 percent, from £15 to £25 million (Parry, Sherlock, and Maingot 1987:277).

Postwar industrialization led to significant growth in the economy, as enormous amounts of revenues accrued from the bauxite and tourist sectors

(Jefferson 1972). But the resources gained from industrialization were not used to boost agriculture, the sector with the most potential for employment. Instead, the newly acquired resources were used for state expansion, which benefited the educated middle class and its upper-class capitalist allies. Despite the economic boom of the period, the high levels of unemployment experienced by the lower classes persisted.

The postwar and early postindependence JLP industrialization strategy lost credibility and the PNP was voted into office in 1972 under the leadership of Michael Manley, the son of Norman Manley. A radicalized PNP came to power in the context of anti-imperialist movements in the Third World, the rise of the Organization of Petroleum Exporting Countries (OPEC), the emergence of black power movements in the Western Hemisphere, and the decline of the United States in the aftermath of the Vietnam War. These events influenced the black lower classes significantly, leading to an open and sharp contradiction between the Jamaican state's commitment to accommodative politics (favoring foreign interests) and the need for social change. The support of the radicalized lower classes catapulted Michael Manley and the PNP to power on the slogans, "better must come" and "power for the people." The PNP subsequently announced in 1974 that it had adopted an ideology of democratic socialism, pitched to the interests of the lower classes.

Overall, Manley's 1972–1980 administrations represented an assertive response to (foreign and local) capitalist domination of the economy. Through programs of a bauxite levy, nationalization, workers' participation, rural cooperatives, and special employment, the PNP had hoped to weaken the economic advance of foreign and local capital and to strengthen its solidarity with the lower classes. Its state-centered policies, however, led to further middle-class dominance of the lower classes, reinforcing class inequalities within the society. Democratic socialism came under pressure from strong conservative opposition in Jamaica (within the JLP and the PNP itself) and the United States, and was in fact ultimately sabotaged by U.S. pressures that resulted in the withdrawal of strategic capitalist resources required by the state.

The 1980–1989 JLP administrations, led by Edward Seaga, saw a clear shift in economic policy toward free market policies sponsored by the International Monetary Fund (IMF). This was most apparent in the JLP's emphasis on export-led development and a greater reliance on foreign private investment. New policies emphasizing private-sector initiatives were developed in such areas as agriculture, tourism, and transportation. Despite an abundance of resources from the United States and its allies, as well as Western lending agencies, Seaga's liberal orthodox economic policies failed to lead to sustained economic growth and increased the disparities between the races and classes within Jamaica. Seaga's JLP was defeated in the 1989 elections, and Manley's PNP returned to power.

The new 1989 Manley-led PNP government shifted away from its democratic socialist ideology of the 1970s. Instead, Manley emphasized accomodative politics and an economic strategy favoring private-sector–led growth. Great economic disparities continued between the upper and lower classes as political disillusionment set in.

Today, the Jamaican political elite faces a dilemma. It is faced with the task of finding a way to achieve necessary economic progress without social change that might undermine the "democratic" order. The tension between dependence on foreign resources necessary to maintain middle-class dominance and the need for rapid socioeconomic changes has its roots in the state expansion and "industrialization by invitation" strategies of the postwar period. The result has been continuous development strategies favoring the interests of the state-controlling middle class and its allies.

DUAL CLIENTELISM:
THE NEXUS OF CLIENTELISM AND DEPENDENCY

Carl Stone's recent contribution (1980) of the concept of clientelism to existing perspectives on Jamaican political economy begins to map the theoretical terrain that needs to be covered to elucidate the complexities of the dependent postcolonial state. In this book, I would like to contribute to an understanding of these processes.

The central feature of Jamaica's political economy is the dialectical unity of domestic clientelism and international dependence. The importance of what has been described as dependency in the literature is not being denied, but it is being suggested here that dependency is more correctly conceived as the external (international) dimension of clientelism. Dependence and clientelism may best be understood as different facets of the same reality; they possess the same pattern of asymmetrical exchanges between superior and inferior. However, the concept of clientelism introduces the critical notion of reciprocity, bargaining, and an exchange of resources—processes that shed light on the way in which external dependence can create political and economic crises for the state.

A theoretical framework that addresses the questions with which this study is concerned is to be found in the work of the underdevelopment and dependency literature as well as the literature on political clientelism and patronage in the Third World. That theoretical framework can be identified in a new formulation, called dual clientelism, which emphasizes connections between internal and external domination and the impact of this interrelatedness on the Jamaican state structure.

Dual clientelism reaffirms Stone's argument that clientelism is the dominant mode of political relations in Jamaica. However, it introduces a new dimension—it recognizes that the Jamaican state is maintained by an elaborate system of internal and external clientelism. "Dual" underscores the point that these processes occur in two separate but converging spheres—in the international arena and in the domestic political system. There is a "layering" of local, national (internal), and international (external) exchange relations. Patronage resources obtained from external capitalist actors determine political behavior and class formation as well as the fiscal viability of the Jamaican state. International business, governmental actors (particularly the United States), and international organizations stand at the apex of this pyramid, as they provide the state with formidable resources, which make it relatively impregnable vis-à-vis any and all domestic actors. Like most developing nations, the state in Jamaica is by far the most powerful institution. Those classes that manage and control the state (and therefore have access to the external resources through external client relations with international patrons) have the best chances of gaining and maintaining dominance in the domestic political arena. This is because Jamaica's political economy is characterized by international dependence.

Clientelism

Patronage is a method of politics in Jamaica, as it is in many other developing as well as industrialized nations. Patron-clientelism has been identified as the dominant feature of the organization of mass support for competitive political parties in the Third World (Scott 1972a). As Stone sums it up:

> Clientelism in the Third World is more than just a device to win votes for competing parties. It is a mechanism by which to institutionalize a power structure that is distinguishable from the class based politics of liberal democracy in advanced capitalist countries, authoritarian military rule in many Third World states and the militarized one-party monopolies of communist states (Stone 1980:93).

Clientelism is defined as a reciprocal exchange of goods and/or services on a personal basis between two unequal parties. A clientelistic political system is based on the exchange of material rewards for political support (Scott 1969, 1972a; Powell 1970).

Stone (1980) was the first to apply the clientelism concept to the Jamaican political system. He indicated that clientelism permeated Jamaican society at the levels of hierarchical structures in the economic, political, and administrative spheres, as well as among party officials, functionaries, bureaucrats, economic managers, and the lower echelons of the society. What is the basis of clientelism in Jamaica? The following quotation may provide an answer:

Vote for me and you might get a job,
Vote for my opponent and if I win,
You probably won't.
Harass my opponent in his electoral campaign and get a handout for a
meal (D. Hall 1968:10).

The effect of the sociopolitical conditions on party political behavior is
clear from the above quotation. This method of politics emerged during the
1944–1962 decolonization period when power was transferred to the dominant
middle-class party leaders. These leaders harnessed the state as a resource from
which to establish a power structure that competed with and paralleled the
power structure rooted in the ownership of the forces of production by foreign
and local capitalist interests (Stone 1980:93). Political power was exercised
in the context of scarcity, poverty, and vast unemployment, as the poor gave
their support to elected officals to avoid political victimization.

Clientelism is most likely to flourish in situations where there is an
inequality of wealth and power because those relationships develop by
definition between unequal parties. With its high degree of socioeconomic
inequality, Jamaica satisfies this condition. If inequalities in access to vital
resources were alone sufficient to promote the expansion of patron-client ties,
such structures would predominate everywhere. A second and more significant
condition of patron-client politics in Jamaica is the absence of institutional
guarantees for an individual's security, status, and wealth. The low level of
stable industrial employment made by the highly capital-intensive strategy of
industrialization in Jamaica means that employment through the state and its
various departments, boards, and corporations becomes even more crucial as a
source of livelihood.

At the mass base of the society, more than half of the poor
(approximately 57 percent of the population is considered poor; see Stone
1973) are locked into patron-client relationships with members of Parliament
(MPs), councillors, civil servants, or brokers for the party leaders,
exchanging their votes for jobs, housing, food, bureaucratic favors, or even a
visa to the United States or Canada. The poor are expected to deliver on
election day, their vote being the payment for the material rewards previously
received. The poor desperately need the scarce material goods and favors
provided by the political leaders in order to survive on a day-to-day basis. The
political leaders tend to deliver only in times of crisis when the poor client
calls upon them. It is the failure or inability to deliver during periods of
crisis that explains the 15 percent shift of voters that often leads to a swing
from one party to another every two terms in Jamaica. The political leaders
of both parties manipulate the resources and so maintain the upper hand in
this patron-client relationship.

The cycle of patronage is perpetuated, as patron-client relationships exist
between the state-controlling middle class and other elites. These
relationships can be explained as a result of the dependence of all social

groups upon national and international agencies with resources. Those in control of these agencies can then exchange such resources for support and/or commitments not to engage in activities that affect their interests.

In developing nations, state power is directed toward the interests of the ascendant state-controlling (noncapitalist) middle class. Domestic capitalists often support the latter in clientelistic relationships, and their interests are protected and promoted in that context. Because of dependency upon state resources, the Jamaican upper class (capitalist class) has been coopted by middle-class contenders for state control (hence their even support of both the JLP and PNP) and has been forced to support a middle-class agenda to maintain their upper-class privilege. This has been done largely through individual personalized relationships rather than through class action.

An inherent conflict exists between international and domestic capital, as the former usually replaces the latter and relegates it to a supporting role at best. Domestic capitalists can be coopted by international capital under conditions where the state is hostile to the interests of foreign capital. This was the case during the Manley regime of the 1970s. The local capitalists had control over strategic capital resources, which were withdrawn (along with foreign capital from U.S. sources), intensifying the economic crisis of the state.

Trade-union leaders constitute an essential element in the clientelistic system because they control institutions geared toward mobilization. These institutions have become the bases for enormous support for the political leaders. Union leaders are extremely strategic in the political economy because they have tremendous power over a large sector of the labor force. For example, in 1974 the BITU, NWU, and TUC membership included 66 percent of the employed labor force. Other smaller unions had approximately 10,000 members (Gonsalves 1977:104). Given the union leaders' control over such large numbers of the laboring population, they have some leverage vis-à-vis the state leaders, whose survival depends on the maintenance of order in the society. In this context, union leaders are given access to government cabinet members, and to crucial policymaking processes. They cannot make policy, but they are given an input into the policy process. Trade-offs are made in the interests of the maintenance of political order.

Rank-and-file union members have access to party leaders and the state resources they control through party institutions. The union leader is dependent on the party leader to make concessions that will be favorable to his followers. The party leader is dependent on the union leader to maintain loyalty to the state among the workers. Thus, there is a reciprocal bond between political and union leaders whereby both interests are served through the instrument of clientelism. Clientelism serves to control the working classes, satisfy the individual interests of union leaders, and maintain support for the middle-class political order.

Bureaucratic elites represent the interests of the ascendant middle class, who benefit from state expansion. They derive benefits from direct access to state resources and through expansion of the state. They have considerable power derived from staffing and controlling state institutions and agencies. When their class interests are threatened, they have the power to sabotage the state-controlling political leaders. At the same time, some bureacratic elites gain access to middle-class status through clientelistic ties to powerful political elites.

Resources gained from international patrons are required to maintain the patronage-based two-party system within Jamaica. The resources have not facilitated public policies with a demonstrable impact on and improvement of the standard of living of the masses of the population. Instead, they have led to increased middle-class dominance of the state, a wealthy and tiny capitalist class, and an impoverished lower-class population whose livelihood is dependent on clientelist patronage for its survival. Under existing conditions of high employment and resource scarcity, the poor have very little choice but to maintain patron-client relations with political leaders. This is because their reality is characterized by dependence, persistent poverty, chronic unemployment, hunger, disease, and other misfortunes. As a result of these apparent vulnerabilities, the lower classes and the poor unwittingly support the middle-class strategy of using patronage to demobilize them. Middle-class dominance is maintained as a result of its strategic international alliances, which provides it with the revenues necessary to satisfy, accommodate, and neutralize strategic social actors via clientelist patronage.

A patron-client analytic approach is valid in the Jamaican context for several reasons. First, patron-client analysis is able to identify the chief mechanisms that limit conflicts and thus regulate and stabilize Jamaican society. Focusing on clientelism provides an explanation of the way in which latent tensions are controlled in the society, thus reinforcing the power of the ruling class and contributing to the equilibrium of the system. Clientelism has provided the cement by which racial and cultural identities are amalgamated within the boundaries of the national political system. There is no doubt that through clientelist politics the individuals, groups, and classes that make up the grass roots of the JLP and the PNP see their immediate and particular needs (e.g., housing, food, employment) partially satisfied. But these interests are secured by means of a process that puts individuals and groups among the working classes and the poor in opposition to one another in the JLP and PNP without ever bringing them together in support of interests they may share in general. Thus clientelism tends to divide the working classes as part of the process of favoring the interests of the middle class.

Second, as an analytic concept, clientelism brings into focus the grass roots of politics, which have received scant attention by political scientists of the Caribbean. Clientelism suggests an essentially rational component in behaviors, which from other perspectives might be viewed as extreme cases of culture-induced irrationality. The submission of low-status actors to high authorities; the reluctance of these actors to form durable, horizontal alliances with their peers; and the general weakness of class and ethnically based associations can all be viewed as results of rational coping devices with which low-status actors maximize their security within a hostile environment (Powell 1970:411).

Third, the idea of a concept that identifies coping mechanisms seems to promise some insight into the question of why Jamaican society hangs together at all. Here, after all, is a system that, by evidence presented by some analysts, should have torn itself to pieces long ago—a society characterized by racial and class polarizations, by distrust and jealousy, and by profound status and class inequalities. Instead, clientelism has been used by the middle class as a mechanism of control and demobilization of the lower classes. Relative order has been maintained in the political economy as the most deprived classes seek advantages through clientelistic structures.

A major weakness of the clientelism concept in its application to Jamaica is that it focuses only on the internal relations of groups within the society and does not pay attention to the international capitalist structure of which Jamaica is an integral part, nor to the ramifications of this relationship. In general, the patronage literature does not recognize that the resource base of patronage lies overseas; instead, numerous authors attribute clientelistic behavior to the people's attitudes and values, but very few identify a linkage between clientelism and the local and international political economy. An analytical focus on dependency complements the patron-client approach by identifying the structure of international relations through which resources are transferred, to be employed by the state-controlling middle class for translating its class power into control of the state.

Dependency

Over the last two decades the shifting focus of development theory has resulted in a large body of literature on dependency in Latin America, the Caribbean, Africa, and Asia. According to Theotonio Dos Santos's (1970:231) much cited definition, dependence is:

> a situation in which the economy of certain countries is conditioned by the development and expansion of another economy to which the former is subjected. The relation of interdependence between two or more economies, and between these and world trade, assumes the form of dependence when some countries (the dominant ones) can do this only as a reflection of that expansion, which can have either a positive or a negative effect on their immediate development.

Early writers on postindependence Caribbean political economies tended to adopt a position closely derived from dependency approaches. The contributors came from different disciplines: George Beckford, Lloyd Best, Havelock Brewster, William Demas, Norman Girvan, Owen Jefferson, Alistair McIntyre, and Clive Thomas from economics; Trevor Munroe from political science; Walter Rodney from history; and Orlando Patterson from a sociohistorical perspective.[4] Most of these scholars were associated with the New World Group, described by one of its members as "a loosely knit group of Caribbean intellectuals whose aim is to develop an indigenous view of the region" (Girvan 1971a:7).

Although the problems of Caribbean dependency were examined in different contexts, the works of the above-mentioned authors can be treated as a class. They all clearly identified the problem of foreign penetration into the political economies of the Caribbean, noting the impact of external influences on local development (Blömstrom and Hettne 1984:98–121). The works of Norman Girvan and George Beckford are perhaps the most representative of the dependency tradition in studies of Jamaican political economy. They concentrate largely on analyses of underdevelopment in the mineral resource bauxite sector and the plantation-agriculture sector.

In his influential book, *Foreign Capital and Economic Underdevelopment in Jamaica*, Girvan (1971a) stated unequivocally that multinational corporate capital promoted economic underdevelopment in Jamaica. This viewpoint was in contrast to that generally held by modernization theorists that foreign investments were instrumental in helping poor countries evolve into a modern socioeconomic system (Harry Johnson 1971:242–252). Specifically, defenders of transnational corporations (TNCs) in developing nations have argued that only the latter had the capital capacity, management, marketing, and technological resources required to promote the requisite economic growth. Moreover, TNCs were seen as the most viable mechanisms for job creation and the transfer of business skills and production know-how in developing nations.

Girvan (1970, 1971a, 1971b) differed sharply from the modernization position in his assessment of the contributions of the bauxite TNCs to the development of the Jamaican economy. To begin with, Girvan argued, the terms on which the TNCs entered Jamaica were inconsistent with the national interest. Foreign investors had 100 percent control over the industry. For Girvan, the problems of underdevelopment could not be solved under those conditions of Western corporate domination. Foreign domination only increased underdevelopment with extremely skewed benefits and costs.

The bauxite sector remained almost like an enclave, better integrated with the external world than with the local economy. Machinery and equipment necessary for mining came exclusively from Western industrialized countries. Managerial and technical employees were drawn mainly from the TNC host country, not from the local population. A relatively small work force of skilled and unskilled labor was created, well paid by local standards. This led to small pockets of a "labor aristocracy" among a much broader mass base of poor and unemployed workers. As the bauxite sector was capital intensive it could employ only a small sector of the work force—a mere 1 percent of the total work force in 1969 (Jefferson 1972).

The rapid growth of the bauxite sector was the single most important factor in the economic growth of the postwar Jamaican economy. There was a signficant increase in government revenues, but, as Girvan noted, those revenues were insubstantial in comparison to the profits made by company stockholders in the host country. Moreover, the government forfeited the customs and income taxes that would have been secured without incentive legislation passed to encourage foreign investment. It was only as a result of a bauxite levy (of 7.5 percent of the selling price of aluminum ingot) imposed by the 1972 Manley PNP government that the tax rate increased significantly over a twenty-year period, from $2.50 per ton in 1972 to $14.51 per ton in 1975 (Girvan 1978:17–26; Keith and Girling 1978:17–26). The negotiations surrounding the levy also resolved the issue of ownership through joint venture arrangements between the state and the bauxite companies. Despite these limited gains, Girvan argued that the state was still entrapped because the TNCs have a vertically integrated industry, maintaining control over all aspects of international shipping, marketing, and production facilities.

Although not rejecting the overall notion of dependence, a number of subsequent writers on the bauxite industry have argued that perhaps Jamaica was an example of "dependent development." Following Peter Evans' (1979) model of industrialization in Brazil, Stephens and Stephens (1985) argued that the Jamaican state was able to establish a sufficiently firm position in the bauxite economy for it to exert some leverage on the TNCs. The suggestion here was that the Jamaican state demonstrated a capacity (denied by many dependency and Marxist theorists in general) to manipulate the operative elements of the international economic system.

Despite Girvan's reluctance to concede that dependent states are not permanently pliable and can renegotiate the terms of dependency, his analyses on the bauxite industry have been an important step away from the dominant modernization perspective of the 1950s and 1960s.

Caribbean plantation-dependency theorists (e.g., Best 1968; Beckford 1972; Mandle 1972) all advance the thesis that the plantation structure of the slavery era dominated all aspects of social life and blocked economic development in the postindependence period. Domestic capital accumulation has been restricted to the boundaries of the plantation, and foreign ownership and control of various stages of production and marketing limit the portion of capital returned to the local economy. Essentially, plantation dependency theorists perceived little structural change in the local economies' 500 years of existence. The modern period in the Caribbean, dating from after World War II, has been labeled "Plantation Economy Further Modified," consisting of the emergence of new export staples such as bauxite, tourism, and petroleum; domestic manufacturing; and an active public sector. However, many of the features of the original "pure plantation economy" (1600–1838) have been strikingly similar to those of the modern period, because many of the new institutions, and particularly the TNCs, have the same characteristics as the joint-stock trading companies under the old mercantilism. Both product and factor markets continued to be fragmented within each Caribbean territory, and mercantilism under the TNCs enforced dependency as under the old mercantilism. Best (1967:1–5) succinctly summarized the similarities in operations between the new and old mercantilism:

> James, it was, I think in *Black Jacobins*, who reminded us that, having landed in the New World, Columbus praised God and urgently inquired after gold. Nowadays the industrialists arrive by jet clippers, thank the Minister of Pioneer Industry and inquire after bauxite. The "Enterprise of the Indies" is still good business.

George Beckford is perhaps best known for his elaboration of the plantation thesis. He has argued extensively that there is a basic continuity of the major features of plantation society, which replicates on a larger scale those of the original slave plantation. The heritage from the pure plantation economy period has continued to paralyze economic development. Beckford identified a number of mechanisms through which the plantation economy generated underdevelopment: (1) the linkage and spread effects of plantation production have been insignificant; (2) domestic food production has been restricted because of the land requirements of plantation production; (3) terms of trade have continued to deteriorate because of inter alia rationalizations of plantation production, which lower the export prices; and (4) the plantation economy is characterized by racial and class divisions (Beckford 1972).

These negative tendencies have their roots in the colonial period, creating the conditions for modern dependency. Caribbean plantation economies were oriented toward serving the capitalist expansion of Europe and thus prevented the development of an internal momentum strong enough to ensure that surpluses were returned to the region. One of the central features of modern dependency—namely, the bias toward the utilization of domestic resources in the production of primary exports—emerged during the colonial period. Indigenous resources continued to be used exclusively at the dictates of capital accumulation in the metropolitan countries. What was consumed through the market was, by and large, imported and did not reflect the needs of the broad population. The Caribbean region has continued to be dependent on a few primary products, which has made it extremely vulnerable to the vagaries of world trade.

The core of Beckford's economic analysis of plantation economies has centered around the issue of plantation-peasant conflict in the post-1838 emancipation period (e.g., 1972, 1980). Typically, plantations were first established in open resource situations where there were extensive lands and suitable conditions for the production of tropical crops. The dynamic of capitalist development then forced the plantation into a closed resource situation. By extending its rights over fertile and well-situated land, it consolidated its dominance over the peasant sector, its potential competition for resources (Best 1968; Stone 1974a; R. Young 1976). The development possibilities of the peasant sector have been frustrated by its weakness in the face of plantation dominance manifested in the distribution of landholding and in control over credit institutions, transport facilities, price and marketing structures, and so on.

Beckford's plantation thesis was both economic and sociological. The sociological dimension included an analysis of the correlation between race and class oppression in plantation society. As Beckford explained, the Caribbean labor regime and the system of production were based on race. Race was instituted into the mode of production and the mode of exchange. Different types of labor had different access to the means of production. It was race that determined whether or not a poor laborer would eventually rise on the social ladder because it was race that determined access to the means of production.

It is this structure, which is a hangover from the plantation era, that has perpetuated in the black masses severe disadvantages relative to the white and light-skinned upper strata of the society in terms of income, employment, education, and ownership of property. Beckford noted that blacks have made some gains in the areas of representation in political and administrative structures and in middle-class occupations. For example, the proportion of blacks employed in professional and managerial occupations rose from 0.1 percent in 1943 to 5 percent in 1970 (Broom 1954). Nevertheless, economic inequality for most blacks has persisted virtually unchanged in the postindependence period (Jefferson 1972). In spite of the gains that have been made by middle-class blacks, the systematic subordination of one race has remained a problem in Jamaica.

The dependency approaches briefly discussed in this section have concentrated on the effects of capitalist and plantation forces in retarding the potential growth and the development of the forces of production in Jamaica, and the Caribbean in general. Dependency provided a relevant explanatory frame for analyzing Jamaica's economic problems in the context of conditions imposed by the world system. However, it ignored the nature of class forces existing in the peripheral economy that inhibit development. There has not yet been an understanding of the dependence of the political structure on external dependency relations. To dismiss domestic ruling classes as mere puppets whose interests are mechanically synonymous with those of metropolitan interests is to ignore the realities of a much more complex relationship.

Caribbean dependency approaches have not yet examined the postcolonial state and the extent to which the state-controlling middle class has separate interests of its own. The insights from Beckford, Girvan, and other dependency theorists can be drawn together to produce a framework for understanding the Jamaican postcolonial state. In this way, there can be a focus on the state and the groups who control it, and their relationships with internal and external forces.

Dual Clientelism

The internal aspect of Jamaican political economy cannot be properly understood unless the international aspect is understood. The structural organization of Jamaica's contemporary political economy emerged from its past relationship with the world economy. The dialectical relationship between domestic and international structures of inequality is thus critical to my framework: hence the marriage of the two concepts of dependency and clientelism.

Dependency scholars and others have argued that countries such as Jamaica, with historically disadvantaged positions in international relations, have little or no chance for development in a capitalist world economy. Indeed, Jamaica has had a subordinate role in the world economy, with its participation limited to primary, raw material production for the British market. In turn, Jamaica imported manufactured goods from the expanding factories of Britain, which favored the latter's industrial revolution. The nature of production in the Jamaican economy was primarily geared toward the satisfaction of metropolitan colonial interests (Clive Thomas 1988).

In the post–World War II period, with the discovery of bauxite, the Jamaican economy diversified, moving away from agricultural dependence to a new dependence on bauxite, tourism, and manufacturing. Payne (1988a) has shown that the reliance on bauxite earnings had an unfavorable impact on the Jamaican economy in the 1980s in terms of reduced government revenues as well as on the performance of the economy. Decline in world demand for bauxite was reflected in the decline in the country's 1982/83 export earnings (Clive Thomas 1988). Jamaica's experience in the 1980s confirmed the perils of commodity concentration for some developing nations. In addition, the new growth sectors (particularly bauxite and tourism) of the postwar period have been effectively penetrated by foreign capital and have become a part of the international capitalist system, with its asymmetrical distribution of power and resources (Amin 1976).

The overall thrust of the dependency historical/structural approaches discussed in the previous section is most important in understanding that Jamaica's underdevelopment was not a historical accident, but rather a result of concrete historical processes. The political, social, economic, and cultural consequences of plantation slavery created conditions of domination, scarcity, dependency, and impoverishment for the broad masses of the population.

Under such conditions the clientelistic social formation emerged in the postcolonial period.

The educated noncapitalist middle class that has controlled the state since independence has been ideologically predisposed to pursue "development" policies through an international framework. Policies based on the transfer of external resources to the state have been consistently pursued by postindependence governments. External resource transfers have not been primarily determined by an economic imperative of industrialization, but rather by the politics of clientelism. State expansionist policies led to a "strong" state with formidable powers in the domestic arena.

International resources have been a significant part of the state's patronage arsenal. The quantity of resources required to maintain an extensive state-centered patronage system has not been available to the local economy. Without access to international resources, a broad-based patronage system could not have been maintained. State expansion has become the thrust of middle-class policies, as it has been an excellent way to gain resources required to maintain clientelism. Those contending for state power have been concerned with choosing ideologies that best allow them access to external resources.

International resources have been necessary for patronage as well as to carry out the normal political and economic functions of government. This increased the vulnerability of Jamaican leaders to actions of external actors. A decline in resource transfers (as occurred during the Manley regime of the 1970s) led to a diminished capacity for state patronage as well as to the PNP government's inability to maintain social and political order. A political economy cannot operate under conditions of breakdown of order. The experience of the Manley regime demonstrated that external resources have become critical for essential functions of governments in developing nations.

As a result of the structural inequalities of the international capitalist system, leaders of developing nations have had difficulty transferring resources to the domestic economy in a value-neutral way. Often, the transfer of external resources has been determined by the willingness of the political elite to maintain existing international relations that favor capitalist or socialist ideology.

The process of accommodating international actors with powerful resources can also be characterized in terms of a patron-client relationship. Both Fidel Castro and Ronald Reagan were patrons of Manley and Seaga in the 1970s and 1980s. However, the resources Reagan transferred to Seaga were far greater than those Castro transferred to Manley. In return, both Manley and Seaga gave ideological support to their patrons in the ideological battle between "imperialism" and "anti-imperialism" in the Western Hemisphere. The patron-client chain has become more complex, as the "super" patrons are now foreign, with no cultural ties to the local society. More of the resources of the domestic economy have been siphoned off for international actors as well as for the ruling middle class and its allies, thus leaving even less for those at the bottom of the ladder.

International capital has served to consolidate the power of the ascendant middle class, but it also has been used by the latter to constrict and restrict the power of the domestic capitalist class. Given the weaknesses of the peripheral capitalist economy (Clive Thomas 1988), the domestic capitalist class has remained relatively underdeveloped, unable to play a leading role in economic development. State expansion policies strengthened the middle class vis-à-vis the capitalist class. Acting in its own interests, the former coopted the latter through a clientelistic relationship in which state sponsorship is guaranteed in exchange for support of middle-class policies required for mass mobilization. In most instances, capitalist interests have been protected in the context of their support for a middle-class agenda. At the same time, the interests of foreign capital (the state's most powerful ally) have often been protected at the expense of local capital accumulation (see Chapter 6).

Representative institutions have played a critical role in domestic clientelism. Strategic material and nonmaterial resources have become centralized in the control of party leaders and redistributed at their discretion to establish and expand groups of followers (see Chapter 3). Since its inception in 1944, party politics has always served a middle-class agenda. In the early postindependence years, the middle-class was able to appeal to the black lower classes, whose members were mobilized in support of a middle-class institutional and policy agenda. The lower classes were successfully convinced that their interests would be well represented.

By the late 1960s, as the lower classes experienced deteriorating economic conditions, they began to participate in party politics in an involuntary way. The resources required for their daily sustenance became linked to political participation. Under conditions of scarcity, high unemployment, and general impoverishment, the lower classes faced limited options. Participation in parliamentary institutions became a requirement for the acquisition of strategic resources. Lower-class acquiescence to party participation has resulted in the persistence of mass support for democratic institutions, albeit by default.

NOTES

1. The notion of the state means different things to different people. Marx and Engels defined the modern state as "but a committee for managing the common affairs of the whole bourgeoisie." For six different images of the Marxian state concept, see Bob Jessop (1977). Weber characterized the state as "a human community that claims the monopoly of the legitimate use of physical force within a given territory" (Gerth and Mills 1958:78). David Easton, typifying the mood of the postwar behavioral revolution, substituted the word

"state" for "authoritative allocation of values" (Easton 1965). More recently, Theda Skopcol offered a conceptualization that includes a definition of the state as an internal and external actor, standing between internal socioeconomic structures over which domination must be maintained and from which resources must be extracted, and a world order, which provides both opportunities and dangers that condition state needs and behavior. I will adopt Skopcol's conceptualization and definition of the state as "a set of administrative, policing, and military organizations headed, and more or less well coordinated by, an executive authority" (Skopcol 1979:25–32). The internal pressures of clientelism and the external pressures of dependency will be illuminated to reveal the uniqueness of the Jamaican state. Models of the modern state were diffused to formerly colonized regions of the world through imperialism. Dominant understandings of the state in the English-speaking Caribbean fall between liberal pluralist (Stone 1980) and neo-Marxist (Beckford and Witter 1980). For valuable analyses of the Caribbean state, see Omar Davies (1986a).

2. See Munroe (1972), Robotham and Munroe (1977), Beckford and Witter (1980), Ambursley (1983), and Figueroa (1988).

3. These figures are for 1970 and are reported in Population Census, *Jamaica Statistics*, Kingston, p. 3.

4. For a representative sample of Caribbean approaches to underdevelopment, see, among others, George Beckford (1972); Lloyd Best (1968); Havelock Brewster (1973); William Demas (1965); Norman Girvan (1970, 1971a, 1971b, 1973); Norman Girvan and Owen Jefferson (1971); Clive Thomas (1974); Trevor Munroe (1972); and Walter Rodney (1967).

2

Decolonization and the Emergence of a Clientelist Postcolonial State, 1944-1962

This chapter analyzes the factors that led to the clientelistic social formation of the postcolonial state that emerged in the post-1944 period. During the 1944–1962 period of decolonization, British and North American investors created the economic conditions for middle-class domination of the postcolonial state. At the same time, the introduction of parliamentary democracy by Britain paved the way for control of the state by the middle class. Party politics served to galvanize lower-class support for politicians representing the interests of the middle class. The economic interests of foreign capitalist investors, the political interests of Britain and North America, and the interests of the Jamaican middle class converged and became represented in the political economy of Jamaica and through the institutions of parliamentary democracy.

The limited analytical attention given to the 1944–1962 period does not accurately reflect its importance in understanding the contemporary political system. Political scientist Trevor Munroe's (1972) pioneering study of the period, *The Politics of Constitutional Decolonization in Jamaica, 1944–1962*, provides an excellent account of middle-class domination of the constitutional process through manipulation, deception, and charismatic leadership. There is a paucity of documentation in Munroe's work relevant to an understanding of why the ordinary Jamaican supported middle-class elites when their values and interests were often divergent. This chapter seeks to supplement Munroe's work in explaining the circumstances that led to the convergence of interests in 1944 with the creation of a democratic parliamentary system. The important question is: How, and under what circumstances, did these divergent interests converge?

ECONOMIC CONDITIONS FOR MIDDLE-CLASS DOMINATION

Generalized discontent over material conditions in the post-1838 emancipation period culminated in labor riots, which rocked Jamaica in 1938

29

(G. K. Lewis 1968; Post 1979). The growing impoverishment of the black population coincided with changing agrarian relations in the 1838–1890 period. The 1846 Sugar Duties Act[1] led to declining sugar prices as it opened up Jamaican sugar to competition from European beet sugar as well as sugar from Cuba, Brazil, Mauritius, Puerto Rico, and Fiji. The plantocracy began to crumble and was gradually replaced by agricultural TNCs, such as Tate and Lyle, as the plantations became more mechanized. As the TNCs brought more and more land into production, using more capital-intensive production methods, they had less need for black labor and less space to accommodate small farms. The demand for labor diminished relative to supply, and the laborers' conditions deteriorated rapidly.

The small farmers became impoverished and displaced. As rural life became less attractive than previously, these farmers began, in desperation, to seek alternative opportunities elsewhere. Avenues of emigration in Cuba, Panama, and Costa Rica were closed temporarily, so many were forced to return to work on the Jamaican plantations. As labor was abundant, the TNCs were able to pay the black laborers very low wages. As their income diminished to a pittance, their insecurity became increasingly more acute. Robotham and Munroe (1977:19–20) noted that in the decade of the 1930s, one-fourth of the population was unemployed, 92 percent of those employed earned less than 25 shillings per week, and out of a total of 200,368 income earners, 184,000 earned under 65 pounds per year. The Great Depression precipitated a crisis in the West Indian sugar industry, which worsened the already deteriorating conditions of the lower classes.

The middle classes, although faring much better than the lower classes, were resentful of the marginal political status conferred on them by the colonial system. They possessed skills that should have allowed them to prosper in a democracy, but their progress was being hampered by racism in colonial society. Their discontent led them to empathize with the lower classes, whose demands were for improvement in their living conditions. An interclass alliance was formed between the middle and lower classes to confront the British colonial power and demand change. Mass mobilization led to labor rebellions throughout the Caribbean. The labor movement that emerged was harnessed by middle-class leadership employing both materialist and nationalist ideology to press demands for change. Charismatic middle-class leaders, such as Alexander Bustamente and Norman Manley, subsequently emerged at the head of organized labor unions and parties demanding better wages, improved working conditions, the establishment of formal collective bargaining procedures, and self-government (Gonsalves 1977).

In response to the riots, which spread throughout the West Indies, the British government immediately dispatched the West India Royal (Moyne) Commission of Inquiry to investigate. The Commission was comprised of social liberals highly influenced by the welfarist current of Fabianism in

Britain (G. K. Lewis 1968:90–93). The Commission urged establishment of a West Indian Welfare Fund, with an annual grant of at least one million pounds for a period of not less than twenty years. It also suggested self-government, extension of the suffrage, the encouragement of trade unionism with adequate legislative protection, establishment of a labor department in each colonial government, and additional industrial and protective legislation, especially minimum wages and a workman's compensation law (West India Royal Commission Report 1989:94, 108).

The Commission's report led to the 1940 Colonial Development and Welfare Act, the precursor of the Jamaican welfare state, which became the basis for middle-class ascendancy (G. K. Lewis 1968:91). Ultimately, efforts to implement the recommendations of the Commission led to the development and expansion of representative governments elected by universal adult suffrage. The recommendations were identical to earlier demands made by Jamaican and other West Indian leaders for a restructured representative government in which they had equal standing with whites.

The recommendations were beneficial to both West Indian political stability and the British economy. With the victory of the British Labour Party (BLP) in the post–World War II era, colonial policy began to reflect the spirit of the Moyne Commission and ultimately led to independence in Jamaica in 1962. The introduction of representative institutions created the facade of democratic participation of the lower classes, thus legitimizing middle-class domination and control of the labor and party organizations. Britain's granting of independence to Jamaica was contingent on middle-class control of the sociopolitical system. Hintzen (1989:42–45) noted that in colonies such as Trinidad, where the political and labor organizations were not yet dominated by middle-class leadership, Britain was reluctant to move the constitutional process along to full independence. Thus, with the introduction of representative institutions, participation was expanded and the newly mobilized lower class was channeled into the middle-class–led JLP and PNP (and their affiliated unions) in a manner that was not disruptive to the system.

British welfare capital expenditure in the West Indies (and in its other colonies) was designed to bolster British investment in those territories. In the face of its significant decline as a hegemonic power, the British state assumed an interventionist role in order to revive its economy. Government resources were placed into colonial primary and industrial production to provide incentives for British firms to invest in the colonial territories. Welfare resources were also used to prevent further riots and breakdown of the West Indian social order. The new resources led to state expansion, the beneficiary of which was a powerful domestic middle class that could be coopted in support of colonial and capitalist interests. The state infrastructure that developed during the 1944–1962 period of tutelage leading to independence was consistent with the interests of North American investors and the strategic and political interests of the United States. The discussion in the next sections turns to these issues.

The 1940 Colonial Development and Welfare Act: The Basis for the Postcolonial Statist Organization

By 1940 the formulation of a new colonial development policy became imperative as part of the measures of state intervention in the Jamaican economy. Among the chief instruments for implementing the new policy was the Colonial Development and Welfare Act of 1940. This superseded the act of 1929, which had provided only a small trickle of aid to the colonies. The 1940 CDWA appropriated 120 million pounds to the colonial governments for a period of ten years. Further supplementary acts of 1949 and 1950 increased the total amount of 140 million pounds and extended the size of the central reserve, thus raising the amount that could be paid in any one year. About 40 percent of the funds from this act went toward education, health services, housing, and water supplies (J. M. Lee 1967:85). Of this sum, approximately one-fifth was allocated to the British West Indies, following the recommendations of the Moyne Commission (Simey 1946).

The bureaucratic organization of colonial government in Jamaica was transferred into a postcolonial statist organization and expanded upon to include functions that were not part of colonial governance. State expansion into economic activities became the channel for clientelistic recruitment, which is now the basis for lower-class domination and control. Populistic demands by the lower classes during the riots led to the expansion of social services administered by the state. Bureaucracies were created for managing social welfare, such as the Jamaica Welfare Limited, the Land Settlement Department, and the Central Housing Authority. The Cooperative Council and the Agricultural Society were also established. In all cases, the educated middle class in control of the new postcolonial state became responsible for organizing the administrative structures established to take over the duties that were performed by the colonial government. The justification was that the prevailing 70 percent illiteracy rate (Broom 1954) for the vast majority of the population made it difficult for others besides the educated class to fill those positions.

The state surpassed the church in matters of social welfare. During the slavery and postemancipation periods the church had always provided welfare services; however, the church was soon overtaken by state agencies in its guidance of the poor. The pastor saw his sphere of influence contract and the allegiance of many of his constituency transferred to others. There was an attempt at collaboration through the appointment of representatives of the Christian Councils to serve on official bodies such as the Social Welfare Committees. The influence of the church on social problems declined, however, as it did not have the resources needed to match those of the state in carrying out welfare schemes.

The state assumed a new role as an agency for promoting the welfare and safeguarding the standards of living of the majority of the population. It was no longer limited to the functions of law and order, collecting revenues, and minimal welfare. Its scope was broadened to take an active part in extensive development programs. The British government believed that sociopolitical order in Jamaica and other West Indian colonies could be maintained only if social and economic reforms were made. It also recognized that the colonial constitutions would have to be revised to facilitate the purpose of the necessary reforms. Thus, at the same time that the social-welfare programs were worked out, efforts also were made to establish representative self-government under a system of universal adult suffrage.

The Penetration of North American Capital and the Formation of the Domestic Classes

In the postwar period both JLP and PNP governments actively encouraged the penetration of foreign capital in the local economy in an "industrialization by invitation" program. The political elite opted for a development strategy based on North American foreign capital to promote social and economic development. It was convinced that what the Marshall Aid Plan and the Western international financial agencies were able to do to help war-ravaged Europe to emerge as a capitalist center of power in less than twenty years could probably be done for developing nations.

The industrialization by invitation policy provided incentives to attract foreign capitalists to establish manufacturing activities in Jamaica. Incentive legislation led to tax-free holidays, duty-free imports of raw materials, accelerated depreciation allowances, and site rental in industrial estates. Under the incentive program, over a ten-year period the number of workers employed by the manufacturing sector was less than the growth of the labor force in a single year (Beckford and Witter 1980:65). Incentives were provided at great costs to the public sector, which lost potential revenues, but the benefits to the government in terms of employment were minimal.

Foreign capital provided the technology for a significant diversification of the economy (Girvan 1971a; Jefferson 1972). Although there was tremendous growth in the economy in the 1950s, reflected in the increases in per capita national income and gross domestic product (GDP), the new growth sectors (bauxite, tourism, and manufacturing) had no links among themselves and developed few links with the agricultural sector. Bauxite, tourism, and manufacturing became the largest sectors in terms of GDP in the Jamaican economy in 1968. However, they reinforced the basic import/export orientation of the colonial economy. All of the imports, raw materials, services, and skilled work force required for these sectors were imported. Much of the manufacturing and bauxite and alumina output was exported. Jefferson (1972:8) noted that "foreign ownership ranged from 100 percent in bauxite-alumina, to 40 percent in sugar and its by-products, 40 percent of transport, communications and public utilities combined and 55 percent of hotel capacity in the tourist industry." Local capital benefited from the new investments, which provided profitable opportunities for merchants selling consumer goods and textiles; entrepreneurs selling services such as entertainment, restaurants, and transport; and real estate speculators.

External economic penetration of the postwar economy reinforced racial and class divisions within the society. In the foreign establishments, the high-level management positions were held by white expatriates or Jews, Lebanese, Syrians, or "Jamaican whites." Middle-management positions went to the browns, Chinese, and Indian professionals. At the bottom were the black workers. Significant class differentiation occurred in the middle and lower classes as a result of foreign investments. The state bureaucracy expanded, leading to the creation of new jobs for the brown and black educated middle class. Highly skilled bauxite workers earned high salaries relative to their counterparts in other sectors. The low skilled and unskilled had access to jobs in factories, hotels, gas stations, transportation, and as domestics in middle- and upper-class homes. At the bottom were the agricultural laborers and the peasantry, who were displaced as large acreages of land were alienated from them and sold to the bauxite and tourist industries. The displaced peasantry migrated to the urban areas of Kingston and St. Andrew and to England. Migration became an escape from the dispossession generated by these forms of foreign capitalist penetration of the economy.

The majority of the black lower classes did not share in the new prosperity of the postwar era. As they were largely unskilled and uneducated, they were not able to benefit from the new jobs created within the private sector and the state bureaucracy. Unemployment remained high, wages low, and job tenure insecure. These conditions were conducive to clientelistic recruitment of the lower classes into the middle-class–led JLP and PNP.

It is important to emphasize that changes in the international economy in the aftermath of World War II facilitated the industrialization by invitation strategy. The United States emerged as the dominant force in the global economy and industrialization by invitation was the thrust of its foreign policy in the Caribbean. In the war and postwar environment, enormous opportunities for investment in the industrial countries emerged and led to tremendous postwar economic growth. The economies of developing nations became important as raw resource producers, particularly of minerals (such as bauxite and industrial metals). It is within this context that Jamaica became locked into dependent relationships with powerful governments, TNCs, and financial institutions of the advanced capitalist countries.

The other main participants in Jamaican financial relations during the mid-sixties were the World Bank, which began disbursements in 1963, and the International Monetary Fund. The Inter-American Development Bank (IADB) and the Caribbean Development Bank (CDB), two regional institutions, also began participating in the 1960s. U.S. aid agencies participated actively since the 1960s through the Agency for International Development (USAID). The World Bank's objective was to provide long-term development loans for specific development projects. The IMF provided short-term balance-of-payments financing as well as the general "seal of approval" required before many organizations would lend money. The IADB played a similar role to the World Bank, providing both commercial and concessional loans. USAID provided soft loans and some grants for various development projects.

Between 1963 and 1973, USAID gave J$11.6 million; the Canadian International Development Agency (CIDA) gave J$12.5 million between 1965 and 1974; CIDA government guaranteed loans were J$18.3 million; the International Bank for Reconstruction and Development (IBRD) gave J$63.3 million between 1965 and 1974; and the IADB gave J$24.3 million between 1970 and 1974 (Kirton 1977:86–87). In order to obtain funds from these agencies, such as the World Bank, for example, "experts" usually were sent to evaluate the present economic policies of the government and those likely to be pursued in the future. In the case of Jamaica, which had been having a rapid turnover of elected governments, the government in power as well as the opposition were evaluated, to ensure the World Bank that a stable government would always exist. International agencies' conditions for loans have always been free-market economic policies and political stability. Because of this, the political directorate of Jamaica, which is dependent on the resources of the international agencies, often complied with their wishes.

The influx of resources from North America substituted for local resource scarcity and provided the economic resources necessary for the maintenance of clientelism in Jamaica. Simultaneously, the major industrialization program enacted with the North American corporations had the effect of creating new social classes among the elites. The middle class expanded to include salaried and professional groups whose activities and survival were directly linked to the state. The middle class struggled for power against the commercial propertied elite, which dominated at the level of production and controlled most of the nationally accumulated surplus. The lower class was accommodated through clientelistic arrangements of the JLP and PNP organizations. This freed the middle-class state-controllers to pursue policies that were exclusively in the combined interests of external investors, local providers of capital, and the middle class itself. Such interests were tied to the intensified penetration of international capital in the Jamaican economy.

THE EMERGENCE OF LABOR
AND PARTY ORGANIZATIONS

The Moyne Commission Report resulted in the formation of a new labor code and labor legislations in Jamaica. Prior to 1938, trade-union organizations met with little success, as the laws did not allow for collective organization of workers, peaceful picketing, or workers' compensation. The British government realized that unless it provided adequate legislation and machinery for the institutionalization of protest, it would be continually faced with massive unrest and continuous social disorder. Thus it decided to establish institutions that would be an outlet for social protest.

Britain amended the 1919 Trade Union Law[2] to permit peaceful picketing, and granted trade unions immunity against actions in tort. In 1939, Britain enacted the Trade Disputes (Arbitrary and Enquiry) Law, which provided for mediation, conciliation, arbitration, and enquiry of trade disputes. Between 1937 and 1941, social legislation was passed relating to minimum wages, workmen's compensation, and shop assistants. Between 1938 and 1946, there were twenty-three active labor organizations registered in Jamaica under the Trade Union Act (Gonsalves 1977). These labor unions emerged independent of party politics, their objective being to level out the economic inequities that had grown up between employers and wage earners since emancipation. Their basic concern was with a better distribution of income and the claiming of certain rights of trade union representation as workers.

A united labor movement emerged out of the 1938 riots, with Alexander Bustamante as the leader of the Bustamante Industrial Trade Union. Other middle-class leaders, such as Ken Hill, Florizel Glasspole, A. Coombs, and Ivy and Amy Bailey, were also responsible for launching the labor movement. Colonial state policy was aimed at consolidating the middle class, whose survival had become linked to the colonial state and whose interest was linked to maintaining the status quo and guarding the stability of the country. Within the general union movement, leadership passed from the semiskilled or unskilled workers to persons of upper middle-class background like Bustamante. The colonial state attempted to resolve the contradiction between itself and the middle class, which aspired for power, by helping the latter consolidate its hold over organized politics. The British hoped that middle-class control would guarantee that the trade unions developed along the "right lines." The middle class gullibly imitated the organization of British trade unions and political parties and directed their own unions and parties in such a way that was pleasing by imperial standards. The new representative institutions were thus not in the hands of those who might overthrow the political order.

By 1940, middle-class control over the labor movement was firm. Munroe (1975) pointed out that at the same time that Bustamante was organizing his BITU, the Marxist Left (also led by the educated middle class) in Jamaica tried to develop the trade-union movement on a socialist basis. The Marxist Left was not able to penetrate the working classes. The most important reason for this was that Marxist ideas were resisted by Bustamante, whose union had massive control over the working classes and thus retarded the spread of those ideas in the labor movement. Organizations such as Millard Johnson's "Black Man's party" and Rastafarian Sam Brown's "Suffrage party," attempting to maintain some autonomy from the educated middle class, were dissolved or were unsuccessful (Carnegie 1973; Munroe 1975).

There was a popularly held view at the time in Jamaica that successful competition for mass electoral support could not be achieved by a party without a well-organized trade-union base. The fact was that in an electorate dominated numerically by propertyless wage earners, trade unions comprised the largest single organized component of the voting population. The PNP thus felt that the future of its party was endangered if a union base was missing; thus it allied itself with the Trade Union Congress, and subsequently established its own affiliate, the National Workers Union.

Incessant interaction occurred between the unions and their party affiliates. Bustamante was the head of the BITU as well as the JLP, and although Norman Manley was the head of the PNP, his son, Michael Manley, became the head of the NWU upon his return to Jamaica from England. Because of the close affiliation between party and union, there was not a sharp differentiation between party policy and trade-union policy, and great efforts were always made to retain an effective liaison between the two. The BITU and NWU were engaged in constant competition to wrest control of a union branch from the hands of its rival, as the winner became the bargaining agent for that specific group of workers in the collective-bargaining process. Party leaders monitored that ceaseless struggle with great care, as they understood that its outcome would strongly affect the campaign strength of their own party's organization in any forthcoming elections.

Once the trade unions merged with the parties, the former were pushed into a backbench position. The labor movement became partially coopted, concerned only with negotiable short-term benefits, and had a very limited potential for autonomous challenge of the existing power structure in postindependence Jamaica. The political parties came to center stage, became electoral devices, and were organized behind the messianic leadership of Bustamante and Manley. Thus, by the late 1950s the nationalist movement in Jamaica had become essentially a bid by the middle class for political power and liquidation of colonial domination.

The two dominant organizations that grew directly out of the 1938 confrontations between labor and employers—the BITU and the PNP—were controlled by the middle class but represented two distinct constituencies. The BITU represented the rural masses, as well as a small element of the propertied classes (traders). The PNP represented the new transforming middle class—that sector of the middle class represented by the intelligentsia, teachers, civil servants, and all salaried state bureaucrats. For the BITU, the central issue at stake in the 1938 riots was the demand by the laboring classes for greater distributive and productive justice. For the PNP, those issues were important, but were "bread and butter" issues that could be resolved only in a context of self-government for the Jamaican people. The real issue from the PNP's standpoint was the carving out of autonomous zones of jurisdiction between an indigenous Jamaican ruling class, the traditional planter class, and the Colonial Office.

Despite these differences in emphases, the BITU and the PNP worked together from the start, although often in an uncomfortable and uneasy alliance. In 1939, the PNP declared itself socialist, adopted a manifesto of the British Labour party, and called for responsible government at the national level, full adult suffrage, Jamaicanization of the civil service, agricultural and industrial development, public ownership of utilities, development and protection of local industry, an expanded educational system, improved welfare services, and support for the trade unions (Sherlock 1980:90–100, as cited in M. Kaufman 1985:48). Furthermore, in 1943 the PNP released a statement pledging that, if selected to form the next government, the party would "end the political power of capitalist domination" while in office. The PNP advocated that "all the existing sources of light, power and irrigation be acquired by the State" (from "Plan For Security 1943," *Jamaica Daily Gleaner*, November 13, 1943, cited in Munroe 1972:42).

In 1942, ideological differences, coupled with Bustamante's own personal desire to be magnificent and powerful within his own right, led him to denounce the PNP and set up the JLP. The JLP was strictly the electoral arm of the BITU. It represented a typical Caribbean trade-union party, and responded to the specific needs of unionized workers and small farmers in the rural countryside. The JLP was not much of a party in the sense of having a well-articulated program, office holders, offices, and conventions, nor did it embrace a clearly defined ideology. However, it did convey a firm commitment to a more orthodox capitalist system with a dominant private sector. Bustamante genuinely believed that this form of economic organization was most appropriate for finding solutions to the problems of poverty and underdevelopment in Jamaica. In the absence of a clear ideology around which party members were organized, the JLP developed in the image and personality of its leader, Bustamante. Scholars of early party organization in Jamaica emphasize the authoritarian nature of JLP party organization (Bradley 1960; Eaton 1975). Candidates for elections were always selected by Bustamante himself, who was often referred to by those around him as "the chief." Bustamante ruled the JLP with a firm hand, without significant participation from cabinet members.

As an affiliate of the BITU, the JLP articulated the same goals as its BITU workers' movement. It maintained its populist mass base among the lower classes (whose major concern was with a distribution of income and the claiming of certain rights of trade-union representation as workers), and won the support of the conservative rural middle classes and significant support from the upper classes of capitalists and large farmers. The JLP won the support of remnants of the conservative white planter classes of the colonial era after their Jamaica Democratic party (JDP) was defeated in the 1944 election, receiving only 5.1 percent of the popular vote (M. Kaufman 1985:50). Since 1949, the planter class has established a lasting relationship with the JLP, as it remains deeply suspicious of the PNP's expressed commitment to socialism. However, a significant percentage of white capitalists also set up a lasting relationship with the PNP, as they were convinced that the PNP would be more efficient economic managers and more likely to modernize the economy.

Like the JLP, the PNP was not representative of a particular social stratum nor of persons committed to a single political or socioeconomic theory. The PNP was established as an alliance of disparate elements united by their common commitment to the achievement of political self-determination. The dark-complexioned middle classes were dissatisfied with a system in which all the top administrative, managerial, and supervisory positions were going to persons from Britain or to persons of white or light complexion. Dissatisfied members of the local economic elite wanted to have new industries that were locally owned and controlled. The PNP's commitment to political self-determination appealed to the protectionist instincts of this sector of the business elite. There was a genuine basis of support for the PNP's nationalist ideas, and the party worked on all these dissatisfactions with the aim of attracting support from those classes that were most affected by imperial political and economic arrangements—professional and clerical workers, business and commercial interests, as well as the urban semiskilled workers and small farmers in the rural areas.

The ideological influence of the middle-class PNP leaders was the Fabian socialism of the BLP. Fabianism emerged in England within the context of the development of a "social democratic alliance" between capitalists and workers (Amin 1976). Out of this alliance came the welfare state, which facilitated the emergence of the professional and educated middle class to political power and gave their leaders control of the state and its distributive functions. The BLP actively supported self-determination for the colonies. It recruited colonial students in Britain and identified capitalism with colonialism and racism. It seemed quite natural, therefore, for the middle class to embrace Fabian socialism. The latent function of Fabianism is the service of middle-class interests through statism. In spite of its acceptance of Fabianism, the PNP continued, as before, to court the support of capitalist interests and did not seek to confine itself to voters committed to socialism, nor did it adopt a socialist program.

The issue of Jamaica's participation in the West Indies Federation (1958–

1961) served to further polarize the ideological cleavage between the PNP and JLP. Norman Manley and the PNP supported the idea of a federation of West Indian states whereas Bustamente and the JLP vociferously opposed it. Bustamante argued persuasively that Jamaica's continued participation in the federation would constitute a severe strain on its limited resources. An attractive alternative would be unilateral independence rather than independence within the federal arrangement. The British government and West Indian politicians, particularly Norman Manley, Grantley Adams, and Eric Williams, believed that for these tiny West Indian nations federation and independence went together hand in hand. Britain supported the idea of a federation, not as a vehicle for self-government but as a concept that would improve colonial administrative efficiency (G. K. Lewis 1968:343–386). Antifederalists, such as Bustamante, were convinced that federation implied British abandonment of its West Indian colonies without economic aid. The Jamaican people voted against federation in a referendum, rejecting the opinions of the British and the majority of West Indian leaders on the issue. The proposal for a federation was the work of British officials and West Indian politicians. There was little popular support behind it.[3]

By 1958, the Jamaican economy had already become incorporated into North American capitalism, and the economic ties with Britain had been significantly reduced. With an infusion of North American resources in the early 1950s, the population had already become harnessed to the clientelistic parties. A federal arrangement under British guidance would seem to offer little potential for economic aid because the British economy was in decline. Unilateral independence allowed Jamaica to align itself politically and economically with the United States. The dependency relationship that resulted from this alliance led to the development of a clientelistic polity.

Most published works on the subject suggest that with regard to policy outcomes, between 1944 and 1972 the JLP and PNP had few differences (Munroe 1972; Stone 1984). Stone (1984) suggested that the only real difference that emerged between the parties in the policy area was the tendency of the PNP to increase both public spending and taxation at a faster rate than that associated with the JLP, and consequently to promote a higher increase in public employment. However, most social and economic policies remained intact during this period after changes in party government. A unified perception of both domestic and international politics facilitated this consensus of middle- and upper-class opinion in postwar Jamaica. Party leaders as well as the upper and middle classes were committed to the "Westminster model" of parliamentary democracy, as were the lower classes who saw it as a means to their political empowerment.

Economic policies reflected continuity for the most part, as did the governing styles of both parties. The lower classes became bound to the parties through personal loyalty to the leaders. In the absence of channels of access to the decisionmaking centers of government, the majority of the poor, nonpropertied people were unable to articulate and aggregate their interests. As a result, the machinery of government was operated to harmonize and conciliate existing middle- and upper-class interests and, where possible, to extrude other interests (this point is developed further in Chapter 4). In the area of international politics, both party governments maintained a pro-Western posture, aligning with the industrialized nations of North America and Western Europe.

LOWER-CLASS/BLACK SUPPORT
FOR BUSTAMANTE AND MANLEY

According to an abundance of reports in the early 1920s, 1940s, and 1950s, Bustamante and Manley were regarded by large segments of the Jamaican population as heroes and heaven-sent saviors of the nation. (See Nettleford 1968; Munroe 1972; Lindsay 1975; and Eaton 1975 for different perspectives on these leaders' relationships to the movement for independence.) On November 21, 1925, the *Jamaica Daily Gleaner* contained a laudatory editorial, which admitted that:

> Manley will win the attention of his audience, whether it be an audience of learned judges, of politicians, of government officers, or of the working public; he will always command attention, for what he has to say is worth hearing, and it is the man with something to say who secures an enduring regard. (p. 10)

In the 1950s, Manley was being characterized as "the principal architect of Jamaican democracy" and as "the Father of Nationalism" (Nettleford 1968). Manley possessed undoubted personal authority rooted in his achievement as a brilliant lawyer in a society where, next to wealth, education determined status and class to a great extent (Foner 1973). Bustamante aroused a very strong following among working-class women, who surrounded him with an undying devotion and a fanatical loyalty. They often sang:

> We will follow Bustamante
> We will follow Bustamante
> Till we die.
>
> Bustamante is a good man
> Bustamante never did wrong
> We will follow Bustamante
> Till we die.[4]

Bustamante and Manley created populist parties based on what political scientist Archie Singham (1968) characterized as a hero-crowd relationship in which participation in the political system is minimal. The distinguishing feature of this type of politics is that the hero is expected to achieve on behalf of the population. How did Bustamante and Manley and the black lower classes develop this dependent relationship? What created this leader-follower relationship? It was the colonial environment, with its culture of dependence on leaders and figureheads; political and economic underdevelopment; and deference to color and class that created the conditions for "heroes" like Bustamante and Manley in Jamaica and Eric Gairy in Grenada to emerge (Singham 1968, Aggrey Brown 1979). Singham (1968:300) described the phenomenon:

> The personalism of the leader's style is dependent on his understanding of the cultural and social patterns of relations. Among the rural people there is a tendency to rely on the elder or spokesman who has "special" skills, e.g., his knowledge of colonial regulations and relationships, and/or his capacity to speak and write the Queen's English which gains such an individual a personal following in this area. The potential leader must be able to exploit this pattern of personal relationships in building his movement. This is why school-teachers and clergymen play a pivotal role in local politics. Another requirement is that a potential leader must be capable of expressing the powerful but often articulate grievances of the masses on a national scale. He uses his personal charisma to claim legitimacy couched in terms of the national interest.

The level of political legitimacy of these rulers had deep roots. The rigid system of stratification, the narrow spread of mass education, and the widespread lack of group confidence among the population all combined to promote an elite leadership in Jamaican society, deriving from the educated middle classes and based on their ability to deal with the colonial masters and get things done on behalf of the masses. Enter thus Bustamante and Manley. In the context of a small-scale society, these leaders provided the necessary personalization of the political system, and by virtue of the esteem in which they were held, even by nonmembers of their party, created a reservoir of political legitimacy that still persists, despite their departure from the current political scene.

Although Bustamante was not white, he was what is known in Jamaica as "light skin," "high color," or "clear skin." In a society in which those having white skin have been traditionally viewed as better than others, and in which whiteness was a pillar of superiority, it would be inaccurate to say that Bustamante's skin color had no effect on the masses' allegiance and dependence on him. This aspect of race must not be underplayed because race/color was an integral factor in the colonial condition. Color was not the only component in Bustamante's charismatic relationship with the laboring class. He was a skillful organizer, he understood the feelings of the underdog, he spoke their language, and he was unquestionably committed to them.

Much more fundamental to the emergence of these middle-class leaders were the economic and political conditions of the 1930s and 1940s. The scarcity of resources worked to intensify political partisanship. Specifically, the failure of postwar economic policy to provide enough jobs meant that any political party in office distributed the available work not randomly, but by rewarding its own supporters first (Girvan 1971a; Jefferson 1972). This patronage system encouraged the perpetuation among the black lower classes of political allegiances that have very little to do with policy considerations. Chapter 3 elaborates on this phenomenon in greater detail.

IMPEDIMENTS TO LOWER-CLASS ORGANIZATION

The postwar organization of Jamaican society was characterized by racial and class inequalities, with the majority of the poor being black, but the political elite did not opt to use racial politics for mass mobilization. (See Munroe 1975 and Campbell 1987 for an elaboration of this viewpoint.) Instead, it used clientelism to harness the support of the black lower classes. Those organizations that were controlled by the lower classes, which attempted racial or class mobilization strategies for mass support, were unable to compete with the middle-class elites for mass support.

Marcus Garvey's Universal Negro Improvement Association (UNIA) used racial politics to mobilize widespread disaffection among the black lower classes, but that organization failed to seriously challenge the emerging political tendencies in Jamaica. The educated black middle classes, to whom Garvey turned for political and financial support, largely ignored his cause and in fact supported continued government attempts to silence him. Frustrated by political developments in Jamaica, Garvey migrated in 1916 to the United States, where, by 1925, his UNIA had an estimated two million dues-paying members. His abilities as a political organizer soon came to the attention of businessmen and government leaders. Garvey was later charged, arrested, and sent to jail for breaking U.S. laws. Upon his return to Jamaica in 1928, he formed the Peoples Progressive party (PPP), the island's first political party, and opened a daily newspaper, *The Blackman*, as the political education arm of the local PPP. In 1930, he organized the Working Man and Labourers Association (WMLA).

Both the WMLA and the PPP fell apart, unable to withstand government political and economic pressures. Garvey's philosophy of racial unity and autonomy for blacks challenged the British colonial system of domination in Jamaica as well as the illegitimacy of British colonialism in general. It is not surprising that Garvey was portrayed in the press as a "dangerous element" who would not be tolerated by the authorities (*Jamaica Daily Gleaner*, February 11, 1925). Garveyism was perceived as a threat to sociopolitical stability in this period, and was dealt with accordingly.

Garvey's limited but powerful impact set the stage for the emergence of

Rastafarianism in Jamaica. His vision of the solidarity of Africans at home and abroad became linked to the Rastafarians' "back-to-Africa" call. The first Rastafari, Leonard Howell, Archibald Dunkley, and Joseph Hibbert, like Garvey, felt the full force of state harassment. Howell and Dunkley were both sentenced to imprisonment in mental institutions for their continuing challenge to the power structure. During the postwar and postindependence years (1938–1972), Rastafarians were stereotyped as insane, violent, ganja-smoking (marijuana) criminals—elements of a depraved subculture.

While the culture of the Rastafari (including language, art, and music) never became the culture of the majority classes in contemporary Jamaica, the movement was and continues to be pregnant with relevant social and political criticism. As a result of its leaders' focus on metaphysics and religion, it naturally refrains from organized political action. (For a full understanding of the Rastafarian movement in Jamaica, see Smith, Augier, and Nettleford [1960]; Hill [1983]; EPICA Task Force [1979]; and Campbell [1980].) Although the issues of racial domination and imperialistic exploitation struck a cord in Jamaica's postemancipation historical legacy, racial politics did not go over well in the post-1938 period. The nationalist movement served to develop in the black masses a sense of "all of us are Jamaicans regardless of colour." The black middle class, in its denigration of Garvey and Rastafarians, portrayed the latter's black politics as racist and "antinational." In the aftermath of a united nationalist movement, the black population was prepared to bargain and collaborate with those forces that seemingly articulated its demands to the British colonial government. Moreover, the PPP and other organizations with racially based platforms were effectively coopted by economic and political pressures of the state as well as the subsequent system of clientelism by the JLP and PNP, which later absorbed Garvey's entire constituency.

Middle-class elites then took control of a competitive two-party system characterized by periodic changes of government between the JLP and PNP (Stone 1973, 1980, 1981a). The party system in Jamaica did not become polarized into racial blocs that limited the tendency to switch partisan supports. This is in contrast to countries where sociocultural homogeneity is lacking, as in Guyana and Trinidad, where the Westminster two-party system leads inevitably to the intensification of conflicts between social groups, which perceive themselves as being politically divided along racial, ethnic, or cultural lines (Ryan 1972; Premdas 1972; Greene 1974; Hintzen 1989).

Race and class divisions have been salient cleavages in the entire history of plantation society in Jamaica. However, the new political leaders manipulated these cleavages, thus affecting their saliency and intensity in the developing party system. The black population was accommodated thus: adult suffrage was granted to them, new occupational opportunities were opened, political leaders were largely black and brown, and lower-class browns and blacks were allowed to have membership with the upper- and middle-class whites and browns in both of the dominant parties. Although the economic resources in the society were not in the hands of the black population, party leaders managed to prevent recurring racial and class rebellions in the political system. Part of the reason is that as the political leaders were predominantly black it was not perceived that ethnic differences converged with power distinctions. The other explanation may be that the lower-class black population, by virtue of its poverty, gave its support to the competing JLP and PNP leaders in order to obtain the scarce resources of the state. With no other options, the black poor had little choice but to support the parties; it was a matter of imposition.

The postwar expansion of the state and subsequent growth of government services greatly increased the supply of political spoils available for dispersion by the political parties. At the same time, the policies of both party governments in the postwar period enlarged the scope of state action (Jefferson 1972; Stone 1980). The parties pushed nation-building goals directly by implementing developmental programs. In return, the state provided spoils essential to the viability and development of the party. A functional synthesis emerged as nation-building and party-building became inseparable and mutually reinforcing.

In order to maintain party followers and system support, the new state was forced to seek additional resources from external sources. Thus, Jamaica's dependence on metropolitan capital became multilateralized, as it shifted away from Britain toward new relations of dependence vis-à-vis North American governments and transnational corporations. The state became the mediator between the resources of industrialized North America and the needs of resource-scarce Jamaica. This condition reinforced Jamaica's dependence on North American resources as well as strengthened the state's capacity to control various social groups. Dependency relations between the Jamaican state and North American capital sources, and patron-client relations between the middle-class party leaders and other social classes within the society, were crucial factors that shaped the character of the postindependence political economy. External dependency and internal clientelism were the responses of the state-controlling middle class to the rapid social, political, and economic transformations that occurred in the aftermath of labor riots in 1938. These issues are the subject of Chapters 3 and 4.

NOTES

1. The 1846 Sugar Duties Act essentially removed protective duties on British West Indian sugar. See Joseph Ragatz (1971:369) and Douglas Hall (1959) for an in-depth analysis of the decline of the Jamaican sugar economy after the 1846 Act, and the social consequences of this decline.

2. The 1919 Trade Union Law was passed through a combination of forces: labor unrest in Jamaica; labor unrest in Britain and the United States, which was

widely reported in the local press; and agitation by trade-union leaders such as Bain Alves. With the passage of the Trade Union Law in 1919, workers were finally freed from criminal penalties related to organizing a trade union (Gonsalves 1977:91–92).

3. For various perspectives on the West Indies Federation, see David Lowenthal (1961), John Mordecai (1968), Jesse Proctor (1956), and Gordon Lewis (1968).

4. Cited in Eaton (1975:118) and Aggrey Brown (1979:101). The origin of the anthem is unknown.

3

Party Politics and
Internal Clientelism

Current portraits of the Jamaican political system suggest a polity that is deep in economic crises, but one in which liberal democratic institutions have taken root (Stephens and Stephens 1987; Manley 1987; Payne 1988a). The democratic label has been too readily conceded to various political processes, as the litmus test for democracy has been the existence of party organizations whose leaders compete for national power in "free elections." Jamaica boasts of having competing parties, an open news media, a free and impartial judicial system, and four and a half decades of continuous constitutional government. For these reasons, the democratic characterization of the party system has generally been accepted by students of Jamaican politics, despite the fact that substantial deviations from the requirements for democracy have been acknowledged (Stone 1980; Edie 1989).

This chapter attempts to delineate and explain the way the party system organizes, constrains, and deprives the majority classes of political choices through structures of clientelism. It was argued in Chapter 2 that the structures of democratic practice (the Westminster Parliamentary Model) provided the channel for the emergence of the educated middle class and its subsequent control of the postcolonial state. Middle-class political leaders have managed to consolidate such power through the clientelistic party structures of the JLP and PNP. Power is in the hands of those who have the technical qualifications to control the state. Control of the state carries with it the power to provide (or withold) security, and to allocate benefits in the form of jobs, food, contracts, and so on. The ties between the political leaders of the middle class and the lower-class electorate are exercised through clientelistic structures, as resources are distributed to the electorate in exchange for political support. Jobs, housing, food, clothes, furniture, and other benefits are distributed to the poor clients and constituents of party elites at the politicians' discretion. Clientelism is the anchor on which Jamaica's "participatory" democracy rests.

The myth is that there is a symbiosis between the formal institutions of democracy and democratic practice. The existence of political parties, frequent elections, and representative bodies does not guarantee representative government. Indeed, Jamaican democracy has been undermined because the formal democratic organizations have been transformed into an instrument of regimentation.[1] This regimentation (disguised as democratic participation) legitimizes the political system and hides its true nature. The conditions have thus been created for domination by those in control of the formal "democratic" organizations.

THE PARTY SYSTEM TODAY

When one talks about the party system in Jamaica, one is referring, first and foremost, to the alternation of the JLP and PNP in government. Despite the potential challenge that third and minor parties pose, the JLP and PNP's position has remained one of unchallenged dominance over the entire life of the party system. The inability of third parties to gain access to state resources, coupled with the substantial support of the JLP and PNP, has ensured their predominance for almost half a century. The Communist Workers Party of Jamaica (WPJ), led by University of the West Indies political scientist Trevor Munroe, exists as a third party that has little chance of forming the government or official opposition, but whose presence cannot be ignored. Other minor parties, such as the Jamaica Democratic party and the United party, existed for short periods and disappeared unnoticed.

The PNP is perceived to be the ideologically liberal party, closely resembling the British Labour party (after which it was fashioned) and the liberal wing of the Democratic party in the United States. The PNP also represents a greater degree of ideological deviance than the JLP, allowing socialists and Marxists some voice in the party. This is perhaps due to its expressed commitment in the 1930s and 1940s to Fabian socialism and the resurgence of that expression in the 1970s. The new PNP government, formed in 1989, has again expelled the radical left from its ranks (D. K. Duncan and Anthony Spaulding have disappeared), since it was almost torn apart in the 1970s by ideological factionalism. The "ideologically mature" PNP continues to publicly express its commitment to egalitarianism (and refrains, on most occasions, from the use of the term socialism) as well as its desire to work with the United States and its Western allies.

The JLP has always been more parochial in its outlook (its anti–West Indian Federation stance in the 1950s exemplifies this position). It is ideologically conservative, and advocates orthodox free enterprise and pro-Western ties. The JLP traditionally draws its support from the rural small farmers, trade unionists in the BITU, semiskilled and marginal urban workers, and the capitalist classes. The PNP has always attracted the bulk of the educated, affluent middle classes, and has received considerable support among urban workers of the lower middle classes as well as the capitalist classes and the professionals that serve them. Because of its advocacy of economic reforms based on government intervention, its identification with dispossessed elements of society, and its progressive anti-imperialist posture, the PNP has also attracted a small articulate Marxist left wing.

Both parties emerged with and continue to maintain multiple class constituencies. They organize and incorporate into their folds citizens of widely differing social class origins. Once recruited as party supporters, however, participation by the masses has been restricted mainly to electoral activity (see Jones and Mills 1976; Beckford and Witter 1980). From 1944, the interests of the incipient domestic capitalist elite have been integrated into party competition. Although there may be minor disagreements, the upper middle classes have supported and have largely benefited from the policies pursued during the 1944–1972 period. The business class represents the wealth of the nation, and has a tradition of giving even support to both parties, assisting with party finances particularly at election time. While in power, each government (PNP or JLP) has access to the management, technical, and business skills as well as the advice of the capitalist elite. The latter has been given considerable influence and leverage, but is still subordinated to the power of the state on whose sponsorship it depends.

The party system has multiple class support but is narrowly controlled by a closed elite at the top of the party hierarchy. Power is concentrated within a select group of members of parliament (MPs) and party office holders drawn disproportionately from the middle-class professions. The PNP has traditionally been less centralized than the JLP and has made strides to expand the channels of party participation. With the existence of organs such as the National Executive Council (a 250-member plenary body at the national level), the PNP is often perceived to be less oligarchic than the JLP. Regardless of what may be enshrined in party documents, when both parties are examined, the close connections between the business elite and the technocratic professionals cannot be ignored and the absence of the lower classes from positions of decisionmaking is revealed. Irrespective of the party in power, it should not be surprising to see a style of government that favors the technocratic middle class that controls the state.

The average Jamaican voter assumes that the JLP and PNP are adversaries. The parties oppose each other in parliamentary debates and at general elections, and are expected to govern the country differently when each has its turn in office. But reality tells otherwise. The politics of the postwar and early postindependence periods was characterized by a contest of personalities or party leaders, rather than ideological or programmatic differences.

The Structure of Party Organization:
The PNP as an Example

The formal organizational structures of the PNP and JLP differ; the JLP is by far more centralized, revolving around the party leadership to a greater extent than the PNP. To the extent that the structure and organization of the clientelistic system is identical for both parties, an in-depth case study of the PNP is presented here. Access to the PNP proved to be less difficult, as the JLP (the government in power at the time of writing) was reluctant to give access to significant party documents or participate in interviews with probing researchers.

Beckford and Witter (1980) presented a diagram of PNP class and formal organization structure, which is useful for this discussion (see Figure 3.1).

The formal structure of the PNP is laid down by the party's constitution. The party proceeds through three general levels—constituency, regional and national—and the structure at all levels follows a similar pattern with variations at specific levels. The general organizational pattern consists of the annual conference, the National Executive Council (NEC), six Regional Executive Councils (RECs), constituency committees, and group structures (PNP 1979).

The constituency groups are the basic units of the PNP at the grass-roots level, and they consist of a constituency secretary, a group leader as well as group members, and a staff tending to the affairs of constituency business. The group is the level of the ordinary citizen-member of the party—the party rank and file—and party officials at this level are expected to be unpaid brokers and party politicians if necessary. The group is responsible for collecting dues, maintaining party members, and narrating group activities to the constituency committees. Group meetings are expected to be held at least once a month.

The intermediate level consists of party organization in regions and constituency zones. Party functionaries who staff intermediate organizations are generally full-time party workers and, unlike those at the grass-roots level, are paid a regular salary. Their commitment is expected to be essentially that of the professional politician.

Nationally there are sixty constituencies, divided on the basis of what the constitution determines. Each constituency has electoral divisions for which parish councillors contest elections every four years in the local government elections. Each constituency has a constituency committee, composed of the constituency secretary, treasurer, and a general staff. The secretary coordinates the activities of the groups within his/her constituency and functions as an intermediary between local organs, regional committees, and the national levels of the party organization.

The fourteen parishes within the island are divided by the PNP into six regions. Six Regional Executive Councils exist for each of the following six regions:

Figure 3.1 PNP Class and Party Formal Organizational Structure

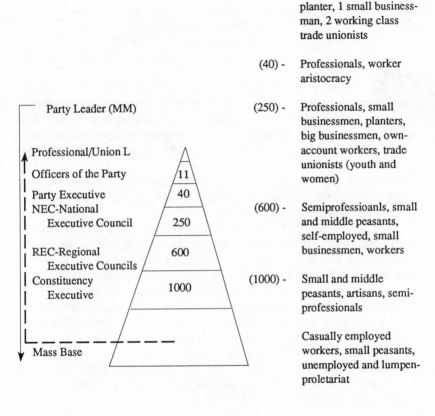

(11) - 7 Professionals, 1 big
planter, 1 small businessman, 2 working class
trade unionists

(40) - Professionals, worker
aristocracy

Party Leader (MM)

(250) - Professionals, small
businessmen, planters,
big businessmen, own-
account workers, trade
unionists (youth and
women)

Professional/Union L

Officers of the Party

Party Executive
NEC-National
    Executive Council

(600) - Semiprofessioanls, small
and middle peasants,
self-employed, small
businessmen, workers

REC-Regional
    Executive Councils

Constituency
    Executive

(1000) - Small and middle
peasants, artisans, semi-
professionals

Mass Base

Casually employed
workers, small peasants,
unemployed and lumpen-
proletariat

Party Groups
1976: 2,000 --► 1979 (early) 500; September 1979:1,200

Line of effective
decisionmaking—
articulation from top
via charismatic leader

Limited upward mobility
from and disarticulation within
the mass base

Source: Beckford and Witter (1980:100).

Region	Parishes
1	Trelawney and St. Ann
2	St. Mary and Portland
3	St. Thomas, Kingston, and St. Andrew
4	St. Catherine and Clarendon
5	Manchester and St. Elizabeth
6	Westmoreland, Hanover, and St. James

The membership of each REC consists of all NEC members, constituency secretaries, party parish councillors, constituency organizers, and representatives of affiliated organizations within the region. The duties of the REC are essentially to maintain stable constituency organizations within each region and to educate the public on party and government programs, policies, and thrusts.

At the national level, the PNP's organization structure consists of a National Executive Council, an Executive Committee, and an Annual Party Conference, which meets each September.

The NEC consists of at least 250 members at any one time. It includes (1) officers of the party—the president, the four vice-presidents, the general secretary, the two deputy general secretaries, and the treasurer; (2) the six members elected to the Executive Committee from the regional conferences; (3) sixty members elected by the regional conferences; (4) members of the parliamentary group; (5) persons coopted to the Executive Committee subject to the council's approval; (6) two members from each recognized constituency; (7) one member from each provisional constituency; and (8) representatives from affiliated organizations.

The NEC is the plenary body of the PNP at the national level, and it has the responsibility of determining general national policy for the party. Its duties include the following (PNP 1979:24):

(a) To ensure the establishment of Constituency Organizations, to maintain and develop the Organization of the Party generally, and to receive reports from Regional Executive Councils from time to time on the state of work in the constituencies.

(b) To protect and enforce the Constituency and Standing Orders of the Party and to take any action it deems necessary toward this end.

(c) To maintain contact and periodic conferences with the Parliamentary Groups on all matters and progress of the Party and to receive an Annual Report of the work of the Parliamentary Groups for submission to Annual Conferences.

(d) To maintain the funds of the Party.

(e) To present to Annual Conference a report covering the work of the Party for the year.

The Executive Committee is a much smaller body than the NEC. It is more of a de facto executive body for the party, expediting party decisions made by the Council. The Executive Committee consists of the officers of the party as defined above; the leader of the house when the party forms the government and the leader of the opposition when the party forms the opposition in parliament; three representatives of the parliamentary group; eleven members elected by the NEC from their number; one member elected by each REC from their number; and representatives from affiliated organizations appointed by the NEC under rule (4). The Executive Committee is presided over by the officers of the party and the party's leader. The party officials are selected by the annual conference. The party leader is the pinnacle of the party organizational structure and is seen as the one single representative of the entire party by the electorate.

In addition to these organs, the national structure of the party includes the PNP annual conference, held each September. The PNP constitution declares that "the Supreme Authority of the Party shall be the Annual Conference" (PNP 1979:22). The annual conference elects the party officials, deals with the annual reports, and discusses financial statements and matters of party policy. It also deals with constitutional amendments if they arise, resolves resolutions, and conducts any other business that the NEC may approve. All members of the NEC and members of the parish councils are entitled to attend as delegates.

All party members are expected to accept the program and policy of the party based on the principles of Democratic Socialism. They should also conform to the constitution and standing orders of the party. Membership of the party is open to all Jamaicans, and can be obtained through a group, an affiliated society, or individual application. The NEC ultimately decides on party membership.

In theory, authority in the PNP flows upward from the group levels of the party organization to the national level, and within any one level from the largest plenary organ to the smallest executive organ. In practice, the flow of party authority is from the party leader downward to the local level (Stone 1980). The party is tightly organized around the party leader and a parliamentary elite. This is the authority structure created with the inception of party politics in 1944, and succeeding generations of both the politicians and the electorate have been socialized into accepting it (Aggrey Brown 1979).

The PNP's mechanisms for nominating and selecting candidates are not stated in its constitution. The reason offered by party officials is that they are not governed by set rules. The party follows the British model, wherein candidates are selected by party organs in closed quarters away from the public. The system of primaries that exists in the United States, for instance, wherein candidates are presented to the electorate, who then vote for one, is absent in Jamaica as it is in Britain. What the party constitution does say about the selection of candidates is that,

> Recognized Constituencies of not less than 2 years standing,
> complying with the provisions of Rule 7 (I) (g) and which shall be
> active and functioning shall in Constituency conferences elect the
> Party's candidate for the Constituency for the House of Representatives.
> (PNP 1979:15)

In the selection of candidates for election to the parish council, the
constitution gives the constituency party machinery more influence (PNP
1979:15).

This absence of stated rules regarding the selection and nomination of
party candidates—an issue of major importance—may simply indicate PNP
conformity with the practice of the British Labour party, its role model.
Another plausible explanation is that the party wishes to exercise its own
unstated norms of candidate selection, which are consistent with maintaining
electoral victory among the Jamaican population.

A review of the occupational backgrounds of PNP members of
parliament and councillors in the period 1944–1983 reveals an enormous
diversity. This suggests that the unstated criterion may not have anything to
do with one's training in matters of public life, or even elite status for that
matter. A possible criterion, which cannot be ruled out in the Jamaican
environment, is that candidate selection is based primarily on the ability to
have electoral influence in a given geographical area by virtue of that person's
prestige, education, or roots in that area.

The PNP constitution has been under constant revision, as the
party appears to be attempting to clarify its ideology internally as well as to
the Jamaican electorate. Most observers and analysts of parties in Jamaica
agree that the PNP organization, in theory and in practice, is more
decentralized and democratic than that of the JLP (Bradley 1960; Robertson
1972; A. Kuper 1976; Stone 1980; Beckford and Witter 1980). However, the
PNP organization still has not been able to rise above the specific
socioeconomic conditions within the Jamaican environment, a situation
that forces it to adapt its "democratic" structure to Jamaican realities.
The party machinery is forced to adjust to the behavior patterns of the
population and the party politicians, which are dominated by patron-client
relationships.

The Structure of Power in Party Organization

The most striking inconsistency in norms associated with the PNP's
democratic and decentralized structure is that of the patron-client arrangements
within and among the different levels of the party machinery. Patron-client
relationships permeate all parts of the party organization (Stone 1980). The
main reason for this is that the PNP is based on a multiple class coalition,
with the dominant classes at the top of the party hierarchy always attempting

to pursue their own interests and actively trying to keep the mass base in check at the same time. The multiple-class coalition, with its inherent conflictual tendencies, is maintained by the party leader.

The model of the PNP apparatus presented by Beckford and Witter (1980) (Figure 3.1) takes the form of a pyramid. The base of the pyramid consists of thousands of members of the party who do not participate in decisionmaking and who therefore can be easily manipulated. The most important intermediate level, the constituency committee, is in charge of recruiting members and expanding the mass base. Its role is extremely important in the pyramidal power structure.

The party leadership controls the power apparatus in the party, and the councillors and MPs who are given the responsibility for representing hundreds of members are given an enormous amount of control over the mass base. They act as key intermediaries in the management of political interactions between the electorate at the base and the party hierarchy and vice versa.

A large constellation of interests is brought together within the party. Electoral results have shown that at the national level the PNP organizes a mass body of citizens of different social classes (Stone 1973, 1981a, 1983). Once recruited into the party, participation in decisionmaking at the national level is limited to only a small number of people. Only very few representatives of the lower classes are represented on the NEC and higher levels in the party. There is little scope for mass participation in important party decisions. The PNP shares these characteristics with the JLP.

The constituency level is the area in which the greatest number of party members participate in the political process of the party. Recruitment of members and political socialization occurs at this level. It is at this level that party leaders must locate their search for electoral support. The formal structure described above shows that at this level no major party decisions are made and party political brokers are most active. Councillors have a major role at the constituency level, a limited role at the REC level, and are practically powerless at the NEC level. They are much lower in rank than the parliamentary group, the professionals, and other party officials. Councillors are peons in the power structure of the party, and are generally looking to members in the NEC and Executive Committee to support their personal ambitions of becoming candidates for the House of Representatives or higher positions within the party hierarchy. Members of the NEC can easily establish clientelistic ties between members of the REC and constituency executive who are dependent on their support for higher level party positions. Councillors are low ranking in the party hierarchy, and their primary role is to interact with the rank-and-file members, as well as the grass roots outside of the party, to solidify party support. The political function of this local government representative will be elaborated upon (subsequently), but suffice to say at this point that the councillors play the role of brokers between the higher levels of the party hierarchy and the mass base in generating party support.

At the REC intermediate level, power brokerage appears to exist, but on a limited scale. The people in this group are powerful in relation to those below at the constituency level. Their influence would particularly be sought if they were members of the NEC. Those who sit on the REC have influence over decisions made at the regional level and would have a strong voice in the allocation of regional jobs and other forms of patronage. For the ambitious members of the REC, their position on this council could lead to more important posts, such as the NEC or the Executive Committee, where real power within the party lies.

The NEC looms large in the internal life of the party. It is a major national organ of the party. The NEC provides the party with a major manageable forum. It gets full media attention when it meets, and the public is generally made aware of the views of that council. The NEC is the forum for intra-elite bargaining within the party. The middle and professional classes are represented fully at this level and it is here that the debate over changes in programs and policies are usually more intense. The final decisions on the direction of the party usually come out of the discussions of the NEC. In theory, the annual conference is the supreme decisionmaking body of the PNP, and the NEC and the Executive Committee are subordinate. In practice, however, much bargaining goes on between the party leaders, the Executive Committee, and the NEC before the annual conference convenes. Factions are formed and alliances are made depending on what can be gained politically within or outside the party. Thus, elite bargaining is supported by intraparty mobilization.

The party Leader is at the apex of the power structure of the PNP. The office has never been the object of intense competition in the history of the party. Norman Manley was unchallenged as leader from the time he founded the party in 1938 until he retired from politics and as party leader in 1969. Michael Manley won the leadership of the party in 1969 after a challenge was made by Vivian Blake. Michael Manley has been leader of the party from 1969 until today. The ability of a party leader—JLP or PNP—to retain that post for long periods, lies in his ability to sustain the multiclass alliance in and outside of the party.

The party structure serves as the single channel through which resources from the state flow to party supporters. Accordingly, the party itself becomes the expression of this inequality in the society. It reinforces inequality by assigning political (particularistic) roles to the elected officials in their relationship with the masses of the electorate.

ELITE-MASS CLIENTELISM

The general assumption of scholars of local government in Jamaica is that its leaders have very little power and have few resources at their disposition (Mills 1970; Nunes 1974). The officials of the central government have more important legislative duties and political power, and the local government representatives are relegated to administrative matters, considered to be of minor importance.

Following the British pattern, the administration of local matters in Jamaica is the task of the parish council, the major local government unit. Local government is charged with the following duties: (1) providing environmental services—roads, sanitation, and water supplies; (2) providing fire brigade, housing, and public assistance; (3) providing services relating to community recreational activities; and (4) providing functions relating to public safety and order and a great number of miscellaneous services.

Local government politics in Jamaica consists of a continuous interaction among the citizens, the councillors, the civil servants, and the MP. As mediators between the central government and the citizens, the MP holds somewhat of a strategic position in this system. The concept of patron-clientelism has never been considered relevant to the study of the Jamaican local government system. Although Mills (1973,) and Jones (1974) do not explicitly use the concept of clientelism in their analyses, they make loose references to the existence of patronage in the local administrative institutions.

The concepts of patrons, clients, dyads, networks, reciprocity, and exchange are nowhere more relevant than at the local government level. The bastion of patronage has always been at this level in Jamaica. In the early period of party politics, Jamaica's patronage system found its fullest expression in municipal and parochial politics. Local government politics was the medium for dispensing party political patronage and largesse, as well as the training ground for budding politicians (Eaton 1975).

The Lower Classes as Clients of the MP and Councillor

The dyad constitutes the primary unit of clientelist analysis. The most important dyad at the local level is composed of the MP and his/her constituent, or the councillor and his/her constituent. (In what follows, use of the masculine is meant to encompass both genders.) The councillor is the key figure at the electoral parish council division level within the parliamentary constituency. Elected by the population within his division, the councillor is also expected to perform, among other things, a representative function. Most councillors, like MPs, end up being social workers, job coordinators, and jacks-of-all-trades for their constituents.

The councillor's status is inferior to that of the MP because the latter belongs to the central government, which controls the local government. The councillor, unlike the MP, does not control or manage resources directly. The ordinary people treat the councillor as a mediator. More than 75 percent of the councillors elected in the 1981 elections lived within their divisions, and so the constituents have had easy access to the homes of the councillors, to which they would bring their problems at all times (General Elections 1981:5–17). The councillor, like the MP, accepts the role given to him by the constituents and is generally ready to offer his counsel to those in need.

The Councillor has two characteristics that are common to all elected leaders in Jamaica. First, he must participate in patronage relationships with his constituents in order to be given support in his bid for reelection. His legitimacy, although sanctioned by election, is often based on some locally rooted tradition of his role as a patron. He is usually a well-known public figure. He is regarded by the people as one who can render services to the community and to individuals. Second, he is closer to their social class than the political directorate in the capital and, at the same time, he speaks their language and he is expected to make gains on their behalf. The councillor is considered by his electors as their personal representative. The people expect elected officials to assist them in finding jobs as well as in their relations with the bureaucracy. The role image that MPs or councillors have corresponds to the expectations of the electors. This is why the most important part of their time is spent in procuring favors for their electors.

The MP/councillor–constituent partnership is based on an exchange of favors: "I vote for you so you find me a job." Each is dependent on the other. When asked what he would do if a person confronted him and demanded that he find him or her a job, a PNP councillor from South Central St. Catherine had this response:

> One has to understand the total situation. Here is a person who may have been unemployed for a long time, and he has helped you to campaign, and so it is natural, only human nature, for that person to expect you to help him. I would have to get it across to him that I don't have an employment bureau out there. What we try to do is to place people. We scout around to see where the jobs are available, and placement is made by sending him with a letter to the manager when we find out that jobs exist. We have relief or crash programs that employ a lot of people. The people need that. It relieves tension.[2]

The MP and councillor are elected representatives of that constituency, and are the only links with the political directorate in the capital. The constituents want them to use their influence to get favors for the constituency. The relationship between the elected representatives and the constituents is asymmetrical but based on reciprocity. The constituents compete among themselves for favors from the politicians and the latter try to grant these favors so that they can be reelected. There is thus an interdependence between the politicians and their constituents.

The councillor spends a great deal of time on nonadministrative matters outside of the parish council. He is expected to be in the council whenever it meets, and if he has other duties, he is expected to carry them out. On the other hand, he is expected to play an active and supportive role in the lives of his constituents. As councillor, he is of lesser status in the party hierarchy than the MP and as such he is seen by his constituents as closer to them, although superior, and as their protector against the bureaucratic red tape of the civil servants.

The councillor and the MP are expected to go beyond the call of duty in helping their constituents. Inasmuch as they do this, they build for themselves a personal clientele of grass-roots people. Their main task is to get votes by developing clientelistic networks. As is commonly known in Jamaica, just how much a constituency gets is closely related to the extensiveness of networks that the MP and the councillor have built and the resources available to the patron through the ties he has developed with the center.

The MPs and the councillors are simply the people who bargain on behalf of the population. Their patronage function cannot be overemphasized. They are elected because they are patrons.

Grant Programs: Who Gets What, When, and How?

The most significant avenue for transfer of patronage resources is through the parish council grant programs. Grants are given out for holiday work, crash programs, work on construction sites, work on highways, and so on. The central government allots a certain amount of money to a particular activity, such as highway construction, for example, in a particular parish or constituency. The total funds are provided by the Ministry of Finance, which then collaborates with the Ministry of Local Government, and the latter allocates the funds to different parish councils throughout the island. The councillors then make recommendations to the civil servants within the parish council, so that the grant money can be distributed to the people.

There are two types of grants with which the study is concerned—a member of parliament grant, and a parish councillor's grant. Both types are allocated through the parish council. The central government gives the MP full jurisdiction over his grant, but generally tells the Councillor specifically that his grant is for jobs at Christmas time, or gully development, or some other restriction. The MP supervises his grant and distributes it over a larger area (his constituency) than the councillor, whose grant is restricted to the people within a smaller electoral division.

The average citizen's perception of the grant system is that it is based on "pulling strings." If the MP is in the upper echelons of the party and has the clout to get money, then he gets it. If he is a junior minister with little or no electoral or political clout, he may have difficulties getting money for the development of his constituency, especially if his constituency is not considered an electorally strategic one. An upper-class Kingston businessman's explanation of the system of grant allocation reflects a generalized opinion within the Jamaican society:

> Each MP has a constituency and he has the power to get the most money into that constituency, and if he has his finger in the right place, and he knows the right man, he can pull a string and do something for his constituency. The money is given out to the people from the constituency area. You may find that if a man is strong in his constituency, whether he is a JLP or PNP, he will be returned because of what he has done for the area. Good examples are Cecil Charlton in Mandeville, Seaga in Tivoli, and Tony Spaulding in Trench Town. They have the clout . . . that's how money is given out.[3]

A long-time PNP supporter and Spanish Town businessman makes a similar argument about the clout of the MP in getting funds for his constituency:

> It is common knowledge all over Jamaica that the Minister of Finance, who is also the Prime Minister, spends money in Tivoli that is half of what is spent in the rest of the island put together. The people in Tivoli are not lacking anything. Shortages never affect them. You can see for yourself, miss, the Ministry of Finance should have a record of the various money spent on all the different constituencies. You can see for yourself why some MPs are always returned even in a period of a massive swing. I give you an example. Recently they had these Pen Relays in the secondary schools, and their athletes were sent abroad to the games, and all the members of the Tivoli High School team went first class. They had first class hotel, first class accommodation, and the pocket money that they had was so much in comparison to the other schools. There was a certain young lady from St. Thomas who was supposed to be in a constituency of one of the Parliamentary Secretaries, and it is alleged that her pocket money for the two and a half days was over US$200.00 and yet you had other athletes from other schools who went up in economy class and had to share hotel rooms, three to six in a room, just to meet the expenses because they did not get that type of allocation from the Ministry and the Bank of Jamaica to afford to live reasonably. This disparity shows the difference between the Tivolian people, the lady from St. Thomas and the others. It is plain to be seen.[4]

The MP's clout has become almost supreme in getting assistance for the poor people. The Spanish Town businessman states succinctly:

> It is only the MP's recommendation that has weight. If the MP does not give the people what they want they vote him out. There is a need for immunity from the people. This "I vote for you so you must find me a

job" must stop. People believe that the MP is there for their individual needs. They shift from party to party when the MP does not do what they want. I have always said, and continue to believe, that legislation should be made that states that it will be unlawful for an MP to recommend a job for a person. But they haven't given it any attention.[5]

It is not surprising that this sort of suggestion would not be given any attention because clientelist hiring and awarding of money on the basis of party affiliation seems to have been legitimated in Jamaican political culture. Several councillors pointed out to the author that "it is a fact that we will have to live with in Jamaica." The issue was once raised on a popular Jamaican radio talk show, when the caller pointed out the obvious unfairness involved when people who brought letters from MPs got jobs ahead of himself and others who were qualified, but were not even interviewed. I was not surprised that the host of the show treated the matter very lightly, stating that jobs were scarce and those with contracts and connections got results. The host then quickly changed the subject and proceeded to ask the caller about his Barbadian origins. The main issue was simply dismissed lightly, as this was the accepted norm in Jamaican society.[6]

The allocation of material rewards by party affiliation is very interesting at the parish council level. It is unfortunate that to date little published research is available on this interesting subject. It is extremely important because it is at the parish council level, with its grant and financial aid programs, that the stability of the two-party system is anchored. The resources are carefully distributed at this level to ensure continued support of party politicians. The lower classes' fear of poverty is manipulated here by the party politicians. They are given financial resources in exchange for their political support.

Resource allocation is based on an intricate informal word-of-mouth system, which can be represented in the following way: First, the councillors tell party activists at the grass-roots level that some jobs are available. Second, party activists are given a list with a specific number of slots indicating how many jobs are available. Third, they come up with a list of party people who need jobs. Fourth, the councillors then recommend those people to the parish council civil servants for the available jobs. Fifth, the parish council civil servants then give out the jobs based on the councillors' "recommendations," which have very little to do with qualifications. In this way it becomes almost impossible to be put on the job list if you are not a party supporter. This in-house system is very painful to the hundreds of people who hang around the parish council doors hoping for a job. They are then forced to become clients of party elites in exchange for resources necessary for their livelihood.

There appears to be an implicit understanding on the part of the people that although the councillors do hand out the money, the amount is determined at a higher level in the central government. It follows then that the main focus for them would be on getting their party elected to the central government, as that is where the real power lies. Local government elections are thus not characterized by the intense participation and violence that characterize party politics at the national level.

Because of the clientelistic character of the party system, those with the greatest material needs and deprivations become most involved in rank-and-file party activism. Their only resource is bringing in the vote, and violence. Interparty hostility and violence emerged in the early period of party politics and was derived from the rage and frustration of the most deprived strata in the society as they fought among themselves for spoils from the party system (Stone 1980). The violence was often orchestrated by the political elites in the quest for political power. It is common knowledge in Jamaica that certain "lumpen" elements (youth gangs) have developed a tradition of mercenary relationships to organized party politics. The politicians of both the JLP and PNP and the Kingston and Spanish Town youth gangs have entered into symbiotic relationships despite public condemnation of violence and accusations against each other. The lumpen proletariat continues to be used to provide defense and protection for contending political groups in exchange for certain patronage benefits. The effect is to divide the lumpen into warring factions of antagonists who contend for control over the territory.

Grass-Roots Activists:
Patrons of the Lower Classes, Clients of the Political Elite

Grass-roots party activists are a very important link between the politicians and the electorate. Stone's data show that party activists are concentrated in the lowest strata of the society. The unemployed, the small farmers, and the lower working class together comprise 81.9 percent of rank-and-file party activists (Stone 1980:100). The literature on parties in parliamentary democracies provides evidence that party activists tend to have a high socioeconomic status, business or professional orientations, and a background of some political ability (Marvick and Nixon 1961; Althoff and Patterson 1966). Jamaican parties do not fit this pattern. The evidence shows that activists are generally found among the less educated and the lower middle classes in both the JLP and the PNP (Stone 1980).

The broker or party activist at the grass-roots level is totally dependent on the party system for his existence. Unlike the justice of the peace, the schoolteacher, and other middle-class brokers, he is a dependent client of the politician, and a patron for the lower-class electorate. The grass-roots activist has many tasks. He funnels all the local problems to the councillor or the MP, whether or not they can solve them. He generally maintains a closer relationship with the councillor, as the MP is less accessible. The activist usually knows the constituency very well, and advises both the MP and the councillor on election strategy. He knows which areas will deliver the votes on election day, and delivers the goods and services to the constituents when the day for "pay off" comes. He has a direct relationship with the people. He is the one who gets the votes for both parties at the local level, on the basis of the goods and services that he delivers to them. Grass-roots activists are also very important before election time. They will alert the candidates to potential rivals and inform them of the latters' plans and maneuvers. Being a politician's client gives these lower-class activists prestige in the eyes of the population. It means that they have connections with politicians and are in a position to help them.

Hurricane Gilbert and the Politics of the Distribution of Aid

In September 1988, Jamaica was devastated by Hurricane Gilbert. The estimated damages were said to be within the range of J$1 billion. There was damage to crops, livestock, poultry, schools, and houses, as well as loss of lives throughout the fourteen parishes. Hundreds of thousands of poor people lost their homes with all of their contents. A large percentage of them had neither land on which to reconstruct their homes nor financial resources with which to start rebuilding their lives.

Humanitarian aid poured into the island from the U.S. and Canadian governments, from Jamaicans living abroad, as well as from the Red Cross and other major aid agencies. As with any sort of resource distribution in Jamaica, aid for the victims of Hurricane Gilbert became entangled in political clientelism and gangsterism. The distribution of building stamps (to rebuild homes) and food and agricultural stamps became a political issue, as supporters of the opposition party often complained that they were omitted when allocations were made in their areas (see the *Jamaica Sunday Gleaner*, February 12, 1989). The JLP government had called in the Jamaica Defense Force (JDF) to carry out surveys across the island to determine whether the claims of the victims were indeed genuine.

There was a change in government on February 9, 1989, before hurricane aid distribution was completed. The former JLP government suspended the issuing of hurricane relief stamps during the general election campaign (late January—early February), as it felt that "the distributions would not have been compatible with the conduct of an election campaign." Donald Hannan of the Ministry of Housing, in a telephone interview with the *Jamaica Sunday Gleaner*, reported that there were problems getting newly built houses on the lands in areas such as Trench Town, Collie Smith Drive, and Jacques Road. Workers were said to be harassed by residents of these areas during the election period (*Jamaica Sunday Gleaner*, February 26, 1989, p. 2A).

Hurricane aid distribution was apparently used to manipulate the electorate. The JLP had been trailing the PNP in the polls since 1982, but regained the lead for a brief period after the 1983 U.S invasion of Grenada.

After the elections of December 1983 (in which the PNP did not participate), the JLP continued to slip in the polls. Between September 1984 and September 1988, the PNP maintained a steady lead of 10 percentage points over the JLP. After the hurricane and the government was able to obtain international aid, the JLP regained about 5 percent of the support it had lost over the past years (see Stone 1989:41).

Many PNP supporters expected the government to reward them by allocating relief to them before others. At the time of writing, thousands of people were still squatting in Jamaica's major sporting facility, the National Stadium, as well as in tents close to the banks of the Yallahs River in St. Thomas. The National Stadium is in a PNP constituency, and the stadium (sports) is under one of the portfolios of PNP Vice-President Portia Simpson. St. Thomas has been a traditional JLP stronghold. The victims in both areas require immediate attention, but a rumor has already begun that MP Portia Simpson's priority is to build homes for hurricane victims in the stadium rather than for those in Fletcher's land or St. Thomas (*Weekend Star*, February 10, 1989, p. 19).

Questions have been raised in the Jamaican media concerning the people's claims that they have no choice but to remain in the relief centers until help comes from somewhere. Some Jamaican observers believe that the people have grown too complacent, and are merely displaying the typical "dependency syndrome" of so many Jamaicans. Members of the church, the government, and private individuals expressed the opinion that some people in shelters could find a place to live if they really wanted to, but preferred to sit back and wait for the government to provide free houses for them (*Jamaica Sunday Gleaner*, February 26, 1989, p. 11C). A poor woman who has been living in a tent in the National Stadium candidly expressed her feelings: "We know they don't owe me any obligation, but we are pleading with people to have some compassion and feeling for us" (*Jamaica Sunday Gleaner*, February 26, 1989, p. 11C). Many of the victims were higglers who lost their goods in the hurricane, and some were domestic helpers who lost their jobs because their employers could not afford to keep them. A few owned the houses they lost, but the land did not belong to them. It seems hardly likely that the poor would willingly stay in these degrading conditions, without adequate toilet facilities, privacy, and electricity, just for the sake of receiving a few dollars. As one of the women said in tears, "Oh God, if you think we could find somewhere to go you think we could suffer here on this cold concrete so?" (*Jamaica Sunday Gleaner*, February 26, 1989, p. 11C).

Hurricane Gilbert's devastation of Jamaica only exacerbated existing problems of resource scarcity. It is inevitable, given the political structure of clientelism that exists, that aid distribution would become incorporated into the patronage system, with the supporters of the party in control of the state gaining access and having priority over supporters of the opposition.

Civil Servants and Patronage Distribution:
Bureaucratic Control Over the Lower Classes

For the poor in general, a very important linkage mechanism between them and the political party is the role of bureaucratic intermediation performed by the party politicians and civil servants working in the state bureaucracy. The MP, or the councillor, upon his constituent's request, intervenes in bureaucratic procedures for his own political ends. The possibility of such intervention can be explained by the slow inefficient nature of the bureaucracy caused by the generalized resource scarcity in the society. In contrast to Weber's (1964) rational, impartial model of bureaucratic conduct, all relationships are highly personalized and politicized, even those related to the most trivial administrative procedure (Presthus 1961; Diamant 1962; Nunes 1976a). The personalization of bureaucratic functions is also related to the fact that the bureaucracy itself has become a basis of patronage in the form of jobs. Thus bureaucratic offices, more often than not, have less to do with qualifications and performance and more with patronage rewards. State-controlling elites can employ patronage (in the form of jobs) to secure the support of members of this group, who in turn use the state as an instrument of accumulation.

For the poor, the necessities of day-to-day life—documents required for admission to school or a hospital, for a passport, for application for a job, and so on—are not easily achieved. It is often only by the personal intervention of an influential intermediary that a poor person can obtain any immediate result. The individual often finds himself confronted with an impersonal, insensitive bureaucracy that treats the poor with contempt. The bureaucracy is manned mainly by people belonging to the middle classes, who traditionally look down on the poorer classes, disadvantaged by their illiteracy. Jobs in the state bureaucracies are the predominant form of middle-class patronage in the society. Access to middle-class jobs in the state sector constitutes a large part of the patronage largesse of the state-controlling elite. This elite directs civil servants to distribute state resources in a manner that satisfies their patronage obligations.

When the civil servant is approached with a letter of recommendation from an MP or councillor, outsiders have asked why does he not ignore the politician's request? Why should preference be given to a particular client of a politician whose case may not be at the top of the priority list? It is possible that the civil servant perceives himself to be dependent on the politician's help for appointments and promotions and possible employment for family members. As a result, the civil servant's fate is dependent on loyalty or at least cooperation with the MP regardless of which party is in power.

The civil servants who are in charge of appointments for clerks, road workers, and manual laborers are usually prepared to respond to a politician's request. The politician is generally very direct and overt in recommendation of particular clients. The civil servant generally interviews the applicants and makes his own choices based on the "recommendation" of the politician. It is considered a small favor to grant the politician's request, as later on his help may be needed to pull strings for a friend or family member, or for promotion. In sum, the civil servant distributes resources and dispenses favors to the lower classes to satisfy the patronage obligations of the political elite, in exchange for a job, a promotion, or preferential treatment for members of his family.

Justices of the Peace, Teachers, Influential Businessmen, Prestigious Citizens (Independent Brokers)

Justices of the peace (JPs), teachers, business owners, clergymen, doctors, and citizens, who are respected by the community, function oftentimes as brokers for the parties. They are respected opinion leaders. They are generally well informed about local, national, and international politics, and can usually offer the politician valuable advice on how to win his seat. These brokers generally know as much, or even more, about the personal lives of the constituents, than the politicians. The poor have a tendency to bring their problems to these respected citizens, and while confiding in them often become dependent on them to find solutions to their problems.

These brokers are not dependent on the party machine for material survival. They are financially independent, but usually have much to gain from the party system. In return for being party brokers, they get status in the community for interceding on behalf of constituents. They get appointed to positions of power, influence, or prestige. In some cases they also get preferential access to state resources such as contracts. This circle of brokers is very important for the external support network of the political leaders. They are like the "ears" of the community, and the opinion leaders as well, so they watch the action of the people and constantly inform the political leaders of their change in attitudes or their maneuvers. The independent brokers are an intermediate link in the chain that leads from the politician to the lower classes.

Conclusion

Modern political loyalties evolved along party lines in Jamaica rather than on the basis of race, ethnicity, or class. However, the basis of this partisan allegiance lay in the access that the parties provided to the material resources of the society. The patronage system that evolved following the Colonial Development and Welfare Acts and the inflow of North American capital played a major role in the partisan conflict that characterized the JLP and PNP during the 1944–1962 period. A party-centered system of patronage acted to exclude from the benefits of the state those who were not party supporters. A combination of patronage and favorable policies and programs ensured middle- and upper-class support. Clientelist mobilization, however, became the basis of lower-class support for the state-controlling middle class.

NOTES

Much of the data in this chapter has appeared in Edie (1989). This analysis is based in part upon seven months of field research in Jamaica: July–August 1982, June–December 1983, and November–December 1986. During that time sixty interviews were conducted with councillors, MPs trade union activists, and well-known members of the private sector elite. About 100 in-depth interviews with party activists and ordinary Jamaican citizens were carried out. The interviews were not conducted in a systematic fashion. They are intended to show the validity of certain clientelist issues that the author wishes to highlight.

1. Percy Hintzen (1990) discusses democratic practice in the West Indies in terms of a system of regimentation based on bureaucratic control of scarce resources as well as coercion. Lower-class dependence upon resources controlled by middle-class political leaders and bureaucrats guarantees support by members of the lower class for these politicians. In the post-1973 period, coercion became a critical element in the state's efforts to ensure political order in many English-speaking nations of the West Indies. See Young and Phillips (1986).

2. Personal interview with PNP councillor, July 15, 1983.

3. Personal interview, July 10, 1983.

4. Personal interview, July 11, 1983.

5. Personal interview, July 11, 1983.

6. JBC Radio talk show, *Public Eye*, July 21, 1983, hosted by Aggrey Brown of the University of the West Indies.

4

Middle Class Domination, External Dependency, and Internal Clientelism, 1962-1972

This chapter analyzes the linkages between the interests of international actors and the noncapitalist state-controlling middle class. The Colonial Development and Welfare Act of 1940 legitimized both statist expansion for welfare purposes and lower-class mobilization into labor and party organizations. State expansion gave the middle class tremendous access to the resources needed to finance its clientelistic structure of power maintenance (see Chapter 2). That structure has been largely maintained by extracting resources from international capitalist actors. The latter includes international business, international organizations, international financial agencies, foreign governments, and international sectors within the local economy.

The terms and conditions of the relationship between these international actors and the middle class were determined by the latter's willingness to maintain the existing structures of international dependency. Both JLP and PNP governments of the 1950–1972 period gave foreign capital the most favorable economic conditions possible to pursue its interests (see Chapter 2). Additionally, international actors were protected from the sociopolitical crises of potential private-sector mobilization and lower-class rebellions. The state mediated class conflicts in the domestic economy to ensure continued middle-class access to external resources. External resources were used to constrict and restrict the power of the domestic capitalist class and simultaneously demobilized the lower class through clientelism, intimidation, and violence. The interests of the middle class, the domestic capitalist class, and international capitalist actors converged in the 1962-1972 postindependence Jamaican political economy. As all these interests were mediated by the state, it became very powerful relative to other domestic actors and had room to maneuver in its relationship with international actors.[1]

THE STATE AND TRANSNATIONALS:
THE BAUXITE INDUSTRY

Foreign ownership of business in the postindependence period in developing nations has become an issue of growing sensitivity. In many instances, foreign companies were allowed to purchase controlling interests in key industries without government review and without giving domestic purchasers some type of preference. Insofar as acquisitions were concerned, the local private sector was at an economic disadvantage vis-à-vis their foreign competitors in the areas of tax treatment, technology, skilled personnel, and capital resources. The dominant view within Jamaica was that foreign direct investment was desirable. Foreign control, on the scale on which it took place during the 1950–1967 period, was inimical to the national interest as it involved selling permanent assets and created a foreign claim on the Jamaican economy. Backed by the emerging capitalist classes, the political leaders made a decision to allow unlimited foreign control of strategic domestic industries. This decision appeared to have been based on Jamaica's overdependence on foreign capital and the political leaders' fear of frightening that capital away.

Perhaps the most significant economic event in the postwar period was the arrival of North American–based TNCs in the bauxite, tourist, and manufacturing industries. Demand for aluminum had been stimulated by the Korean War and the space exploration program. Companies participating included Aluminum Company of America (ALCOA), Aluminium Company of Canada (ALCAN), Kaiser, and Reynolds. Massive inflows of capital also led to the establishment of branch-plant manufacturing. Many TNCs set up manufacturing subsidiaries in Jamaica, often in joint ventures with the state or the local private sector. Familiar names such as Firestone, Exxon, Colgate Palmolive, and Del Monte set up alongside existing British companies, such as Bata Shoes, which chose to remain. Sheraton, Hilton, among others, scrambled for control of the hotel industry. First National City Bank, First Chicago, and Citizen's Bank arrived in the same period to join Barclays, Bank of Nova Scotia, and Royal Bank of Canada—British and Canadian banks that had been around for a long time.

Transnational corporate capital was invited into the Caribbean because the needs of the state-controllers and the foreign investors coincided. The former was committed to capitalist accumulation and the latter was interested in accumulation in the form of access to the resources of the state. The middle class's desire to expand the state sector and the TNC's interests in gaining cheap labor and making huge profits coincided to create the basis for alliance.

Underlying these seemingly apparent common interests are two contradictory interests. First, the TNC bourgeoisie wanted to bring its technology, skills, and expertise to Jamaica in exchange for cheap labor and an increase in its global profits. Second, the Jamaican middle-class rulers desired state resources to satisfy developmental functions and to employ state control of the economy to maintain dominance over other social classes. On the surface, these two goals do not appear contradictory. The contradiction lies in the structure of the exchange relationship between the TNCs and the political directorate whereby TNCs not only expropriate surpluses created in developing nations, but also eliminate potential bases for local capital accumulation through the international political and economic structures they monopolize and control (Girvan 1978). The global interests of the TNCs were often in conflict with the political interests of the state in developing nations.[2] To head off conflict, the Jamaican political elite accepted the terms dictated by the bauxite TNCs, as it feared that retaliation could lead to withdrawal of investments.

The Politics of Accommodation

Capital investments made by the four largest North American bauxite companies—Kaiser, Reynolds, ALCAN, and ALCOA—have been the largest single source of investment and capital flow into the postwar economy. This import of capital was accompanied by the purchasing of more than 600,000 acres of Jamaican farmland to carry out bauxite mining. The aluminum industry quickly grew to one of the wealthiest international industries and became the largest export industry in Jamaica, accounting for 47 percent of its exports in 1968 (Girvan 1971a; Jefferson 1972) and one-tenth of its GDP. Bauxite TNCs controlled 100 percent of Jamaican bauxite alumina production and were the largest single source of taxes paid to the Jamaican government.

The U.S. government made a decision after World War II that national reserves of strategic minerals should be stockpiled. With the decision to depend on imported bauxite, U.S. aluminum companies turned their attention to Jamaica. The island soon became a key link in the companies' strategy to internationalize their operations, and became the major supplier of bauxite to North America.

Labor was cheap and abundant in Jamaica. In 1953, the unskilled bauxite worker earned an average of about 13 pounds a week, just slightly more than the sugar cane cutter working full-time during the harvest (Manley 1975:115). Because there was relatively little skilled labor in Jamaica, the companies could control the training and set wage scales for skilled workers. But worker militancy soon forced the companies to raise wages well above the Jamaican average. The companies still had an economic advantage, however, as even with the wage increases they were paying the bauxite workers in Canada and the United States significantly more than their Jamaican counterparts. At that time there was not a single union specifically for Jamaican bauxite workers.

During the period between World War II and 1972, the aluminum companies dominated the bargaining situation in Jamaica (Huggins 1965). The strength of the companies was fortified by the existence of many partnerships among the leading enterprises in the extraction of bauxite and the production of alumina. Agreements linking Kaiser with Reynolds, Pechiney with Kaiser, Alusuisse with Pechiney, and other such pairing characterized the structure of the aluminum industry.

From the point of view of the bauxite TNCs, Jamaica gained technological and managerial skills, much needed capital, government revenues, and foreign exchange. The problem was that the bauxite industry was capital intensive, which meant high labor productivity and hence a high demand for skilled personnel. The bauxite industry employed approximately 1 percent of the Jamaican labor force in 1976—approximately 6,000 workers out of a total employed labor force of 883,600 (Department of Statistics 1976:15). At the level of the highly skilled occupations, the industry imported its own expatriate staff. Thus it displaced more agricultural labor than it employed skilled labor. Bauxite production in Jamaica was profitable to the companies because the costs of extracting the ore was extremely low relative to the price received for the final product.

Revenues accrued to the government were a "drop in the bucket" in comparison to the billions of dollars of profits returned from the Jamaican subsidiaries. In 1968, the Jamaican government received 18 percent of its tax revenues from the bauxite industry. In the same year, taxation was based on a price of J$7.50 per ton, whereas the U.S. companies reported a value of US$15.00 per ton (J$1 = US$1.10) to U.S. customs authorities (*Jamaica Bauxite Institute Digest* 1, 3 (1976):16). The companies consistently undervalued the price of Jamaican ore, which lowered their tax payments to the government. The government could have developed fiscal policies to combat this problem, but it opted to acquiesce to TNC demands, as it feared retaliation that would cripple an economy experiencing incipient industrialization.

National policy during the period was geared toward satisfying the claims of the TNCs while hoping to secure enough revenues for the state-controlling elite to exercise control and maintain its dominance over other social groups. The state opted for a strategy of cooperation and conciliation. Its acquiescence was based on its perception that any negative action on its part might lead to a severe economic crisis because Jamaica had now become dependent on bauxite exports.

Jamaica's bauxite was important to North America only in the short run, as alternate sources could be found (although initially inconvenient and expensive) in Brazil, Guinea, and Australia. Jamaica's ore was not as unique as the calcined ore found in Guyana, nor was Jamaica as central to the global operations of the TNCs as was Guyanese bauxite to ALCAN. The political climate within Jamaica was one focused on political sovereignty and independence from Britain. Economic nationalism was not yet a salient issue in local politics. Furthermore, because the economy was experiencing unprecedented growth, the middle classes were expanding and the government appeared to have sufficient revenues for clientelist patronage to the poor. The government was not yet pushed to seek additional revenues to accommodate the disenchanted and disaffected classes. The state then had the option to pursue a policy of conciliation and collaboration with the TNCs.

In an alliance with the emerging local capitalist classes, successive PNP and JLP governments passed legislation (e.g., the Bauxite and Aluminium Industries Encouragement Law) granting incentives to foreign investors as well as to local private capital. Governmental power was used to stimulate industrial growth with the formation of state agencies such as the Jamaica Industrial Development Corporation (JIDC), whereby foreign investors, the local private sector, and the state were all actively involved in economic policymaking.

Bauxite industry directors were placed on various advisory boards and government committees, as the political directorate had very little knowledge of the industry. The politicians relied exclusively on the information given to them by the officials of the international aluminum industry, although there were competing information sources available to them among economists at the University of the West Indies. This close relationship between the political leaders of both JLP and PNP governments and the bauxite companies ensured the latter's dominance in matters of bauxite policy during the 1950–1972 period.

If a developing nation produces a strategic proportion of a commodity, in whose absence from the international community crisis is sure to ensue, then that nation is in a position to exercise leverage vis-à-vis powerful TNCs. In 1971, the Guyanese Peoples National Congress was able to dictate the terms of the bauxite TNCs' involvement in its economy, and for at least five years thereafter was able to use the productive assets from bauxite to the benefit of its economy. This was successfully done because at the time Guyana produced 80 percent of the world's calcined bauxite, and it had the management and organizational resources required to run its nationalized operations (Hintzen 1989). Jamaica was not in a position to do as Guyana. Although the state in developing nations can make the ultimate decisions on what the conditions will be for the operations of TNCs in its economies, it remains vulnerable to certain international realities, which often force it to comply with the ultimate wishes of the TNCs.

Jamaica's bauxite policy since 1974 has shown important differences from the period of the late 1950s to 1974, when the industry was unambiguously set up to pursue policies favorable to the interests of the North American companies. By contrast, in the post-1974 period, when the changing interests of the middle-class–led PNP government and the companies diverged, faced with the issue of its own survival, the government was forced to attempt to make its wishes prevail. However, as the end product clearly shows, the transnationals' control over the international aluminum industry limited the PNP government's ability to bargain effectively (this will be discussed at length in Chapter 5).

United States Interests in the
Post-Independence Jamaican Political Economy

During the 1944–1962 period of decolonization, both JLP and PNP governments remained firmly committed to the ideas of representative government and free-enterprise capitalism. Before granting Jamaica its independence in 1962, the British introduced funds from the Colonial Development and Welfare Act to revitalize the local economy. These funds later facilitated the transition to independence. This active intervention by the colonial power ensured that the political elites who gained power were those sympathetic to Western interests.

Bustamante and Manley, socialized into British values, readily accepted the ideas of liberal democracy and capitalism. As there was every chance that one of them would continue as leader of the postcolonial state, there was not much concern on the part of the British that those interests would be jeopardized. Jamaica opted to stay in the British Commonwealth, with the Queen of England serving as its titular head of state. Its legal and political/administrative institutions remain tied to the British judicial and the Westminster/Whitehall systems.

The ideology of the JLP government was consistent with both British and U.S. interests. At the time there was opposition to the Jagan government of British Guiana, and Britain and the United States were busy preparing for its ouster. Apart from this, all the governments of the West Indies were warmly received. Although intimate relations were not developed between JLP leaders and U.S. presidents Kennedy, Johnson, and Nixon, Bustamante was a reliable anti-Communist, often denouncing Castro's Cuba and Marxism's atheism (Eaton 1975). After the victory of Castro's forces in 1959, the United States was determined not to have "another Cuba." With a two-party tradition firmly established for eighteen years in Jamaica and the nonexistence of any meaningful third-party threat (Communist or otherwise), the United States expressed little concern.

Jamaica, like the other English-speaking Caribbean nations, was viewed simply as a part of the Latin American/Caribbean region that was within the U.S. sphere of influence. The United States took its predominance for granted, and policy toward the region was drawn up on an ad hoc basis in response to specific crises within its cold war framework. Britain still regarded Jamaica and its other former colonies although politically independent, as its "own." The ex-colonies themselves opted to remain in the Commonwealth rather than seek the benefits that could possibly have accrued from political association with the United States.

For the Jamaican leaders, the relationship with the United States was strictly economic. Bustamante and Manley understood that Britain was declining as a hegemonic power and was not in a position to take care of the needs of its ex-colonies. The economic shift away from Britain toward the United States was based on self-interest. The United States had emerged as the dominant force in the post-1945 global economy, and both Bustamante and Manley had little hesitation in aligning with a superpower. They felt that, as a small nation emerging from colonialism, Jamaica could reap benefits from a relationship with the United States, particularly if it catered to the latter's anti-Communist interests. Jamaica had not yet developed an international role of its own, and it was merely an object of external pressures. Both Bustamante and Manley disregarded the nonaligned movement in the Third World, opting instead for a pro-Western alliance. In the eyes of the United States, the Caribbean had a subservient place in its hemispheric system. The United States paid relatively little attention to the region, particularly the English-speaking nations, which appeared to be relatively secure and politically stable.

The U.S. government has had a conscious policy of trying to keep the Caribbean within the Western capitalist bloc and within its sphere of influence. Between 1962 and 1972, Jamaican leaders maintained friendly relations with U.S. presidents and members of Congress, and consistently held a pro-Western foreign policy, voting in support of the U.S. position in international forums. JLP leaders Alexander Bustamante and Hugh Shearer both believed that friendly relations with the United States would guarantee the much-needed aid and investments critical for domestic development efforts. The leverage that the United States was able to gain through its financial aid package gave it the means to influence Jamaica's foreign policy with Cuba and other Communist nations. In accordance with U.S. wishes, Jamaican leaders of the period refrained from establishing diplomatic relations with Cuba until Michael Manley came to power in 1972.

ECONOMIC RESOURCE ALLOCATIONS: POLITICAL AND SOCIAL DETERMINANTS

Satisfying Private Sector Interests

In contrast to dominant theories in Jamaican political economy, which posit the domination of politics and economic life by business interests (foreign, local, or a combination thereof; Munroe 1972; Beckford and Witter 1980; Davies 1986), I argue instead that the private sector is influential with regard to the policies projected by the state but is subordinated to the latter in a patron-client relationship. The causes of this clientelistic relationship lie in three interrelated factors: (1) the weakness of the capitalist class in the postwar period; (2) the "industrialization by invitation" program of postwar development, which perpetuated the subordination of local class forces to the needs of foreign capital and the state controllers; and (3) the expanding role of the state in the postwar economy.

The capitalist class that emerged in this period was a coalescence of remnants of the white planter classes of the colonial period and an urban bourgeoisie consisting of Jewish, Syrian, Lebanese, European, and Chinese entrepreneurs. Industrial developments led to the emergence of entrepreneurial ethnics endowed with strategic resources in the manufacturing, banking, retail, import, export, construction, real estate, and agricultural sectors. This class is conspicuous in its concentration in minority ethnic groups. Blacks are noticeably absent. The fact that twenty-one families account for more than half of all corporate directorships and 70 percent of all corporate chairmen serves to convince most observers of their overriding presence (Reid 1977:24). Fifteen of these families, of Jewish and Arab origin, represent an important segment of effective capitalist-class leadership among the rich in Jamaica. (These are the families of Matalon, Ashenheim, Hendrickson, Facey, Mahfood, Issa, Hart, Henriques, Desnoes, Geddes, deLisser, Clark, Rousseau, Stewart, and Kennedy.)

This group of family interests were able to take advantage of the opportunities offered by state expansion and the "industrialization by invitation" program. A significant handicap at the time of its emergence was that it was a nonblack capitalist class without cultural links to the black majority classes. The capitalist class did not attempt any relations with the black population outside of the marketplace. Throughout the postwar period up until 1976, it appears to have been content with its image as an apolitical class. Its evolution was dependent on its relationship to the state. In this sense, it can be accurately described as a "dependent" class. It was dependent on the state for public subsidies and loans for creating a climate in which private enterprise could prosper. Although the capitalist class was ultimately weaker than the state, because of its monopoly in certain key sectors of the economy it was able to influence public policies in its own favor, as it posed a significant threat to governments who feared that private-sector retaliation could lead to a withdrawal of capital and destablization of the political system. Thus, there was a convergence of interests between the state and the local capitalist class, which was reflected in the substantial overlap of public policies and private business interests.

A truly private sector did not exist in the post-independence 1962–1972 period in Jamaica. It lacked the requisite resources for autonomous capitalist development. It did not have sufficient capital to invest without a maximum guarantee against losses, and has always preferred to invest in sectors producing rapid, short-term gains to more risky uses of its capital. As a result, productive investment was disproportionately the result of foreign and state intervention. The private sector was dependent on state assistance in the form of direct public investment, government programs of incentives and subsidies, and legislation that provided opportunities for enlarging its wealth.

The political leaders had a significant role to play in local capital accumulation. Although local capital holders had control over significant pockets of the economy (agriculture, manufacturing, communications, distributive trade, real estate, construction, and so on), they were not sufficiently autonomous to bargain on an equal basis with the political leaders. The political leaders controlled access to all forms of public resources and thereby had the power to determine the success or failure of the individual economic actor. As a result, a clientelistic relationship was formed between the local capitalists and state-controlling party leaders, whereby the latter was given support in exchange for access to the channels of capital accumulation. As Italian scholar Pizzorno correctly put it, "economic credit generates a political debt, . . . the criterion of maximization is not the productive efficiency of the credit conceded, but rather the solidity of the bond of gratitude established and the type of service which will be made available in return" (Pizzorno 1974:330). Clientelism as political currency became more important than economic development in the larger society.

Government policies of the postwar and early postindependence period clearly favored private-sector interests over lower-class interests. Both JLP and PNP development strategies involved harnessing foreign capital investment to stimulate growth as well as creating a domestic capitalist class in the nontraditional (nonagricultural) sectors of the economy, albeit under state control. In partnership with North American capital, successive party governments pursued policies designed to promote expansion of a capitalist class around import-substitution, manufacturing, tourism, corporate finance and banking, real estate, and construction. These policies led to an overall growth in the economy and a considerable rise in the level of industrial activity. This necessarily led to an increase in the power domain of the capitalist class that dominated the urban sector.

The cost of private-sector prosperity and capital accumulation was political domination by the state. Lacking sufficient resources to become autonomous entrepreneurs, the private sector's only option was to accept state patronage and sponsorship in order to fulfill its objectives of capital accumulation. State legislation giving incentives to manufacturers boosted private-sector confidence. The Industrial Incentives Law and the Export Industry Encouragement Law, both passed in 1956, led to the independent growth of firms producing almost exclusively for either the domestic or for the export markets. Simultaneously, state agencies such as the JIDC were set up for the purpose of building a manufacturing industry in Jamaica. The JIDC was launched by the JLP under the leadership of a black Jamaican, Robert Lightbourne, as managing director, and N. N. Ashenheim as chairman of the board. Similar agencies such as the Small Business Corporation (1956) and the Development Finance Corporation were later established, and between 1950 and 1967 were used by members of the private sector to accelerate their move in the wholesale/retail trade, formerly dominated by English planters.

The manufacturing, import/export, wholesale/retail, and construction sectors all came under the influence of the local private sector. The "21 families" had an aggressive presence in the industrial sector, with this pattern continuing in the contemporary period. By 1960, the manufacturing sector, in which local capital had significant representation, was the leading contributor to GDP, contributing 13.2 percent at factor cost (current prices) increasing from 6.5 percent in 1938. Manufacturing continued to be the leading sector until 1970 when mining, quarrying, and the refining sectors, buoyed up by large increases in the output of bauxite and alumina, took over as the leading sector. In 1970, manufacturing was at 13.5 percent, mining 16.8 percent, and agriculture 8.3 percent (*Economic and Social Survey* 1970:14). During the 1953–1970 period, the overall increase in the manufacturing sector was J$98.7 million. The industries that showed the largest increases were chemicals, cement, furniture, metal products, paper products, and a variety of other manufactures.

Reid's (1977) study showed the extent to which the local capitalist class benefited from the growth of the postwar economy. For example, Desnoes and Geddes, a family corporation, accounted for virtually the entire beer and stout production in the country's exports in this period. Carreras, an associate company of Carreras U.K. Ltd., in association with Hart and Ashenheim family interests, dominated 80 percent of the cigarette industry. Pulp, paper, and glass were produced under the control of an alliance of Ashenheim, Geddes, and Henriques on one board and Henriques, Desnoes, and Geddes on the other board. The Jamaica Flour Mills accounted for 82 percent of the islands's total requirement of flour consumed in 1971, and reported in that same year a profit of J$1,192,149 after three years operations. The Hart family members are the largest local shareholders, and chair the board of directors of the Jamaica Flour Mills.

The intrinsic limitations of this phase of Jamaican industrialization must be borne in mind. Jamaican industry consisted essentially of the production of textiles, pharmaceuticals, processed foodstuffs, furniture, clothing, alcoholic beverages, tobacco, cigarettes, printing, paper products, and automobile accessories. The capitalist class made high profits from manufacturing activities, but the production of those goods had little power to generate sustained economic growth. The unemployed labor force (largely agricultural workers) could not be absorbed, as the manufacturing sector was capital-intensive.

The capitalist class accumulated much personal wealth, but in order to prosper it had to accept political domination by the state. Black middle-class support was effectively translated into the management of capitalist interests. In the colonial era, state power was used to prevent local capitalists from becoming active in areas that would compete with foreign capitalists. The postcolonial state had a similar policy. It gave tax advantages and incentives and it implemented legislations that would make Jamaica attractive for investment by private foreign interests. State power was used to ensure that economic development and the private economic interests of the Jamaican capitalist class would not pose a competitive threat to foreign interests. The opening up of the economy to foreign interests thus limited the scope of local capital while strengthening the state.

The Agricultural Sector: Attempts at
Small Farmer Accommodation

The rapid economic growth that took place in the postwar economy led to major structural shifts in the economy as well as in class power. The government's "industrialization by invitation" program brought enormous income and investment opportunities for the business classes as well as jobs for the professional and bureaucratic middle classes. The bauxite, manufacturing, and tourist industries flourished, and by 1968 those sectors surpassed agriculture as the sector contributing the most revenue to GDP and export earnings. In 1950, the agriculture, forestry, and fishing sectors contributed 30 percent to GDP, falling to 6.7 percent in 1970. Also in 1970, the mining sectors contributed 12.6 percent, and manufacturing 15.7 percent (*Economic and Social Survey* 1970).

When figures for government expenditure for policy items as a percentage of gross national product (GNP) are examined, data available for 1970 reveals the relative importance accorded to each sector: trade and industry, 0.4 percent, communications, 2.7 percent, and general administration, 5.0 percent (Stone 1980:237). By the late 1960s, agriculture's contribution to export earnings sank from about 50 percent to less than 20 percent, clearly reflecting a lack of government priority (Jefferson 1967:114). What is significant here is not only the decline of the agricultural sector, but also the increase of the state's capital and recurrent expenditure within the public sector from 10.8 percent of GNP in 1960 to 40.5 percent of GNP between 1960 and 1976 (Stone 1980:234).

As both JLP and PNP governments were committed to an industrial development strategy linked to foreign capital, it is not surprising that by 1964 government expenditure was concentrated disproportionately in the urban/industrial sectors. The government was influenced by its desire to satisfy its noncapitalist middle-class constituents as well as the capitalist classes, its newly found political ally.

Given the relative strength of the more organized upper and middle classes, it was predictable that the small farmers and low wage sectors of the population would not have had their interests accommodated in those limited policy outputs available in the postwar period. The small farmers were in a weak position relative to other classes, as the only resource with which they had to bargain (the vote) was coopted in the two dominant political parties and their affiliated unions.

Control and monopolization of fertile land by big planters and foreign landowners has been an obstacle in the development of a vibrant and dynamic peasant sector in the postemancipation period. Numerous studies done by noted Caribbean agricultural economists and policy analysts (see for example, Beckford 1972; Stone 1974; Clive Thomas 1974) pass favorable judgment on the economic potential of the peasantry, but express pessimism about the future of polices based on shoring up the big estates. In the absence of mass trade union and mass party pressures on JLP and PNP postwar and postindependence governments for redistributive policies (in agriculture and other policy areas), agricultural policies continued to accommodate the views and interests of the capitalist classes, without whose cooperation the postwar industrial development strategy would have collapsed.

Beckford (1972, 1980) has written extensively on the subject of the past and present conflict between the plantation and peasant sectors and the negative developmental impacts inherent in that conflict. He pointed to the inequalities in resource endowments between the peasant and plantation sectors, the absence of linkages and spread effects in plantation production, the monoculture nature of plantation economy, the monopolization of land by the plantation system and its subsequent underutilization, the bias toward low-skill labor resources in plantation production, and the low income in the plantation economy. The total effect of these characteristics, in terms of the Beckford thesis, is the persistence of poverty in the Caribbean region (Beckford 1972).

Competing class interests of the big planters and small farmers provided the main basis of governmental agricultural policy in the postemancipation era. In the 1838–1938 period, colonial state policy reflected a clear and exclusive preference in favor of big planter interests while ignoring and often exploiting the small farmers. This was predictable because the colonial assemblies were planter-controlled or planter-influenced, as were the Crown Colony regimes.

The 1938 worker-peasant riots accounted largely for the shift in the direction of the colonial state's agricultural policy in the post-1938 period. Other related factors included the economic decline and consequent weakening of the dominant planter class, the growth of state power exercised by the colonial bureaucracy at the expense of the planters' political influence, and the increasing differentiation between imperial British and local planters' economic interests (Stone 1974b:150). The British government (under the BLP) adopted a welfare-oriented public policy perspective.

By 1949, according to Stone's study, per capita recurrent expenditure in agriculture rose to US$0.78 per annum from $0.12 in 1939. Capital expenditure in agriculture rose to $230,000 per annum in 1949–1950.

Simultaneously, the functions of the Department of Agriculture had been broadened to undertake service functions with respect to the small farmers. As a result, the technical and administrative staff increased by 100 and 600 percent, respectively. Additionally, a program for the settlement of small farmers on new land was implemented and increased the number of small farmer allotments to 26,000. Furthermore, advisory committees were set up to formulate new plans for agricultural development, which for the first time included an emphasis on domestic food crop production in contrast to the earlier focus on planter-dominated export crops such as sugar and bananas. For the first time the government also became engaged in the production and planning of domestic food crops and extended its marketing functions in the distribution of food imports and the export of nontraditional food products (Stone 1974b:150–151).

The subject of the land tenure system of overcultivated and uneconomic miniplots and large undercultivated estates (mainly owned by foreign companies) was the single most important issue to mobilize workers and peasants in the 1938 labor riots. In 1938, only 8 percent of the agricultural land of the country was owned by the small farmers, who made up 84 percent of the farming population. This represented the worst hillside land and unproductive soil available. Farms of under five acres in size (constituting the bulk of the small farmers) represented 71 percent of all farms in the country, but together they occupied only 12 percent of total farm acreage. On the other hand, plantations represented less than 1 percent (0.7 percent) of all farms, yet these occupied 56 percent of total farm acreage (Beckford 1972:48).

The worker/peasant coalition militantly protested this unequal pattern. Their demands in calling for more miniplots, utilities, services and infrastructural development were arguably modest. Given the apparent political leverage of the workers and peasants in the new political coalition that emerged in 1944, why wasn't the land question resolved? Why were there not genuine structural changes in the land-tenure system? Part of the reason was that, despite its good intentions, government policy in the agricultural sector enhanced the power of the state instead of placing the small farmers in a stronger position vis-à-vis other social groups. For example, the settlement schemes designed to give land to the landless were counterproductive. The land that became available for settlement was no longer required by the plantations for their own use (because of its poor quality) or alternatively was mountainous Crown land previously in forest. Redwood (1972) estimated that of all the land settlements launched by the government between 1929 and 1949, only 4 percent was situated in the most fertile aluminum soils. The government program also encouraged the establishment of undersized farms, as the politics of settlement dictated that each property acquired be divided between as many persons as possible (to ensure many votes). Landholdings of five acres or less proved to be uneconomical, often forcing the farmers to seek outside work to supplement their incomes.

Leadership among the workers and peasants may also have had significant bearing on the lowering intensity of peasant demands in the post-1938 period. Upper middle-class farmers (big planters) provided much of the leadership for the rural farming community. The big planters shared common interests with transnational agricultural capital, and were often in direct conflict with the interests of the small farmers.

Given middle-class dominance and control of the structure and operation of political institutions in the period of decolonization, the small farmers were unable to develop the capacity to organize collectively and articulate their interests in the political arena to manipulate government policy to their advantage. Associations formed to express peasant demands in the post-1938 period were all led by rich farmers or businessmen. They included the All Island Banana Growers Association, the All Island Cane Farmers Association, the Citrus Growers Association, the Jamaica Livestock Association, the Sugar Manufacturers Association, and the Jamaica Agricultural Society.

The class character of the leadership represented a preponderance of rural middle-class leaders, a small but influential presence of big planters, and a supporting "middle peasant" subelite. These agricultural associations were more in the nature of extensions of the state bureaucracy than independent interest groups. They were heavily dependent on state subsidy, and the leadership often performed functions as brokers between the poor, uneducated small farmers and the distant state bureaucracies. The associations were essentially coopted into the patron-client political system, with its patterns of dependency, elitism, social deference and inequality, which completely neutralized its potential interest-group role.

Between 1944 and 1962, the British colonial state established an Agricultural Policy Committee charged with the responsibility to advise on the following specific areas of agricultural policy reform: utilization of land, soil, and water resources; settlement of land; production, processing, and marketing of plant and animal products; improvement of rural amenities; cooperation between producers; collaboration of producers' organizations with government; and coordination of government services concerned with rural development. Of the eleven local members of the committee, seven were planters and businessmen, one was a civil servant, the chairman was a colonial official, and the other two members were Bustamante and Manley leaders of the multiple class JLP and PNP (Stone 1974b). The intention of the British government was to build an agricultural policy reflecting colonial definitions of development within a framework of planter/business class consensus and supported by the two leaders of the political parties for the purpose of mass legitimation.

The agricultural organizations and the Agricultural Policy Committee were highly imperfect instruments for securing the interests of the small farmers. The latter had to compete with the rich planters as well as the highly organized manufacturing and commercial interests in the urban-industrial sector for the scarce public resource and policy benefits. Although the small farmers had potential political power in the number of votes they could provide, the state was able to keep them calm and stable by effectively neutralizing them through state-controlled welfare-oriented agricultural policies pitched to their interests. The report produced by the Advisory Committee (reinforced by reports from foreign "experts") provided the basis for agricultural policy during the period of decolonization and in the postindependence period up to the early 1970s.

Policy diagnoses for this period revealed a bias in the analyses of Jamaica's land-tenure problems. Pessimism was repeatedly expressed about the viability of an "inefficient small peasantry," and recommendations were often made to assist the small sector and for technical and organizational improvements in the Ministry of Agriculture. This bias resulted in policies designed to salvage an allegedly "backward" peasant sector. Small farmers were given loans, subsidies, and marketing facilities, and infrastructure was placed in rural communities to facilitate the marketing of goods.

The only new policy direction undertaken in the postindependence period of the sixties was the JLP government's decision to extend the land authorities to the entire island, to extend the scope and operation of the government marketing services through an expanded marketing corporation, and to shift from subsidies to loans as a basis for financing small-scale agriculture. The impact of these policies was limited. First, the administrative control of the government's schemes rested with the government ministries, whose charge it was to minister to the needs of the small farmers on terms decisively controlled by the government bureaucrats. The government sought to increase the efficiency and welfare content of the capitalist market mechanisms in agriculture without transferring control or administrative power to the small farmers while subjecting them to the whims of the civil service technocracy. Second, the impact of loans and subsidies was limited in that it excluded the more needy and impoverished who lacked capital. Landless farmers were given small holdings under the land settlement scheme provided that they could come up with an initial down payment. The more needy and impoverished would be excluded because they would not have the capital.

Rich planters were allowed to acquire larger holdings with the help of government loans that came from British financial sources. Between 1946–1947 and 1967–1968, J$56.4 million was allocated to small and middle farmers in the form of credits and subsidies. Many farmers were reluctant to use the credit facilities because of fears that the requirement of putting up land titles as security for repayment involved a high risk. Much of the subsidy and loan funds was used for consumption rather than investment purposes because of the shortage of cash income among the small farming community (see Stone 1974b).

Neither JLP nor PNP governments of the 1944–1972 period were willing to dismantle the system of skewed land distribution by seizing lands held by foreign companies and big planters and redistributing them to small farmers. The JLP and PNP governments recognized that the land-owning sector of the capitalist classes, unlike its urban, managerial, and commercial counterpart, would be more threatened and resistant to state policies that appeared to be raising the productive capacity of the peasant sector. The clientelist strategy insulated the political leaders from mass mobilization against their policies, which favored upper- and middle-class interests. This therefore meant that the state was able to avoid policies that would compromise foreign interests. The consolidation of power required a strategy that would guarantee inflow of foreign capital necessary for state domination, and at the same time unify all social classes around the state. The Colonial Development and Welfare Act of 1940 and the new investments from North America offered the resources and opportunities that were used to fortify such a strategy based on clientelism.

State Expansion, Patronage, and
Middle- and Lower-Class Clients

As mentioned in Chapters 1 and 2, the postcolonial state had an increasingly active role in the social, economic, and political institutions of Jamaican society. In the postwar period, in both industrialized and developing nations, the state assumed a leading role in revitalizing capitalism and promoting economic development. This strategy was associated with a welfare public-policy orientation common in the Scandinavian countries, in the social democratic parties of Western Europe, in Canada, and during the "New Deal" period in the United States.

Ideological considerations were less important because both the JLP and PNP governments of the postindependence period viewed the public sector as the principal vehicle of social change. Between 1950 and 1967, successive governments pursued "industrialization by invitation" programs to attract revenues from overseas and simultaneously expanded the public sector. The latter was intended to deliver some of the state's resources to its middle- and lower-class clients. The capitalist classes benefited significantly from the growth in the industrial sector whereas the standard of living of the lower classes remained unchanged. Expanding the public sector was the state's way of catering to middle- and lower-class demands, while still maintaining control over them. Having benefited from state protection and sponsorship, the private sector did not express opposition to a policy that would have normally appeared to them to be directed against capitalist interests.

The state intervened in the agricultural sector, implementing policies that led to development of rural infrastructure, institution of marketing services for agriculture, and extension of credit to small farmers. Between

1946 and 1968, US$56 million was allocated mainly to small and middle peasants in the form of credit and subsidies. Between 1949 and 1969, the clerical and administrative staff of the Department of Agriculture expanded from 60 to 351, and the technical staff increased from 93 to 676. This new state-policy thrust in agriculture from the late 1940s through the early 1960s represented an increasing role in agriculture for the state. Credit and cash flow support for small farmers formerly supplied by shopkeepers, rich planters, and product dealers were replaced by the state's provisions of credit, technical services, loans, and other services (see Stone 1974b).

The public sector embarked on a major expenditure campaign aimed at improving health care and health services and expanding the education system. As a result, all health indicators reflected dramatic changes in the quality of life of the population; for example, life expectancy levels changed from 61 in 1950 to 70 in 1970, and infant deaths per 1000 live births decreased from 81 in 1950 to 36 by 1970 (Department of Statistics 1951, 1962, 1971). Official government data suggest that literacy rates increased from 55 percent in 1951 to 65 percent in 1970. This improvement in literacy was linked to increased expenditure in education and expanded educational facilities.

The state's extraordinary expansion of its administrative and welfare structures was matched by an equally aggressive corporate expansion of the state into the private sector. Government corporations were set up during the 1950–1967 period of industrial expansion in manufacturing, bauxite, tourism, and other service industries. The Jamaica Development Bank and the Urban Development Corporation were later established to assist the JIDC in industrial policy. State resources were used to subsidize the costs of new investments, as the state became an instrument of the development of capitalism in the post-1945 period in Jamaica, replacing the dominance of the economy by English planter interests.

Conclusion

Public sector expansion provided for improvements in the educational and health care systems as well as assistance to small farmers in the agricultural sector, but its real function was to strengthen the state and, consequently, the middle class. It gave the political leaders full control of the resources obtained from overseas, to be used as a part of the state's patronage largesse to be distributed among its lower- and middle-class clients. In this way, the maintenance of the status quo was guaranteed. The strategy of multiple class clientelism enabled the state to placate members of the powerful private sector and win their support while assisting them in the process of capital accumulation. Public sector dominance has been therefore critical for sociopolitical order in that strategic classes were accommodated by the state in return for political allegiance.

NOTES

1. For the past two decades, debate among radical neo-Marxists has focused on the "relative autonomy" of the postcolonial state. Some argue that the postcolonial state cannot be independent of foreign interests and cannot therefore be used in the interests of the nation involved. Others argue that the state is "relatively autonomous" with some power to set limits to the power of foreign capital and bargain with it. The first coherent advocate of this position was Hamza Alavi (1972). Dozens of articles have been written on the subject. For example, see Leys (1976), Von Freyhold (1977), Shivji (1976), and Stone (1977a).

2. For different perspectives on the bauxite TNCs in Jamaica, see Stone (1977a), Stephens and Stephens (1985), and Manley (1987).

5

The Manley Period: Democratic Socialism, Ideology, and Dual Clientelism, 1972-1980

In developing nations, the state is faced with demands of powerful domestic and international actors as well as the demands of its middle- and lower-class clients. The state must attempt to meet all those conflicting claims if the elites controlling the state hope to stay in power. The state must have a capital budget for financing its development and welfare programs. It also needs the resources to maintain law and order. The competing economic claims are as pressing because they pertain directly to the survival of the government. First, powerful domestic and international actors in developing nations view the state as an instrument of economic accumulation. Because the state is so "strong" relative to other social groups, it can set the terms of economic participation and income distribution. If the state is forced to accommodate powerful interests, it is forced to employ state resources to cater to the economic demands made by these powerful actors. Second, patronage claims are made by upper-class as well as mass clients. Upper classes in control of strategic resources make claims that must be met if their political loyalty is to be guaranteed. At the mass level, patronage is used as an instrument of control by the regime. Under the conditions of inequalities in the control of wealth, income, and power, patronage serves to mediate the incipient conflict between the masses and the middle and upper classes for income redistribution.

It is this formulation of state-society relations that forms the basis for Chapter 5. This chapter examines the 1972–1980 period of the Manley PNP government. It departs from current literature on the period (e.g., Stone 1981b; Lewin 1982; Girvan and Bernal 1982; Ambursley 1983; Stephens and Stephens 1987; Manley 1987; Payne 1988a) in that it argues that the ideology of democratic socialism emerged in Jamaica as a strategy to justify the patronage largesse of the state, extend and deepen state control of the lower classes, and develop a pattern of international alliances to counter U.S. hegemony. The PNP government defined its ideology of democratic socialism as a declaration of intent to protect the poor and to correct the inequities of the Jamaican political economy. Because Jamaica's political economy is characterized by international dependence, democratic socialism also called for a restructuring of the existing international economic order, which favored the wealthy industrial nations of Western Europe and North America and locked the developing nations into a dependency syndrome. Western capitalist governments, particularly the United States, and international lending agencies and organizations, as well as private foreign investors, all opposed the PNP's new philosophy.

The upper classes, most of the upper middle classes, and lower classes mobilized into the JLP's clientelist party base all opposed democratic socialism. In the final analysis, the policies were not congruent with the government's ideological declaration, and therefore the government was not able to retain the support of the lower classes, those to whom the ideology was pitched.

As discussed in previous chapters, the role of the international sector is to provide resources to the state that are used in part to maintain its patronage structure. Patronage resources available through control of the state are critical in upper-, middle-, and lower-class support of the political order. When the state-controlling PNP elites elected to adopt democratic socialist policies detrimental to the interests of strategic international actors and their domestic allies, then the international sector retaliated by withholding its resources. The government was defeated largely through the crisis created by capital being withheld by the United States and international lending agencies. The withholding of capital decreased the patronage granting capacity of the government. When the state then lost its capacity to maintain an effective patronage system, the electorate opted for a new political directorate in the JLP, which appeared to them to have access to patrons with greater resources.

THE IDEOLOGY OF DEMOCRATIC SOCIALISM

The new PNP government enjoyed considerable popularity when it was swept to power in 1972 after a two-term rule by the JLP, winning forty-seven seats in Parliament to the JLP's thirteen. The PNP had support from a broad sector of the population, consisting of the traditional middle classes employed in the state sector; critical sectors of the capitalist classes, which favored state protection of the local economy from external capital; and a broad segment of the urban working classes, as well as the militant and unemployed youth and the Rastafarian element, which rejected Western capitalist society as "evil."

By its own description, the PNP was, from 1974 onward, a party committed to establishing a democratic socialist economy in Jamaica (PNP 1979). This was, of course, not a novel development, as the PNP had since its emergence in 1938 aligned itself with the democratic socialist Fabian ideas of the British Labour party. However, during the 1940s and 1950s the Marxist members of the PNP were purged from the party, and socialism was no longer emphasized in PNP party doctrine (see Chapter 2).

The transformation to democratic socialism was in fact driven by economic nationalism and welfare statism. The PNP Manifesto captures this:

> To accomplish our objectives, the economy must be subject to the control of the working people, thus ensuring that exploitation is eventually abolished and that their interests predominate at all times, above all other interests; for it is the people, who, through their sweat and toil produce the goods and services essential to the development of the economy . . . in the transition to a democratic socialist economy, the State sector leads the way in planning, directing and transforming the economy structure (PNP 1979:26).

The weakened position of the United States (after its defeat in Vietnam, Cambodia, and Laos) and its subsequent move toward a more isolationist and less interventionist international role led to the electoral victory of Jimmy Carter, who emphasized nonintervention. This was a significant external factor that provided the context for Manley's emergence to political dominance. Manley's popularity within Jamaica was based on the perception by the masses that their lot could be cast with the emergence of "Third World-ism" and nonalignment as counters to Western hegemony. The policies that emerged from democratic socialism were state expansionist and inevitably led to increased power for the middle classes. This is the reason that the PNP was able to galvanize middle-class support for its socialist programs up until 1977. This also explains how the state was able to justify its clientelistic role vis-á-vis the lower classes.

PNP foreign policy strategy was based on the very same notion of expanding the state. The dependent postcolonial state in many developing nations has not been able to extend its sovereignty beyond the political to include economic sovereignty and autonomous economic decisionmaking. Adherents of democratic socialism generally adopt foreign policy strategies that support the right of a sovereign nation to pursue the collective needs of its citizens even at the expense of the perceived economic and security interests of the Western nations. The PNP insisted on the right of developing nations to pursue economic relations where they are in fact the beneficiaries. The objective, always phrased in developmental terms, was to allow the state to develop the capacity to protect and promote the collective needs of the society.

In the search for resources, Manley indicated that Jamaica's position would be one of nonalignment.[1] Many developing nations are members of the nonaligned movement. The majority have friendly relations with the United States and do not suffer from the retaliatory assault that was inflicted on Jamaica. The problem for the United States was Jamaica's relations with

Cuba and the increasing influence of the latter there. Moreover, Jamaica actively supported the Eastern bloc in its voting at international forums. The JLP opposition, in response to PNP policies, declared itself pro-Western and pro-capitalist and aligned itself with the U.S. government and conservative political leaders in the U.S. Congress. Political divisions within Jamaica became identifiably linked to the international competition between capitalism and socialism, as politics became enmeshed with external actors who controlled the resource base of the internal networks of clientelism.

The PNP government's domestic and foreign policies arising out of its democratic socialist ideology had two aims: (1) to gain more wealth from the international system, and to counter U.S. hegemony, and (2) to use the wealth gained to strengthen and expand the state's dominance over all social groups in the domestic political arena. International responses to PNP policies will be examined next.

INTERNATIONAL RESPONSES TO DEMOCRATIC SOCIALISM

The Third World

During the decade of the seventies, PNP leader Michael Manley's dynamic Pan-Africanist and activist Third World leadership was compared to that of Gamal Abdel Nasser of Egypt and Kwame Nkrumah of Ghana. The PNP's foreign policy was anchored on the realities of its domestic scene. It realized that in order to maintain its dominance in local politics, it had to manipulate its external environment to its own advantage.

Manley therefore sought to rally together more than 120 developing nations in the struggle to overcome economic underdevelopment, and to speak with one single voice in making demands upon the industrialized nations of North America and Western Europe for a New International Economic Order (NIEO). Demands included a greater role for the developing nations of the Third World in the management of the global monetary system; greater technology transfer from the rich nations (the North) to the poor nations (the South); greater access for manufactured goods from the Third World into the North and the eradication of discrimination against Third World manufactures; more predictable and higher prices for Third World commodities; renegotiation of the Third World's massive external debt; and regeneration of codes of conduct for the activities of transnational corporations. (See Demas 1978 and Denoon 1979 for a detailed discussion of the issues pertaining to the NIEO.) After having established himself through the NIEO issue as an able spokesperson, leader, and champion of the poor and downtrodden, Manley easily sought and won various chairmanships and vice-presidencies in the Non-Aligned Movement, Socialist International, the Group of '77, and the International Bauxite Association (IBA).

NIEO was not the only international issue that catapulted Manley into the limelight. Nonalignment was another subject on which he spoke and acted with passion. Manley was forceful in fashioning a foreign policy of nonalignment that ran counter to U.S. interests in the Western Hemisphere. There were deep ties with Cuba at the government and party levels, as well as with democratic socialist parties in Western Europe. Within the Caribbean, support was given not only to Cuba, but also to the Sandinistas in Nicaragua and to Maurice Bishop in Grenada. There was moral support for the Palestine Liberation Organization (PLO), denunciation of apartheid South Africa accompanied by sports boycotts, and there was support for Cuban troops in Angola.

These political developments were conditioned by Manley's firm belief in the practical usefulness of developing multilateral relationships in the world. His government boisterously and courageously refused to be allied blindly and permanently with either side of the Cold War to the exclusion of the other. Manley was sending a clear message to the mighty United States that Jamaica was a sovereign nation and would retain the autonomy to judge world affairs as it pleased, and under no circumstances would it become a pawn in the East-West rivalry.

Manley's anti-imperialist and anticolonialist posture gave him high marks in the Third World. Although he was viewed as "a petty bourgeois nationalist" in many leftist circles (see Lewin 1982; Ambursley 1983), he had the respect, friendship, and support of Cuban President Fidel Castro. Manley has written and spoken about the ideological rigidity of Marxism-Leninism and the reasons that he rejects it as an ideology of political and economic change. Although Castro acknowledged that Jamaica was not on a path to "scientific socialism," he was impressed with Manley's efforts in the areas of health, education, and social welfare. He gave practical support in the form of doctors, engineers, and technicians to assist in training health personnel and constructing schools, roads, and hospitals. Manley courted Castro, and Castro courted Manley. This courtship was of concern to the United States as well as the local capitalists and a small percentage of the working classes in Jamaica. Manley was not bothered by their uneasiness. He traveled with Castro in the latter's airplane (both dressed in a "kareba"—a nonconventional Third World suit) to a meeting of the nonaligned movement in Algeria in 1977. Manley's relationship with Castro gave him some leftist legitimacy in the Third World (as well as with the Communist Workers Party of Jamaica), but it further isolated Jamaica from the United States.

In the English-speaking Caribbean, Manley allied with political leaders in Guyana, Barbados, and Trinidad and Tobago and called for Caribbean unity, particularly in economic affairs. Manley, Forbes Burnham, and Maurice Bishop were regarded as prominent spokespersons and champions of Third World causes. All three leaders spoke in United Nations (UN) forums with much candor, giving firebrand support for anticolonial and anti-imperialist causes.

In radical and progressive circles in Africa, Manley became as popular as such Caribbean predecessors as activist historian Walter Rodney, Pan-Africanist Marcus Garvey, and reggae king Bob Marley. African students and intellectuals often invited Manley to give guest lectures at major universities such as Cairo University, the University of Lagos, Dar-es-Salaam University, and the University of Zimbabwe. Manley also reciprocated by inviting Julius Nyerere, Kenneth Kaunda, and the late Mozambican President Samora Machel on state visits to Jamaica. Third World students living in the United States, Britain, and Canada still constantly seek him to address their organizations.

Notwithstanding Manley's enormous popularity in the Third World, some observers there viewed his radicalism as unnecessary, and as Guyanese political scientist Festus Brotherson, Jr., put it, "incalculably expensive" (Brotherson 1989:19). Manley sought foreign capital to implement his democratic socialist policies and programs at home, but his socialist rhetoric and radical foreign policy posture led to diminished Western foreign aid and investment. His friends in the developing nations certainly could not provide financial backing to fill the vacuum created by the departure of Western capital. This ultimately led to the defeat of his government in the 1980 elections.

The United States and International Financial Agencies

The 1976–1980 period was that of the Carter administration. However, U.S. policy on Jamaica during that period was being shaped primarily by the Republican party with an extremely activist role by Ronald Reagan and those conservatives such as Jessie Helms who were cultivating Reagan for the presidency. Jamaica was chosen as an example of the expansion of Communist influence in the Western Hemisphere and where such influence should be eradicated. It was the conservative Republicans who financed and actively supported the Seaga campaign (Manley 1982).

With a population mobilized on the basis of political clientelism and substantial U.S. financial backing, the PNP government still pursued its socialist line over the objections of the United States. Perhaps Manley believed that the United States should be forced to accommodate his brand of socialism, which was practiced in Western Europe and was not the Marxist-Leninism of the Soviet Union or Cuba. Instead, the United States put significant pressure on Jamaica to ensure that democratic socialism failed and that the PNP government was voted out of office. The U.S. press ran negative advertisements during 1976–1977 to discourage tourists from visiting Jamaica (its impact on the tourist industry and the economy will be discussed later in this chapter). The United States ensured that the IMF imposed stringent rules of eligibility for assistance—rules that would create severe hardships for the PNP government's lower-class clients and therefore would discredit "socialist" economic policies. Economists Keith and Girling (1978) and Girvan (1978) also observed that the United States frustrated Jamaica's efforts to sell bauxite on the world market (after the Jamaican government's 1973 levy on the companies) by encouraging the bauxite companies to choose alternative sources in Sierra Leone, Guinea, and Australia. The Central Intelligence Agency (CIA), the intelligence arm of the U.S. government, allegedly trained opposition supporters to be saboteurs, who staged strikes and committed acts of violence and murder in an effort to bring the government to its knees (Manley 1982). Efforts at destabilization, whether documented or not, must be taken into consideration, as U.S. history in the Caribbean region confirms that this is often a useful and successful strategy. The extent to which it was the basis for the Manley defeat will always be arguable.

Manley believed his socialism to be "democratic" and of the moderate variety, rooted as it was in anticolonialism and nonalignment. Although it was fairly certain that his radicalism could be reconciled with Jamaica's national interests, the confrontation with the United States could not be avoided. The confrontation came, and the consequences were negative for Jamaica.

PNP DOMESTIC POLICIES

The Bauxite Levy and State Expansionism: The Politics of Confrontation

In the context of growing economic nationalism at home and among developing nations in general, the Manley government felt that the environment was conducive to pursuing a more aggressive (yet still accommodating) policy with the bauxite companies. It understood that in order to maintain the state's dominance internally, it had to secure a transfer of a larger share of the surpluses of the bauxite industry to the government. In order to secure its own survival, the PNP state-controllers were forced to exercise political expedience and secure the transfer of a larger share of the surpluses of the industry in the name of the country's lower classes. The stated intent was that the government would reallocate the surplus to other sectors of the society for the benefit of the lower classes.

Despite the fact that Jamaica had a relatively diversified economy, bauxite brought in the greatest source of revenue. The government realized that there were some risks involved in trying to secure a larger share of the surpluses generated by the bauxite industry. In its efforts to do so, the government employed what it perceived to be the least offensive of the alternatives available to it. The solution that it found appeared to be the best strategy to manage the conflict between the claims of the bauxite companies and the need to prevent economic crisis that would threaten its ability to maintain power. Nationalization was ruled out, although it was recommended by some of the government's expert economic advisers (Girvan 1978). Instead, the government imposed a production levy on all bauxite either exported or processed in Jamaica. The levy was set at 7.5 percent of the selling price of the aluminum ingot instead of the previous method of computing the tax based on the artificial profit negotiated between the government and the companies. As a result, the tax rate increased 480 percent between 1973 and 1975, from J$2.50 to J$14.50 per ton. At about the same time, the government began negotiations with the companies to take over majority ownership of their mining operations (see Girvan 1978).

Direct benefits went to the middle-class state bureaucrats and intellectuals who dominated the PNP government, as well as the capitalists in the commercial sector. The latter gained a foothold in bauxite production for the first time in the history of the industry in Jamaica. The newly created Jamaica Bauxite Institute (JBI) was placed under the directorship of Meyer Matalon, a member of the Matalon industrialist family and one of Jamaica's leading capitalist entrepreneurs and long-time PNP supporters. The JBI was staffed with intellectuals and state bureaucrats closely aligned with the PNP, who were given these jobs in exchange for their political support. Additional resources gained from the levy were used to create social welfare programs to expand the state's capacity to maintain a clientelist relationship with its lower-class mass clients. The lower classes provided critical support for the state in its confrontation with the bauxite companies, but they did not gain substantial benefits from the increased resources. The gains that were made from the levy indicated to the lower and middle classes that the PNP government was indeed capable of gaining resources for the state. It was this perception that increased lower- and middle-class support for the PNP during the 1973–1974 years.

The government hoped that these limited attempts at state control over the bauxite industry would provide the additional revenues needed to carry out its development program outlined in the national budgets of 1973 and 1974. The bauxite levy received strong backing from the private sector, trade unions, and the population at large. As the industry was 100 percent foreign owned, and one of the few remaining sectors in which local capitalist interests did not have a share, it was not surprising that the local capitalists supported the government in its struggle for greater control of the industry. The capitalist classes subsequently opposed state expansion in all other sectors of the economy where the state attempted to assert its dominance.

The PNP's "bauxite offensive" failed for several reasons. First, the companies imposed a political cutback on production between 1975 and 1978, as reflected in a decline in bauxite's contribution to the GDP over the 1975–1978 period. Jamaica declined as the world's largest producer of bauxite whereas Guinea, Sierra Leone, and Australia increased production. Second, there was a recession in the industry worldwide, and this brought with it a budget deficit and a balance-of-payments crisis as the PNP government continued to spend money on its social welfare programs necessary for the maintenance of its government in power. The PNP was forced by 1976 to cut back on its spending. With this cutback, the government had very little chance of achieving the goals it set in its national budget and economic development plans of the period. The government was immediately faced with antigovernment demonstrations as a result of continued high unemployment, poverty, inflation, and food shortages among the lower classes. The government's ability to allocate economic resources was so limited that it found itself unable to stave off endemic economic crises that threatened its own survival. Third, the PNP probably could have succeeded with its bauxite levy if there was no retaliation from the U.S. government as well as the companies. U.S. government officials, such as Secretary of State Henry Kissinger, policymakers, and Congressional leaders, as well as the press vehemently opposed the bauxite levy. U.S. public officials were convinced that the Jamaican case would set a precedent for the formation of numerous other raw material cartels against the developed countries. Others held the view that the PNP's actions were part of an expropriation strategy that is consistent with socialist and Communist policies (Cuthbert and Sparkes 1978).

The U.S. press presented a picture of the United States "under siege" by Third World countries. Exaggerated reports of violence in Jamaica dominated the front pages of the press in many large cities in North America. Tourists were advised to seek vacations in other Caribbean islands. Revenues from the tourist sector declined significantly over the 1974–1976 period (Cuthbert and Sparkes 1976). The bauxite companies themselves retaliated with economic pressures. They filed suit with the World Bank's International Center for the Settlement of Investment Disputes, contesting the legality of the levy, while they began to transfer bauxite and alumina production from Jamaica to other countries.

The final joint-venture arrangements made between the Jamaican government and the companies were by no means threatening to the latter's power. Kaiser, Reynolds, and ALCOA negotiated separate agreements, but they all followed the same pattern. Essentially, four main ideas dominated the agreements. The government was to purchase all company-owned lands at "book value," and the government would also guarantee the companies a forty-year supply of bauxite from lands it will lease back to the companies at 7 percent of the purchase price. The government was to purchase 51 percent of the mining operations, with the option of buying a share of any alumina refining plant for "book value." The companies were to retain management control of the joint ventures through ten-year management contracts. The production tax paid to the government was fixed at 7.5 percent for eight years instead of 8.5 percent, as initially announced. These arrangements did not put the government in a dominant position vis-à-vis the companies. In fact, some analysts argue that it still left the companies in charge (Girvan 1978; Keith and Girling 1978; Ambursley 1981; Lewin 1982).

Bauxite policy since 1974 has shown important differences from the period of the late fifties through 1974, when the industry was unambiguously set up to pursue policies favorable to the interests of the North American companies. By contrast, in the post-1974 period, when the interests of the PNP government and the companies diverged, the government, faced with the issue of its own survival, was forced to attempt to make its wishes prevail. However, as the end product clearly shows, the transnationals' control over the international aluminum industry limited the PNP government's ability to bargain effectively.

The Jamaican bauxite policy reveals the dilemma of governments of developing nations faced with economies dominated by transnationals whose local subsidiaries cannot be immediately nationalized. While efforts at economic self-determination must be made in the face of nationalist political demands, and state control of transnational operations are demanded, the government is forced to pursue the least offensive strategy through a fear that stronger measures may provoke negative and retaliatory measures from the companies concerned. In the final analysis, the negotiated end product demonstrated that the state's bargaining position was just as weak after its efforts at control as it was before then (Girvan 1978).

State Expansion, Patronage and Agricultural Reform:
Project Land Lease and the Landless People

> Of all the areas of the Jamaican society, it is in the rural life that the most backward and oppressive conditions prevail. With 60% of the country's total population still living in the countryside, income for each employed person in agriculture averages only 1/3 of the national average between 1960-72. Widespread illiteracy and cultural exploitation, malnutrition, unemployment and underemployment, poor housing, and health conditions are the lot of the country's people (Robotham 1977:45).

The predominant reason for the desperate conditions quoted above is the increasing concentration of landownership in Jamaica. According to the 1968/69 agricultural census, 300 of the largest landowners with properties of 500 acres or more owned 40 percent of the island's farmland. The number of small farmers owning between 5 and 25 acres had dropped from 53,000 to 37,600 in the decade after 1958, while the number of farmers with 5 acres or less increased by 10,000. In 1972, those with 5 acres or less made up over 70 percent of Jamaica's farmers, but occupied only 11–16 percent of the total farmland (Robotham 1977:45–46). These were the statistics that the PNP faced when it came to power in 1972.

In March 1973, only several months after taking office, the government announced that legislation providing for agricultural reform was ready to be submitted to Parliament. Several months later, Agricultural Minister Keble Munn outlined in Parliament two Government Green Papers, jointly prepared by the government and the Inter-American Development Bank. The aim was to implement a major land reform program designed to reduce social pressures in rural areas and to increase the amount of land under cultivation. The PNP stipulated that the state would undertake land-lease programs, agricultural and livestock credit programs, road construction, irrigation and drainage works, cooperative farming where desired, and initiation of research into the economic use of irrigation for various crops. Proposals were made relating to a wide range of services: extension; marketing; soil conservation; research on sorghum, soya beans, rice, and maize; expansion and improvement of the services offered by the Cooperative Department; and establishing in the Ministry of Agriculture a Soil and Water Conservation Unit to facilitate on-farm activities.

The aspect of the government's agrarian policies that was most important to its democratic socialist program was Project Land Lease. Legislation in the form of a Land Development and Utilization Act had been passed by the previous JLP government in 1966 to force the utilization of agricultural lands or free idle lands for those who wanted to cultivate it. The government bought 100,000 acres, but only 50,000 were actually parceled out to small farmers (Kaplan et al. 1976:248). In 1973, the PNP government insisted on introducing the very same policy under its Land Lease and Land Reform Program.

Project Land Lease was designed to settle Jamaica's land question. The exercise of settling landless people was a typical example of the sort of compromises that the PNP made to try to accommodate and neutralize strategic groups to achieve stability and maintain its multiclass alliance within the existing liberal democratic system. Project Land Lease had three phases. Land Lease I involved leasing small plots of land for five to ten years from the government, which also provided the new farmers with credit for all major soil conservation, seed, harvesting, and transportation costs. Land Lease II was similar to Land Lease I but the government provided the new farmer with leases up to forty-nine years. Land Lease III was a cooperative farming program in the sugar industry where community-structured organizations were to be set up to satisfy the basic needs of the community.

Project Land Lease served primarily as a service to the middle class via state expansion. The consequence of the government's land reform was not only to provide Jamaica's landless people with land but also to preserve middle-class dominance by placing the potentially disruptive rural poor under the administrative control of the government. The rapid developmental efforts were carried out under the direction of the government and the party. The land-lease programs were substantially incorporated within the existing patronage system as a part of the state's largesse. As economic historian Robert Bates (1983) argues in his book on agricultural policies in Africa, public programs that distribute farm credit, seeds, fertilizers, and public lands become instruments of political organization in the countryside of Africa. The same process was in existence in Jamaica. JLP supporters charged that land was given exclusively to PNP supporters, and managerial and supervisory positions to party activists (EPICA Task Force 1979; Ambursley 1981). State resources were used to regiment the population. While the government tried to initiate an expansion of the class of small farmers, it simultaneously subjected them to close administrative control. Recognizing that these new landowners, with their newly acquired property, would have the incentive to support the political system, the government sought to guarantee this support in several ways. It saddled them with heavy debts from government loans, thus forcing them to comply with the wishes of the state or lose their newly acquired property. This fear served to neutralize the small farmers.

Through Project Land Lease, the government was also able to neutralize the rich landowning class through state appropriation of their assets for patronage, while tying their interests much more firmly to the state. In this way, a very powerful opposition to middle-class dominance could be eliminated. Project Land Lease entailed a PNP government commitment to purchase land from the landowning class each year for the rest of its term in office. For those farmers who wanted to leave the island, or perhaps shift their investments into other sectors of the economy, the government created a market through which they might liquidate their assets, compensating them for the losses they would suffer as a result of Project Land Lease.

From the point of view of former landless people, Project Land Lease brought better opportunities to them and enhanced their contribution to Jamaica's economy. The official government figures indicated that between 1973 and 1976, more than 47,000 small farmers had been allocated 10,000 acres of arable land on a 49-year leasehold basis. By 1980, the government reported that under the three land-lease programs it placed more than 21,000 small farmers on 39,500 of the 42,500 (gross) arable acres of land it had acquired (Manley 1982). Stone's (1977a) study of the attitudes and perceived benefits of the tenant farmers gives some indication of just how much better off these farmers were as a consequence of their involvement in Project Land Lease (see Tables 5.1, 5.2, and 5.3).

Table 5.1 indicates that 51 percent of the tenant farmers interviewed felt that they were better off economically because of their involvement in Project Land Lease, compared to 13 percent who thought nothing had changed and 36 percent who felt that they were worse off. The highest number of negative evaluations came from the more educated farmers with higher levels of pre–Land Lease incomes and a higher proportion of landowning and thus higher aspirations. Those with positive evaluations of the program cited the sense of dignity and independence that comes from own-account farming as the most important benefit of Land Lease (see Table 5.2).

The PNP government was able to provide access to land and working capital for the small farmer who had become displaced as a result of land concentration in rural Jamaica. This created social and political stability as well as loyalty to the government. At the same time, the small farmers recorded an increase in domestic food production for the 1974–1977 years. The proportion of food import declined from 14 percent of total nonfuel imports in 1973 to 10 percent in 1980 (Stephens and Stephens 1987:237).

In spite of the contribution that Project Land Lease made to domestic agricultural production, a significant 49 percent (Table 5:1) had yet to receive tangible benefits from the program. The most negative evaluations of the scheme had to do with the shortage of cash to meet land preparation expenditures and to hire labor (see Table 5.3). Thirty-five percent of all farmers complained of the shortage of cash for hiring laborers. Another significant complaint concerned the inadequacy of the land allotted to the farmers. Stone (1977a:125) reported that 74 percent of the tenant farmers indicated a desire for a larger allotment, as the majority of the existing allotments were insufficient to provide adequately for the income and subsistence needs of the tenant farmers and their large families.

The 51 percent majority of positive evaluations of personal economic improvement from the scheme up until 1977 is a good record considering the host of organizational problems that ensued as a result of the speed with which Project Land Lease was implemented. The cash problem was due in part to the diminishing supply of capital available for social problems as a result of the 1973 OPEC-induced oil crisis. Project Land Lease was to be financed from foreign aid as well as from revenue obtained from bauxite production. Obtaining foreign aid became difficult as Michael Manley's socialist rhetoric, Third World activism, close friendship with Fidel Castro, and state expansionist policies infuriated the U.S. government. The United States encouraged and pressured lending agencies such as the IMF and the World Bank into withdrawal of their capital between 1976 and 1980. The dependence on foreign loans and aid to finance public-sector programs such as Project Land Lease peaked by 1976, reducing the government's ability to resist pressure. In a maneuver familiar to many developing nations, the multilateral lending agencies, acting in concert, withheld aid and encouraged the PNP government to rationalize its agrarian strategy. The JLP opposition, supported by private sector interest groups and international donors, called on the government to liberalize the domestic market to private enterprise and to move away from state investment in agriculture. The economic crisis was so severe, and the onslaught on the government—from both inside and outside

TABLE 5.1 Tenant Farmers' Views of Improvement

View of Relative Improvement	Percentage of Tenant Farmers
Better off	51
Conditions same	13
Worse off	36

Source: C. Stone (1977a).

TABLE 5.2 Tenant Farmers' Views of Benefits Received

Precise Benefits Received	Percentage of Tenant Farmers Perceiving Benefits
Increased employment	15
Increased cash income	22
Increased availability of food for family	16
Sense of dignity from land tenure	28
Knowledge about farming	13

Source: C. Stone (1977a).

TABLE 5.3 Complaints by Small Farmers

Complaints	Percentage of All Farmers With Complaints
Shortage of cash	35
Water supply and internal road	12
Inadequacy of land	11
Low AMC prices	10
Absence of building on farms	7
Burdensome terms of credit payment	8
Administrative delays and failures	11

Source: C. Stone (1977a).

the country—was so intense that it was left with little room to maneuver. The government was forced to retreat from its agricultural policy and to abandon most of its social-welfare programs.

Despite the government's seemingly good intentions, it became captive of policies that enhanced the power of the state and did not in fact place the small farmers in a stronger position vis-à-vis other social groups. The small farmers have in fact become more dependent on state and party bureaucrats. The changes that did occur emerged largely from state intervention seeking to increase the efficiency and welfare content of the capitalist market mechanisms without transferring control or administrative power to the small farmers.

Special Employment Program

In 1972, the government introduced the largest Special Employment Program in the history of Jamaica, using public sector resources to hold down unemployment levels. These jobs were referred to as "crash programs" or in the Jamaican vernacular as "bullo work." These programs were not productive, but designed as service work that could not generate income for debt repayment. Many of the programs were wasteful and brought loud objections from the middle classes. People were often seen collecting the minimum wage of J$20.00 while sitting idly by the street side. There were reports of people collecting checks for others not employed in the program. As expected, in various constituencies these programs were incorporated into the patronage system, through the methods outlined in Chapter 3, and jobs were distributed according to political loyalty.

Private Sector–Public Sector Reallocations, Lower-Class Economic Demands, and Fiscal Crisis

The government embarked on economic policies designed to redirect resources to the state sector from international economic actors embedded in the Jamaican economy as well as from local capitalists.

Nationalizations. During its first term in office, the PNP took over Barclays Bank, the Jamaica Public Service Company (the island's only utility company), the Jamaica Omnibus Service, foreign-owned hotels and sugar estates, and Radio Jamaica, without any opposition from local private-sector interest groups. But when the government attempted to acquire an interest in the cement and flour companies, traditionally monopolized by two powerful local capitalist families, the private sector reacted with outrage. It was acceptable to shift foreign assets to the state sector, but unacceptable for the state to try to secure a share of the construction and flour industries. Friction began when the state attempted to encroach on the power domain of the private sector.

Government Enterprises. With its democratic socialist policy, the government began to seek meaningful participation in the management of export-import trade and marketing of major agricultural crops. These have been traditionally the preserve of the private sector. The PNP also began to impose import and tax restrictions, which further upset the business community. Government agencies such as the State Trading Corporation (STC) and the Sugar Industry Authority (SIA) were established, and the importation of necessities such as staple foods, drugs, and timber for the construction industry and sugar marketing came under their control. These government enterprises are said to have been unprofitable drains on the national budget, thus preventing a more meaningful use of public resources on other activities.

PNP domestic policies were not breaking new ground, as since the early sixties it has been common in developing countries for the state to use its resources to promote economic growth and to redress the colonial legacy characterizing the economies. The interventionist state that evolved was reinforced by the pressures on the government to meet the basic needs of the poor through public sector budgets. The question has been raised as to whether it was wise for the PNP to have pursued state interventionist policies, which generated massive fiscal deficits and inflationary pressures that led the country into eight consecutive years of negative growth. Many find it difficult to understand the speed at which the economic situation deteriorated in the seventies. From the viewpoint of economic theory, perhaps it was a serious mistake for the PNP to pursue the policies it did, and to postpone their adjustment in the face of economic crisis. But its economic policies emerged from political constraints resulting from pressures by the state's lower-class constituents for change.

In the 1970s, all countries in the Caribbean Basin (except perhaps Trinidad and Tobago) reflected the problems and performance of small, petroleum-importing, dependent economies facing unstable world markets. In the face of the OPEC-induced oil crisis, which led to a massive increase in oil and energy related costs, Jamaica and most non–oil-exporting developing nations experienced rising inflation from the early seventies onward. Attempts by Caribbean governments to maintain high levels of imports and high living standards for the middle classes in the face of declining export earnings led to increased foreign indebtedness. Another misfortune was the decrease in North American demand for bauxite and alumina and the decline in the tourist industry. Because of the heavy dependence on bauxite and tourism as foreign exchange earners, Jamaica's terms of trade deteriorated sharply between 1975 and 1977. In addition, in response to the government's democratic socialist policies, there were changes in the country's access to borrowing. As a result it had a huge foreign debt, which was only exacerbated by its expansionist policies.

It seems plausible to suggest that a combination of external events and domestic policies generated the negative growth trend of the seventies. External events cannot usually be controlled by political leaders, but public-policy choices are certainly made by these leaders. Some scholars (e.g., Stephens and Stephens 1987; Looney 1987) suggest that PNP domestic policies, by increasing the relative role of the public sector in allocating and controlling resource flows in the economy, represented an inappropriate response to the external pressures on the Jamaican economy. The demands of regime survival compelled the Manley government to embark on a major public sector expenditure campaign that led to increased state dominance of the economy. Public expenditures soared from 1975 on, and deficits began to appear with large-scale budget overruns. Much of the government's resources went to pay public-sector employees, and the benefits reaching the lower classes were minimal. Central government expenditure as a percentage of GDP increased from 12.1 percent in 1970 to 22.1 percent in 1977 (World Bank Tables 1980, cited in Stone 1986:88). Public-sector workers and staff doubled from 57,000 to 107,000 in the five-year period between 1968 and 1973 (Stone 1986:89). The rapid expansion of the state's administrative apparatus and its capacity to deliver these equity-oriented programs demanded that it increase its tax dollars. In order to achieve the necessary resources, the government imposed burdensome taxation on the middle and upper classes and resorted to excessive external borrowing.

After one and a half years in office, inflation and the worldwide recession threatened to severely dislocate the PNP's newly announced reform programs under democratic socialism. The economy was hit by an increase in domestic inflation, fueled mainly by the escalating costs of imported oil. Table 5.4 shows the general deteriorating economic conditions faced by Jamaica as well as other Caribbean states during the 1973–1977 period.

During 1973–1974, the Jamaican economy came under several influences that adversely affected its performance. Important among these were declining inflows of private capital investments in the mineral (bauxite) sector, depression in the world market for aluminum, and persistent inflationary pressures in Jamaica's trading partners (the United States, Britain, and Canada). The immediate effect of these factors was reflected in sluggish investment growth, rapid inflation, and deterioration in the balance of payments. Nevertheless, the national economy continued to expand, but the improvements were insignificant in terms of growth in real output per capita. Such economic growth as was reported reflected the contributions of the manufacturing, tourism, construction, and public administration sectors. However, the island's balance of payments was in deficit, with foreign exchange reserves depleted to the extent of J$43.6 million as a result of the continued growth in the trade deficit and the decline in capital inflows.

By 1976, Jamaica's balance-of-payments position had weakened considerably, as shown clearly in Table 5.5. The proximate causes of this critical balance-of-payments situation included significant outflows of capital

TABLE 5.4 Gross Domestic Product for Selected Caribbean Countries, 1973–1977

Country	Annual Growth Rates, GDP (in percent)					GDP in 1977[a] (in US$ million)	Per Capita GDP in 1977[a] (in US$)
	1973	1974	1975	1976	1977		
Barbados	3.1	-2.8	1.3	3.8	4.7	303.4	1,248.70
Dominican Republic	12.1	6.9	5.6	6.4	3.3	4,168.3	837.30
Guyana	2.2	4.5	7.3	1.8	-3.7	208.0	250.90
Haiti	3.0	3.4	1.3	4.3	2.5	896.6	189.20
Jamaica	-2.6	-2.1	-1.0	-6.9	-5.0	2,497.3	1,203.50
Trinidad & Tobago	-0.3	-1.2	1.0	5.7	4.1	1,510.8	1,328.70

a. Measured in 1976 constant dollars

Source: W. Raymond Duncan (1978). Figures for GDP and per capita GDP were provided by the Statistics and Quantitative Analysis Section of the Inter-American Development Bank, Washington, D.C. Annual growth rates were calculated on the basis of the numbers supplied.

from the island by the industrial and commercial classes, who opted for the protection of their capital in North America; a decline in the level of foreign investments; and a low level of earnings from both visible and service exports. Net reserves stood at negative J$181.4 million at the end of 1976 (*Economic and Social Survey* 1977:46). Accordingly, a new import policy was adopted in January 1977 under which a ceiling of J$600 million was imposed, with approximately J$200 million allocated for petroleum products (*Economic and Social Survey* 1977:46). In order to prevent large-scale unemployment in the manufacturing sector, the government later revised the import ceiling of J$845 million, as a result of external lines of credit, and a standby loan facility from the IMF and other international financial institutions.

A critical aspect of the balance-of-payments problem was the government's external public debt. Table 5.6 shows the sizable growth of Jamaica's debt from 1969 to 1975 in comparison with other Caribbean countries and the staggering proportions of this debt between 1976 and 1977. The Jamaican government was finally forced by the balance-of-payments problems to enter negotiations with the IMF for an infusion of capital. Fearing at the outset that the fiscal and monetary measures proposed by the IMF would jeopardize his development goals, Manley took the lead in mobilizing public opinion in a vigorous campaign against "imperialist pressures attempting to destabilize Jamaica." This maneuver had prevented him from seeking necessary aid from the IMF since 1974 when the economic crisis began, and discredited him later when he was forced to accept the IMF's "stabilization" aid program.

The balance-of-payments difficulties threw the Jamaican economy into severe crisis. The crisis had not yet reached major proportions in 1976 and so the PNP was returned by the working classes for yet another term of democratic socialism. Stone's data show that a large percentage of the domestic capitalist elite had withdrawn its support for the PNP by 1976 and had switched to the JLP (Stone 1981b). The U.S. government and U.S.-based financial sources had cut investments substantially since 1975. It is reported that some parent companies in the United States even refused to lend to their local Jamaican subsidiaries (*Journal of Commerce*, December 13, 1976). The results were very crippling for the Jamaican economy. Jamaica did receive some credits and aid from Western Europe, Eastern Europe, the Caribbean Common Market (CARICOM), and some Latin American countries, but none of these sources could fill the gap left by U.S. financial sources.

When the PNP was reelected for a second term in 1976, the basic contradiction between the upper class of capitalists and the political leaders of the PNP surfaced in full force. From the beginning of 1977, the PNP was faced with adamant opposition from all sources. Many PNP industrialists who had formerly supported the administration's efforts to reduce poverty in

TABLE 5.5 Balance-of-Payments Summary, 1968–79 (in J$ million)

Items	1968	1969	1970	1971	1972	1973	1974	1975	1976	1977	1978
Current account balance	−86.0	−103.0	−127.2	−93.4	−117.3	−164.3	−151.8	−257.0	−275.2	−61.9	−73.5
Capital movement (net)	+117.0	+98.5	+134.1	+112.1	+59.8	+124.7	+221.1	+189.9	+41.5	+51.7	+45.4
Government extended borrowing	+11.7	+10.3	−1.2	+4.0	+18.6	+33.4	+81.9	+112.4	+72.0	−5.4	+151.2
Identified private capital	+105.3	+88.2	+135.3	+108.1	+41.2	+91.3	+139.3	+77.0	−30.0	+57.1	−145.8*
Allocations of SDRs	—	—	+5.3	+4.7	+4.7	+4.7	—	—	—	—	—
Net errors and omissions	−6.3	−6.8	+5.4	+13.0	−9.2	+11.9	−15.2	−6.5	−6.8	−4.4	—
Overall surplus/deficit	+29.6	−11.3	+17.6	+36.4	−43.6	−27.7	+54.1	−73.6	−238.1	−14.6	−68.1

*Includes net errors and omissions
Source: Bank of Jamaica Annual Reports, 1968–1977.

TABLE 5.6 External Public Debt of Guyana, Jamaica, and Trinidad and Tobago (in Millions of U.S.$)

	1969			1971			1973			1974			1975		
	Debt	Per-centage of GNP	Per-centage of Exports	Debt	Per-centage of GNP	Per-centage of Exports	Debt	Per-centage of GNP	Per-centage of Exports	Debt	Per-centage of GNP	Per-centage of Exports	Debt	Per-centage of GNP	Per-centage of Exports
Guyana	63.9	27.9	44.4	144.1	53.6	88.0	166.9	55.9	104.4	202.4	49.0	68.7	237.6	50.6	61.8
Jamaica	123.9	11.3	26.6	147.9	10.6	27.2	306.0	16.6	48.4	474.9	19.7	48.9	647.4	22.9	58.3
Trinidad and Tobago	76.0	10.2	12.8	91.3	9.9	25.1	145.1	11.3	25.6	161.1	8.6	14.7	155.5	7.0	11.6

Source: World Bank, World Debt Tables, Vol. 1 (1977), pp. 220, 221, 81, cited in Anthony Maingot (1979:280).

the society, fearing that further reform could lead to the elimination of the private sector, withdrew their backing.

During 1977, in the midst of the economic crisis, the PNP attempted to restore the confidence of the private sector by abandoning many of the reform measures it had previously sponsored. The acceptance of the US$74 million IMF standby loan is the best example of this conciliatory approach. Faced with criticisms from both moderates and conservatives within the PNP and the unrelenting opposition of the JLP and the private sector, by mid-1978 it had become apparent to the government that it was no longer able to govern effectively. In an effort to assuage tempers and reunify the party before the 1980 elections, D. K. Duncan, a radical grass-roots politician with a base among the urban youth, was removed as general secretary of the PNP, and his Ministry of Mobilization was cancelled. However, the schism created within the party and the middle classes set in motion by all the events of the 1974–1978 period had become unbridgeable. Antigovernment resistance from landowning and commercial groups in both parties continued to mount steadily.

The PNP's conciliatory tactics not only failed to win the confidence of the disaffected private sector, but compounded its problems with the working classes and the poor, who perceived its actions as contrary to their interests. Explosive conflicts erupted between capital and labor, the major issue under contention being wages. The government had made a major concession to the working people by increasing the minimum wage in 1975, but then it turned around and allowed the industrialists to make adjustments with price increases. Both the PNP-supported NWU and the JLP's BITU led many strikes against the government. The government retaliated with antistrike legislation, and opposed major increase in wages. This furthered the conflict between government and labor. The government was now caught in an antagonistic position vis-à-vis its working class supporters and their labor unions.

Political violence escalated in the urban areas of Kingston and St. Andrew at an abnormal rate—even for Jamaica where a certain amount of violence is always expected. The security forces had joined the partisan struggle and no longer maintained order. Sections of the security forces were said to have been persuaded that their continued existence was at stake and that they would be replaced by Home Guards, Brigadistas, and People's Militia.[2] Without the support of the security forces, an important arm of the state, the government was unable to discharge its major obligation to protect the people and provide law and order. Large-scale violence engulfed the society. More than 800 people were reportedly killed in political violence between January and October 1980. The PNP government was perceived to be inept and weak in the eyes of all social groups, as sociopolitical order broke down.

The IMF negotiations began in a political atmosphere that was already becoming increasingly charged with conflict between the JLP opposition, the private sector, and the PNP government. Because the IMF was brought in to solve what had become a national economic crisis, the issues were approached by the PNP government as involving the country as a whole. It was the IMF versus the people of Jamaica, according to PNP government rhetoric. The private sector separated itself from the government in the conflict with the IMF, making it clear that its interests were more in line with those of the IMF. The JLP party leader, Edward Seaga, had also begun to have private negotiations with the IMF members, as the JLP shared the IMF opinion that PNP mismanagement was responsible for the economic crisis.

The IMF issue increased the conflict in the extremely charged and violent bipartisan atmosphere that had evolved in the post-1976 period in Jamaica. "Imperialist" (pro-IMF) supporters were lined up against "anti-imperialist" (anti-IMF) supporters inside the PNP and in the society at large. At first, the PNP bitterly accepted the fact that the IMF option was the only way out for Jamaica in its balance-of-payments crisis. It then accepted the US$74 million standby loan in 1977. The IMF stated that wage increases, exchange rate (overvalued), fiscal deficit, monetary expansion, restriction on trade and payments, state economic activities, price controls, and lack of business confidence were responsible for Jamaica's economic crisis (Girvan et al. 1980). The IMF's credit line was explicitly conditional on the institution of a program of anti–working-class measures. The conditions imposed included a wage freeze, a near 40 percent devaluation of the Jamaican dollar, and a drastic cutback in public spending.

In order to gain access to the IMF's resources, the PNP was told that it had to agree to a program of adjustment whose main elements would be drastic cuts in real wages, severe compression of demand, and retrenchment in the public sector. Such policies would alienate the poorer classes—precisely those groups who formed the broad urban bases of support for the PNP's social and economic initiatives—while appeasing those middle- and upper-class groups who opposed its democratic socialist programs and policies.

While much discussion was taking place within the government on the issue of the IMF loans, the capitalist classes took a stand against the government and supported or agreed with the criticisms that the IMF leveled against the PNP. It is interesting to note that the same capitalist classes that supported the government in its confrontation with the bauxite TNCs was now supporting the IMF against the government. In the case of the bauxite levy, the private sector felt that huge benefits would accrue to it in whatever deal the state made with the companies. However, in the confrontation with the IMF, the private sector turned against the state, which in its view had become too interventionist and anti–private sector, and joined with the foreign forces against the government.

The IMF realized that the political situation in Jamaica was not conducive to a national mobilization effort by the government against the organization. Alliances were shifting quickly within the PNP itself, and the government was barely able to hold itself up in the face of the serious economic problems it faced. The IMF took advantage of the political climate and intensified its pressure on the PNP government. Having won the confidence of the private sector and the JLP party leader, the IMF, as well as the private sector, withheld capital from the state, thus tying the hands of the government. The poor people and the unemployed, who relied on the government for their livelihood, could not bear the hardships created by the shortage of capital and turned against the government. This points up the conflict between an ideology (democratic socialism) designed to create support for the government and political mobilization based upon state clientelism.

The PNP's acceptance of the IMF's credit terms created serious and deep ideological divisions within the government and party, and the government's relationship with the IMF became ambivalent. The PNP was now unable to organize and mobilize its support around a clear political line because with every set of IMF negotiations, the party became more ambivalent and more indecisive in its course (Girvan and Bernal 1982).

The IMF agreed to a two-year standby program for Jamaica, which fell short of its own views on what was required in the areas of exchange-rate adjustment and wages policy, but which, in return, insisted on a tight fiscal program. The economy lived up to nearly all the IMF strictures set for it on the first loan (on public expenditures, public borrowing from the banking system, and the level of foreign exchange earnings), but it had failed to meet one condition: it had not kept to a ceiling of J$355 million in domestic bank assets. That ceiling had been exceeded by 2.6 percent (*Economic and Social Survey* 1977:47). The IMF immediately suspended the program, insisting that Jamaica negotiate an agreement under the Extended Fund Facility, which would involve major and drastic economic adjustments.

In order to obtain the May 1978 IMF loan, major devaluations of the Jamaican dollar were carried out. In addition, a package of J$180 million of additional indirect taxes was imposed, price controls were lifted, and it was planned that the price level would rise by 40 percent in the first year of the program whereas wage increases would be limited to 15 percent (Girvan and Bernal 1982). These measures had an immediate and drastic effect on living standards. In 1978, real wages fell by an estimated 35 percent, the share of labor income in the national income fell from 55.2 to 52.3 percent, and average real per capita consumption declined by 13 percent (*Economic and Social Survey* 1978:40). The balance-of-payments deficit, after improvement in 1977, widened by US$40 million in 1978 and by another $78 million in 1979, owing mainly to increases in outflows for interest and repayment on private and official debts. The overall investment rate remained at about 12 percent of GDP, and real GDP declined at an annual rate of 2 percent in 1978 and 1979 (*Economic and Social Survey* 1980:40).

Economic conditions worsened even with the IMF loans, and Manley decided to make a sudden shift back to his leftist position for the 1980 elections. D. K. Duncan was reinstated as general secretary of the PNP, and Manley's leftist rhetoric began once more. In December 1979, Jamaica failed by a substantial margin the performance tests for the second year of the IMF agreement, and the Extended Facility Program was suspended. The IMF officials defined the problem as one of fiscal mismanagement and demanded J$300 million in budget cuts (about 20 percent of government expenditure excluding debt service) as the condition for a waiver of the performance tests and the approval of a modified agreement. The charge of fiscal mismanagement had been a recurrent theme of the political line of the JLP opposition, and the JLP, along with the Private Sector Organization of Jamaica (PSOJ), called for the resignation of the PNP leadership and the holding of general elections.

The PNP had made two IMF agreements in less than a period of three years, both of which ended in failure. Harsh austerity was imposed upon the people, unemployment continued to escalate, foreign exchange was virtually nonexistent, and the shortages of basic food goods continued. Opinion within the PNP had been badly divided some three years before and then swung strongly in favor of a break with the IMF. The PNP broke off relations with the IMF in March 1980, and announced the beginning of an "alternative self-reliant economic path." As a consequence, the conservative Finance Minister Eric Bell resigned and was replaced by Hugh Small, one of the known PNP leftists. However, the switch back to the Left was too late to change the order of things. By 1980, the majority of the electorate had come to regard the PNP as a party incapable of managing the Jamaican economy and incapable of resolving the conflict between the different groups contending for the resources of the society. The PNP was defeated in the 1980 elections—the JLP got the largest margin of victory in Jamaican history in terms of constituencies: fifty-one seats versus the PNP's nine seats. The margin of victory in popular votes was 18 percentage points, which reflects relatively even support given to both parties.

CONCLUSION:
DEMOCRATIC SOCIALISM EVALUATED

The 1980 elections were of very great significance both within Jamaica itself and in the Western Hemisphere. The United States watched cautiously, waiting to see if democratic socialism would be given a third term in Jamaica. No other elections in the history of the island had such international attention. The elections were to provide a climax to the violence that had engulfed the island since January 1980, which took the lives of more than 800 people. For all concerned it was a relief that it was over.

The convergence of ideology among the local private sector, the JLP opposition, foreign business, international lending agencies, and the U.S. government was a very important factor in the defeat of the PNP government. Another critical factor was the loss of support from the government's lower- and middle-class clients. The interests of these groups converged under the single objective of removing the PNP government, but they all had different reasons. The state's dependent clients wanted leaders who could manage the state and give them access to its resources. The JLP opposition wanted to recapture the state and restore Jamaica to a capitalist path. The domestic economic elite wanted to maintain the capitalist status quo, which gave it a predominant role in the economy. The United States was (and still is) committed to maintaining its hegemony over the Western Hemisphere, which means preventing the spread of anti-imperialist regimes (be they socialist or Communist) in the area at all costs. These interests converged and defeated the PNP government largely through the crisis created by capital being withheld by the United States, Canada, and the international lending agencies. The government's declaration of democratic socialism was extremely beneficial in giving the state the best chance to maintain dominance in the domestic political arena. Clientelistic ties between the upper and middle classes, the masses, and the state were maintained because all social groups were dependent upon institutions and agencies with access to international resources.

The PNP placed emphasis on (1) redistribution of income from rich to poor nations, (2) state ownership and control through state appropriation of the productive assets of the foreign enterprises, and (3) joint ventures with foreign enterprises. The policies and programs that emerged from this framework were consistent with the interests of the middle classes of the state sector. Under democratic socialism, resources of the private sector were placed in the patronage arsenal of the ruling PNP. State control of the economy released jobs formerly occupied by private-sector workers to state employees. Welfare programs for the poor demanded an expansion in state administrative structures, thus yielding prestigious new jobs to middle-class bureaucrats. Business allocations in the imports/exports sectors were made to capitalists as well as lower-class supporters. In exchange for all this, any ruling party has guaranteed mass support for the political order. In transferring those state resources obtained from external sources to the private sector, upper-class capitalist support is also secured.

Capitalist support for the PNP broke down when the latter was no longer able to accommodate these economic actors in the face of their opposition to the new nationalist economic demands of the masses. Since independence in 1962, successive JLP and PNP governments protected the interests of the privileged private economic sector as well as those of foreign economic interests. The PNP's declared ideology of democratic socialism led to a fracturing of that old relationship between the state and the privileged private sector. With a significantly larger share of the country's economic resources under its control, the state can act to effectively demobilize the private sector and neutralize its political significance.

The PNP did not evaluate the costs of its decision to gain control over the economy. It did not anticipate that powerful domestic and international actors might resist such efforts and use their resources to challenge its policies. Nor did it want to pursue the international strategy necessary to ensure the continuation of this economic activity.

The Manley government employed tactics similar to those in many other developing nations in its attempt to resolve the conflict between the economic demands of state functions and economic obligations that come tied to the terms of sociopolitical order and regime survival in developing nations.[3] It lost out in the end, as the democratic socialism pitched to the interests of the lower classes did not result in income redistribution to the lower strata nor in significant expansion of benefits of health, education, and welfare. Indeed, the standard of living of the lower classes declined dramatically between 1977 and 1980 (Stone 1987). PNP support among a small portion of the lower classes was sustained during that period by clientelist appeals by party leader Manley and others in the upper echelons of the PNP, but a significant portion of PNP supporters defected to the JLP and voted the PNP government out of office.

Democratic socialism was employed to justify programs that have been directly beneficial to the middle classes. One might therefore have expected these groups to be committed to the PNP's declared program of democratic socialism. Yet congruence between the declared ideological position and those of the middle and upper classes was low during the 1977–1980 period. The middle and capitalist classes had begun to link the country's declining economic fortunes to the PNP's Third World activism and socialist policies, and had begun to pressure the government to return to a more moderate position. The greatest concern was with the PNP's foreign policy, aligned as it was with Cuba, socialist parties in Western Europe, and its visible anti-imperialist position. Middle-class ideological commitment to capitalism became translated into support for the procapitalist JLP. That party, although in opposition, consistently articulated procapitalist programs. Upper-class occupational groups and members of the private sector who benefited from expansion of the capitalist sector during the post–World War II period aligned themselves with the JLP.

State expansion was the thrust of the PNP's democratic socialist policies. It represented an attempt by the middle-class state-controllers to extend sovereignty to the economic realm in seeking state autonomy in economic decisionmaking. The PNP government viewed its policies as measures necessary to overcome foreign and domestic capitalist domination over the Jamaican economy. The measures were not revolutionary, as the U.S. and Jamaican print media would have led all of us to believe, although they were the most sweeping and comprehensive measures yet undertaken in independent Jamaica.

Assuming middle-class hegemony in the domestic arena, the PNP tried to use the power of the state for the aggrandizement of its own social class. In orchestrating the seizures of foreign and local assets, the state used those resources to consolidate clientelist rule. However, the government was undermined by the weaknesses of the state caused by its ultimate dependence on external capital. When the dislocations engendered by democratic socialism coincided with a broader economic crisis, namely the recession in the international system, the Western lending agencies were in a position to insist, as a fundamental condition for any assistance to bankrupt Jamaica, that these democratic socialist economic policies be abandoned.

The saga of the Manley government shows two images of the Jamaican state: (1) the state as a patronage domain for elite and mass clients, and (2) the state as dependent on external patrons of the Western capitalist economic system. The aspirations of the lower classes were considered in the government's policies, but only insofar as those aspirations were brought under state control. Initially, the policies were designed to curb the naked greed of the local capitalist classes without expecting retaliation on their part. The government failed to realize that external capital interests, Western powers (especially the United States), and local capital all had the power to block its efforts. The leverage of the domestic and international economic actors was strong enough to impose a rollback on the government's social-welfare programs. Many conclude that the PNP inflicted its own wounds by pursuing policies that brought it to a position of massive dependence upon its Western creditors.

The capacity of the PNP government to redistribute resources is linked to the fiscal viability of the state and autonomy in economic decisionmaking. Fiscal viability depends on continuous flows of concessional development assistance and the state's capacity for economic growth. State autonomy in Jamaica would have been at its highest during the postwar period of economic boom, when both the Jamaican and international economies were in periods of expansion. Conversely, it would have been at its lowest in periods of international recession as well as during periods when the government spending programs were dependent on infusions of international public capital.

NOTES

1. Nonalignment is a derivative of the idea of nationalism in developing countries. It is seen as a part of the general assertion of a "Third World personality" in world affairs. Nonalignment is also a function of bipolarity, an

indirect by-product of the Cold War. Some Western writers believe that nonalignment is simply a profitable short-term Machiavellian strategy employed by the newly developing countries to enjoy the best of both sides in the current East-West conflict. John Foster Dulles of the United States, for instance, equated neutrality with immorality. See, for the tenets of nonalignment and the details of the nonaligned conference in Cairo in June 1961, L. Radovanovic (1961) quoted in Colin Legum (1962: 60).

2. The Home Guards were neighborhood groups introduced by the PNP as a supplementary security force. This was an attempt by the government to mobilize the community on a nonpartisan basis to help the security forces in the fight against crime. PNP opposition said the Home Guards idea was a Cuban/Communist device, and likened it unto the Brigadistas and People's Militia of Cuba (Manley 1982:85).

3. For an excellent discussion of the political and economic costs of regime survival in developing nations, see Hintzen (1989) and Noguera (1990).

6

The Seaga Period: Liberal Capitalism, the Dependency Crisis, and the Persistence of Dual Clientelism, 1980-1989

Chapter 6 examines the 1980–1989 period of the Seaga JLP governments. Despite adequate access to foreign capital for financing its domestic programs, the JLP was unable to achieve developmental transformation. Although advocating free-market policies, privatization, and export-oriented growth in the local economy, the government allocated resources to the state sector in keeping with its own survival needs due to the compelling demands of political clientelism. Clientelistic policies geared toward maintaining strategic middle- and lower-class clients preempted choices that were consistent with structural adjustment policies favoring local and foreign entrepreneurs. At the same time, the JLP's commitment to a free and open market collided with the interests of the manufacturing sector of the local capitalist class, which was unable to withstand foreign competition. Political considerations prevented use of foreign resources for developmental transformation, as these resources were allocated into the urban sectors of the economy and particularly in the state bureaucratic apparatus. Like those of its predecessor, the Seaga governments' policies were determined by the politics of clientelism. Ideological differences, governing styles, and class alliances were overridden by the embedded character of dual clientelism and changes in international economic and political support for the two administrations.

THE JLP AND IDEOLOGY

Since the inception of party politics in the late 1930s, Jamaican politics has been rife with ideology (see Hart 1972). The 1970s was the first time, however, that ideology served as the basis for such massive international intervention in the political economy of Jamaica. The JLP accepted the ideas of liberal orthodox economic theory, emphasizing a dominant role for the private sector in the economy. It argued that the expanded economic role the PNP had given to the state contributed to its failed policies in the 1970s. With little empirical evidence to substantiate its claim in the Jamaican context, the JLP insisted that private ownership was more efficient than public ownership,[1] and that it was only through a free market that the economy could be provided with the necessary incentives to move forward.

In the area of foreign policy, the JLP's posture represented a complete shift away from the Third World activism of its predecessor. The Manley PNP government closely identified with Cuba and the Third World and became a champion of the poor in international forums. In the case of the JLP, such a posture was ruled out at the very outset. Rather, it mounted attacks on socialism in general, launched a boisterous campaign against the Bishop regime in Grenada, and broke diplomatic ties with Cuba. The JLP's relations with other Caribbean nations were primarily economic. Seaga sought and established ties with Venezuela, Mexico, and Puerto Rico—nations that had the resources to offer assistance to Jamaica's economic recovery program. Seaga rebuffed the Nicaraguan Sandinista regime, supported the Central American Contadora approach to peace in the region, and argued in favor of the recommendations of the Kissinger Commission on Central America.[2]

The primary justification for the JLP's ideological position remained a desire to closely associate with the United States—the government that would enable Jamaica to acquire the aid, capital, and technology it required for economic recovery. JLP leader Seaga was not concerned with renegotiating the dependency relationship that defined Jamaica's linkage with the international capitalist system. He did not seek an autonomous developmental strategy, remaining confident in his ability to maneuver the geopolitical Cold War setting to extract the most from his relations with the United States.

The JLP's ideological vocation placed the free market at the center of its domestic preoccupations. The government was determined to obey the economic laws of the market, although they intersected the need to finance its clientelistic processes of power maintenance. It embraced the capitalist classes and their traditional values of efficiency, stability, gradualism, and sound financial management. The JLP's trade unionist base of support became subordinated to business interests, as the latter were brought closer to the centers of economic policymaking. As a result, public policy outcomes favorable to business interests dominated the political process.

INTERNATIONAL RESPONSES TO THE JLP GOVERNMENT

The Third World

Given the enormous popularity of Michael Manley in the Third World, it is safe to conclude that Seaga's victory was a bitter pill for supporters of the PNP to swallow. Not only was Seaga perceived as an ideological reactionary, but his racial origin (a white man of Syrian-Lebanese stock) remained a negative factor, often evoked by skeptical observers in developing nations. The author was often hard pressed to explain a white man's accession to power in an approximately 90 percent black and brown population.[3] Seaga was widely perceived as a leader who was willing to support the objectives of the propertied classes at home and abroad at the expense of the collective interests of the majority classes in Jamaica. Breaking diplomatic ties with Cuba in 1981 and supporting the 1983 U.S. invasion of Grenada served to further weaken Seaga's image in the Caribbean and the Third World in general.

In leftist circles, Seaga was viewed as a "surrogate" for U.S. interests in the Caribbean (Beckford and Witter 1980; Figueroa 1988). He attempted to demonstrate his independence in casting Jamaica's vote for black majority rule in South Africa in international forums, and supported the Law of the Seas Treaty. On both issues, Jamaica's interests and perspectives diverged from those of the United States. However, overall Seaga attempted to maintain political distance from "Third Worldism," while pursuing his foreign policy in a bilateral relationship with the U.S. government.

The United States and International Financial Agencies

The 1980 national elections were of great significance both within Jamaica and in the Western Hemisphere. The U.S. government had a stormy relationship with the Manley administration, particularly during the Ford period. Although the Carter administration appeared to be less hostile to the PNP, it was no secret that it wanted to see the PNP voted out of office (see Manley 1982, 1987; Payne 1988a). Seaga's electoral victory was received with jubilation in international capitalist circles. The *Financial Times* editorial cited by Ambursley (1983:98) was representative of the international capitalist response:

> The first and perhaps the most important deduction to be made [from the election result] is that, despite the worst foreboding of the prophets of doom, the island, like much of the Commonwealth Caribbean, is a functioning pluralistic democracy. The people's will, as expressed in the ballot box, is still paramount. Jamaica is therefore an example to other countries of the region, from Cuba in the north to Guyana in the south, where effective democracy is non-existent or gravely ailing (*Financial Times*, November 4, 1980).

Amidst accusations of sabotage, the democratic transfer of power was applauded by international capital sources as an obvious invalidation of charges of their involvement. Jamaica was immediately targeted as a candidate deserving special financial assistance to "halt the spread of Communism in the Caribbean." The island was portrayed as a "structural adjustment showcase," which proved that free-market policies and liberal democratic political institutions could thrive under conditions of economic underdevelopment. For his anti-Communist rhetoric, his pro-U.S. posture, and his commitment to free market policies, Seaga was rewarded with considerable inflows of foreign aid.

As a result of his "special relationship" with President Ronald Reagan and members of the private sector in the United States, Seaga was able to reestablish ties with the IMF—ties that had been broken in the summer of 1980 by the Manley government. In 1979, the PNP rejected the IMF demand that it reduce public-sector expenditures by J$300 million and lay off 11,000 workers. By April 1981, Seaga was able to reach an agreement with the IMF under terms far more lenient than the PNP was able to acquire. The IMF issued new loans of US$698 million over three years, with a 10 percent allowance provided for the application of the quarterly tests that the economy had to pass (Girvan et al. 1980:144–155).

The IMF "seal of approval" enabled the government to obtain more that US$350 million from a consortium of Canadian, Japanese, West German, and Venezuelan banks, as well as the World Bank. The British government resumed an export credit guarantee of US$11 million to insure exports to Jamaica, a facility which had been withdrawn from the previous PNP government (Edmondson 1983:593). In the first three years of the JLP government, Jamaica received an amount equal to 65 percent of all U.S. assistance to the country for the last thirty years (Clive Thomas 1988:232). In 1982, Jamaica was the third largest per capita recipient of U.S. aid, surpassed only by Israel and El Salvador. Table 6.1 shows the sudden increase in U.S. support for Jamaica from 1980 to 1981.

TABLE 6.1 U.S. Economic Assistance to Jamaica, 1980 and 1981 (in US$ million)

	1980	1981
USAID	2.7	12.9
PL 480	10.0	17.1
ESF	0	41.0
OPIC	0	51.0
EXIMBANK	0	21.4
Housing Guaranty	0	15.0
Totals	12.7	158.4

Source: *U.S. Overseas Loans and Grants and Assistance From International Organizations*, 1983. Annual Report of the Chairman of the Development Coordination Committee, Statistical Annex 1, cited in Barry et al (1984:187).

In response to the JLP government's new promotional activities to attract foreign investors, a committee of British businessmen, a Jamaican–West German Economic Committee, and a Jamaican-American Business Investment Committee were established between 1980 and 1981. During that first year, more than 400 proposals were received from foreign investors. In addition, Reagan generated momentum in Washington to support Seaga's concept of a "mini Marshall Aid plan" for the Caribbean, later worked out in the formulation known as the Caribbean Basin Initiative (CBI). As a result of the support gained in the United States for the Reagan-Seaga CBI, Jamaica received another US$50 million, and a total of US$150 million in aid was promised for 1983 (Payne 1981:437). The World Bank estimated that over the 1981–1984 period, the Seaga government had obtained (from all sources) approximately US$2,000 million in concessionary financing (Clive Thomas 1988:232).

These high aid levels were a direct reflection of the perception of the nation's position as a stable pluralist democracy with a pro-Western foreign policy and a deep commitment to "Reaganomics." External financing came with tight policy strings attached, including IMF-imposed short-run macroeconomic management and medium- to long-term structural reforms encouraged by the World Bank. U.S. financial support was used to back IMF policies and press for a more market-oriented economy; at the same time it guaranteed support for the Nicaraguan Contras and U.S. hostility toward the Bishop regime in Grenada. Foreign assistance compromised Jamaica's foreign-policy autonomy to a great extent, with the Seaga government reasserting its independence on the issues of the Law of the Seas and black majority rule in South Africa without incurring serious penalties.

JLP DOMESTIC POLICIES

Stabilization Policies, 1981–1984:
Overcoming the Legacy of Democratic Socialism

The economic toll of the 1972–1980 years had been very high. In 1980, real per capita disposable income fell 30 percent, from J$1,019 in 1974 to $717 in 1980. Over the same period, per capita consumption expenditure in real terms fell 25 percent, from $737 to $557, while per capita wages in real terms fell 25 percent, from $588 to $440. Despite expansion of public-sector employment, the overall decline of the economy increased unemployment from 23 percent in 1972 to 28 percent in 1980. Import dependence increased from 46 percent of the GDP in 1974 to 53 percent in 1980. Gross capital formation fell from 26 percent in 1975 to 16 percent in 1980, indicating the dramatic fall in investment activities. Dependence on foreign borrowing to finance savings increased from 30 percent in 1969 (under the JLP) to 63 percent in 1976 (under the PNP) to 68 percent in 1980 (again under the

PNP). Domestic savings in real terms fell by approximately 35 percent between 1969 and 1980 (Stone 1987:64).

For the JLP, the above statistics resulted in these significant problems in the economy: a balance of payments crisis; inadequate public savings and excessive public investment; sluggish performance of both the agricultural and the industrial sectors; an over-regulated and over-bureaucratised economy; and an unfavorable investment climate for domestic and foreign capital (Davies 1986; Looney 1987; Stone 1987).

To overcome these problems, the main economic measures adopted included the following:

1. Negotiation of IMF loans of over US$625 million over the 1981-1983 period, and over US$700 million in non-IMF loans to reduce the budget deficit and address the balance of payments problem;
2. To stimulate public savings and decrease public investment, the government targeted public enterprises to generate current account savings equivalent to 2 percent of GDP in fiscal year 83/84; and, public investment expenditures were to be maintained below 15 percent of GDP in each year of the structural adjustment program;
3. To increase the development of the industrial sector, the government created the Export Development Fund and the Kingston Free Zone; increased the activities of the Jamaica National Export Corporation and the Jamaica Export Trading Company; and liberalized the import licensing system;
4. To increase the development of the agricultural sector, the monopsony powers of the External Marketing Organizations (EMOs) were abolished; the sugar cooperatives established during the PNP years were abolished; some of the government-owned factories of the National Sugar Company (NSC) were divested; the local price of sugar was increased by 30 percent; subsidies to the local condensary were eliminated; and, the NSC staff was reduced by 650 at the end of 1982, with another substantial reduction planned over the next three years;
5. To address the problems of an over-regulated and over-bureaucratized economy, the most immediate measures introduced were government rationalization of industrial institutions and the removal of the monopsony powers of the EMOs;
6. To attract domestic and foreign investment, the Jamaica National Investment Promotion Ltd (JNIP) was set up to assist potential foreign investors by guiding them through red tape; all commercial arrears were eliminated with IMF assistance; the import licensing system was simplified, with automatic issue of licenses to exporters for all their import needs when financed through export certificates; the Export Development Bank (EDB) was expanded, becoming the main source of foreign exchange for imports required by exporters. (Looney 1987:195-226)

The IMF Loans and the First Phase of Adjustment

Like the PNP, the Seaga government economic strategy was centered on foreign borrowing to stabilize the economy and promote growth. The assumption was that Jamaica was not capable of financing its developmental projects from internal sources. As a result of his conservative ideology, Seaga was able to attract bilateral funding from the United States, Canada, Western Europe, and Japan, and multilateral funding from the World Bank and the IMF.

Table 6.2 indicates the tremendous growth in Jamaica's external debt between 1980 and 1987. At the end of 1985, the total official debt was US$3.4 billion, with commercial banks accounting for 12 percent of total debt, bilateral loans 42 percent, multilateral loans 3.9 percent, and other loans 7 percent. By 1987, the total debt had increased to US$3.5 billion, or 133 percent of GDP, with debt owed to multilateral institutions amounting to US$1.3 billion, or 37 percent of the total stock of debt and roughly 50 percent of GDP. Bilateral creditors were owed US$1.8 billion, or 57 percent of the total stock of debt, and commercial banks US$0.4 billion, or 11 percent of total debt outstanding (Table 6.2).

TABLE 6.2 Creditors by Institutional Category, 1980, 1985, 1986, and 1987 (in US$ Million)

	1980		1985		1986		1987	
	Debts Outstanding	%	Debts Outstanding	%	Debts Outstanding	%	Debts Outstanding	%
Commercial banks	440	25	393	12	389	11	400	11
Official (bilateral loans)	420	27	1417	42	1634	45	1800	51
Official (Multilateral loans)	620	36	1313	39	1498	42	1300	37
Others	204	12	232	7	56	2	—	1
Totals	1684	100	3355	100	3577	100	3500	100

Source: Bank of Jamaica, cited in N. Davis (1988:158).

The government signed an IMF Extended Fund Facility agreement in April 1981, providing for a loan of US$650 million over three years. In addition, it received US$48 million from the Compensatory Financing Facility to offset shortfalls in traditional export earnings. The bilateral and multilateral aid led to the temporary and superficial economic growth that Jamaica experienced between 1981 and 1982. Economic aid from the United States jumped from US$38 million in 1978–1979 to US$208 million in

1981–1982. In that same period, multilateral aid went from US$174 million to US$302 million. More than 67 percent of World Bank loans to the Caribbean went to Jamaica in 1981–1982. The total loans for 1982 amounted to $133 million, more than the island received from combined World Bank lending in the entire period 1946–1978. More than half of this amount went for a structural adjustment loan to reorient Jamaica's economy toward export industries and away from production for the internal market. However, private capital and foreign investment continued to be relatively static (Barry et al. 1984:346). With these abundant resources, the government was able to create an atmosphere of prosperity. Most of the import restrictions of the Manley period were lifted, as luxury items and basic consumer goods were readily available. Roads were repaired, professionals began to return, and the private sector became optimistic once more.

The IMF loans were a centerpiece of the government's recovery program, intended to ease the burden of its external debt and to ultimately restore the economy to a state of equilibrium. Implementation of IMF policies were swift and immediate: prices were increased on all imported items including oil, a liberal import policy was instituted, subsidies to basic foods were reduced, interest rates were increased, credit was restricted, and public sector spending was decreased as some public sector resources were reallocated to the export sector.

These policies were instituted to meet IMF targets for reduction of current account deficits. The JLP government agreed to retain an overall central government deficit at the level of 6.8 percent of GDP in fiscal year 1985/86, with a further reduction to 4.0 percent of GDP in 1986/87. In order to increase domestic resources, the IMF required government reductions in expenditures equivalent to $128 million per fiscal year. The government responded to that request by laying off more than 6,000 state employees and eliminating critical social services as well as relief programs set up by the previous government (Davies 1986b).

Although the government was convinced that its IMF-inspired policies were more appropriate than those pursued under democratic socialism, politics primarily determined its fiscal policies. The government realized that it had a choice between alienating a significant percentage of the middle and lower classes by increasing prices, reducing food subsidies, and decreasing public-sector spending, or risking foreign exchange scarcity by not imposing these sanctions. Given the severe economic difficulties that Jamaica experienced as a result of foreign exchange scarcity, it is not difficult to understand why the government considered external capital sources to be the greater danger in the short run, although it had no guarantee that its stabilization policies would stimulate growth in the long run. The JLP government remained optimistic about economic payoffs for its stabilization policies, assuming that the international environment would remain favorable.

IMF officials paid little attention to the role of the Jamaican political leaders in shaping economic policy. Although committed to liberalizing the economy and making greater use of the market, the state-controlling leaders had good political reasons to oppose reduction in public sector expenditures because they clearly had much to gain from a system in which resources for survival were controlled and allocated by the state. Market-oriented policies required not only a new ideological orientation in the government, but a political strategy for handling the transition and the capacity to dismantle the clientelist political coalitions that characterized the party system. The latter has not occurred.

The inflow of foreign capital was expected to offset the political damage caused by the JLP's adjustment policies, and set the stage for the economic miracle that was expected under the Seaga administration. Both the government and IMF officials were so encouraged by the financial support that Jamaica received between November 1980 and December 1982, and by the investments promised, that they made unrealistic projections of economic growth in the economy. Table 6.3 provides a comparison of the production projections made in the Extended Fund Facility agreement with the IMF and the actual achievements.

TABLE 6.3 Projected and Actual Production Achievements, 1981–1984

Sector	Actual Production					Target for Fiscal Year 1983/84 (from IMF Agreement)
	1980	1981	1982	1983	1984	
Bauxite/alumina (million tonnes)	12.1	11.7	8.4	7.7	8.9	18
Sugar (thousand long tons)	242	198	196	193	190	330
Bananas (thousand tons)	33	19	22	23	11	120
Non-traditional exports (US$ million)	111	126	144	153	137	220

Source: Davies, 1986b:93.

It was envisaged that the state's revenues would increase enormously through export earnings generated by the bauxite and agricultural sectors. However, the government quickly discovered that export earnings were ultimately dependent on conditions in the international market. The projections were off base, as in none of the critical areas was the target achieved. The bauxite sector was perhaps the most disappointing. The government announced in June 1981 that bauxite production would be increased from the 1980 figure of 12.1 million tonnes to at least 26 million tonnes in 1983/84; alumina production was to be similarly expanded from 2.4 to 8.6 million tonnes as a result of a proposed joint venture between the state, ALCOA, and several Norwegian firms to expand ALCOA's refinery in Jamaica (*Jamaica Daily Gleaner*, June 1, 1981). Far from expanding as anticipated, decline in the international demand for bauxite, coupled with changing production techniques, led to a fall in bauxite production to only 7.7 million tonnes in 1983 (Table 6.3). Government revenue from the industry fell accordingly from US$206 million in 1980 to US$137 million in 1982 (*Economic and Social Survey* 1983:9.3–9.5). Seaga capitalized on his friendship with Reagan and appealed to him for assistance. Reagan responded in December 1981 by ordering 1.6 million tonnes of Jamaican bauxite for defense stockpile, sidestepping regulations for competitive purchases. The impact on the industry was softened by Reagan's action, but the purchase could make only a limited contribution to the balance of payments because the United States insisted on paying for the bauxite, in part, by the barter provision of agricultural products (Payne 1988a:116). The government also negotiated two barter deals with General Motors and Chrysler, exchanging bauxite for vehicles (Barry et al. 1984:349).

The poor performance of the sugar and banana sectors aggravated the balance-of-payments problems caused by the fall in bauxite production. Sugar production declined by 46,000 tons between 1980 and 1982, and banana production by 11,000 tons over the same period. Yet, the JLP government made no substantive policy changes regarding its dependence on commodities whose prices were determined by shifts in the international market. Diversifying the agricultural sector could have created more jobs and increased export production; however, such policies would have required allocating resources to the rural middle and lower classes and perhaps encouraging settlement in those areas. As the urban industrial classes formed a central part of the political coalition in the state in 1980, their overwhelming influence prevented the government from pursuing economic policies that could have led to developmental transformation.

Political imperatives led to the government's implementing liberalized import policies, which allowed luxury items (such as Mercedes Benz, Volvos, BMWs, VCRs, videos, and satellite dishes) desired by the upper and middle classes to enter the country at an unprecedented rate. The JLP had to reward those middle classes that guaranteed its 1980 victory by allowing them to have access to the luxury goods that were not available during the 1976–1980 period. The importation of these goods had an adverse effect on the trade balance, leading to an increase in the trade deficit from US$213 million in 1980 to US$500 million in 1981 to US$595.4 million in 1983 (Davis 1986b:85, 98).

Although the new inflows of foreign capital enabled the government to record an upward trend in the economy away from the negative growth of the seventies, the majority middle and lower classes still found themselves unable to meet their basic daily needs. Table 6.4 shows the situation in the overall Jamaican economy in 1984. Despite positive GDP growth in the 1981–1983 period, the levels were marginal. In the case of unemployment, it dropped only 0.6 percent, and the high levels remained.

TABLE 6.4 Key Socioeconomic Indicators, 1981–1984

Variables	1981	1982	1983	1984
Unemployment (%)	26.2	27.0	25.8	25.6
Youth unemployment (%)	48.0	50.7	46.6	47.7
Rates of growth				
(a) GD	2.5	1.0	2.0	–0.4
(b) Agriculture	2.3	–7.9	7.3	10.0
(c) Mining	1.3	–29.0	0.6	0.7
(d) Manufacture	1.1	6.4	3.2	–6.4
(e) Construction	0.4	15.9	6.3	–5.4
Housing completions				
(number)	2304	6229	4514	3040
External Debt (US$million)	2237	2757	3275	3237
Inflation (%)				
(Consumer Price Index,				
December to December)	4.6	6.5	16.7	31.2

Source: Davies (1986:101).

The costs of servicing the external debt had virtually eliminated half of the declining export earnings and the fiscal budget. Although the primary beneficiaries of its policies were the country's upper classes, the government still had to continue the Jamaican tradition of allocating resources for lower- and middle-class patronage. As a result, the public sector continued to absorb a large share of the national budget: in 1981, central government expenditure was 42.8 percent of GDP as compared to 43.1 percent in 1980. The public debt held by the Bank of Jamaica increased by J$100 million in 1982, indicating that the distribution of bank credits continued to facilitate public sector access to resources (Looney 1987:222).

Public-sector resources were insufficient to increase employment opportunities, as were private-sector and foreign economic activities; hence the unemployment rate continued to hover at 27 percent (Stone 1987). The lion's share of public sector resources was allocated as patronage to government supporters. The government did not have a compelling desire to circumvent the patronage system and create a developmental program that would have provided steady employment and upward mobility for the lower classes. Instead, it continued policies that strengthened the state sector and guaranteed support from its dependent clients.

There was some effort at job creation in the form of the Human Employment and Resource Training (HEART) and Solidarity programs, funded by J$10 million of state monies and US$10 million from USAID. This increased public-sector expenditures and increased the labor force that the government employed. In order to subsidize the HEART program, a system of payroll taxation was imposed whereby private-sector employees whose monthly payroll exceeded J$7,222 were required to pay a 3 percent tax on the total wage bill and the tax collections were to be placed in the HEART trust fund. The tax collections were used to assist with financing training programs in the areas of continuing education, cosmetology, business, agriculture, construction, crafts, and garments. The government reported HEART tax collections of J$5.5 million in fiscal year 1982/83, increasing to J$21.9 million in 1984/85 (Alm 1988:477–496).

Programs such as HEART and Solidarity were attempts to incorporate the secondary school levels into government employment. The approximately 250,000 unemployed of the Manley era had not been absorbed. Solidarity was intended to accommodate the projected 13,000 youth each year who were unable to participate in training at the level of the HEART program. In 1986, the government reported 8,023 students in training with an additional 14,850 to be enrolled at the end of 1986. Solidarity reportedly had 10,000 participants in its first year, ending November 1986 (*Budget Speech* 1986:49). Evidently, the government was unable to put a dent in the unemployment figures, and the picture continued to be bad (relatively worse than under the previous government).

At the same time, the JLP's economic policies, with their emphasis on export-oriented growth, foreign investment, and privatization, were benefiting the private sector and the professionals employed by them, who stood to gain from expanding opportunities created by the new access to international financial markets. As mentioned, the private sector is disproportionately white (Arab and Jewish origin) with a small number of Chinese and East Indians among them. Free-market policies favored this group, whereas public-sector expansion provided patronage resources for the black and brown lower classes as well as employment opportunities for the white, black, and brown middle classes employed in government organizations. Seaga had hoped that this strategy, which benefited all classes, could have consolidated support for his policies and his government. This was not the case, as both domestic and international factors created severe economic problems that led to a balance-of-payments crisis and the dismantling of the government's domestic political coalition.

Balance of Payment Problems:
Shift in Domestic Political Alignments

Despite his commitment to free-market policies, Seaga, like the democratic socialist Manley, was unable to substantially reduce public expenditure. The reasons were primarily political, having little to do with mismanagement and inefficiency. Jamaican political leaders have always used populist and clientelist policies oriented to their political objectives. Both Manley and Seaga understood that they must meet the public-sector service demands of their voters. Despite ideological differences, they both implemented policies that created majority interests committed to the preservation of a dominant state.

Immediately after the Seaga government came to power, it set about dismantling many of the efforts made by the previous government toward expanding political participation and democratizing the society. The new government embarked on an apparent crusade against some of the "populist" programs established under democratic socialism. The Worker Participation schemes were scrapped without any effort to assess their potential. The Sugar Cooperatives' Program (said to be very unpopular) was disbanded and labeled as an abysmal failure without any effort to make it more administratively viable. The sugar lands were instead turned over to Tate and Lyle interests on a management contract basis, which guaranteed the foreign managers large payments in foreign exchange. The Food Farms, Project Land Lease, and the Community Enterprise Organizations (CEOs) were all scrapped, perceived to be wasteful efforts, and were not replaced by any similar policy initiative. In addition, the Home Guards (designed to mobilize community support for fighting crime) and the Community Councils (set up to provide a channel for citizen's participation) were dismantled. Although the latter was not replaced, the Home Guards were replaced by wardens hired in rural areas to help cope with mounting problems of crop and livestock theft. This alternative turned out to be ineffective (Stone 1986:136).

However, the government did maintain some of the existing policies and attempted to implement some populist programs of its own. Some state agencies were maintained, such as the State Trading Corporation, whose name was changed to the Jamaica Commodity Trading Corporation (JCTC) instead of transferring its business to the private sector. Employment opportunities continued to be created for government supporters in the JCTC. Although this enhanced the capacity of the state to control the population, it meant that the political opposition bases continued to shrink during this administration.

In 1985, social welfare services such as the Food Aid Program were launched. Food stamps (free of cost) were provided to 200,000 indigent persons and 200,000 expectant mothers with pre-school children. In addition, 600,000 school children were promised free school lunches (*Budget Speech* 1984/1985). Demonstrating that it could be as innovative as the PNP in the area of education, the JLP established the Education Tax in 1983 to advance educational goals such as increasing teachers' salaries and constructing buildings. Total taxes collected in the first eight months of its imposition (August 1983–March 1984) totaled J$10.8 million, and in 1984/85 it more than tripled to J$35.1 million (Alm 1988:477–496). It has been argued that the government's excessive spending on populist programs precipitated a fiscal crisis in the economy in late 1982 and early 1983. Although it was widely perceived that the stabilization and adjustment policies had been drastically applied, the government faced balance-of-payments problems by early 1983. Although government spending certainly contributed to the government's problems, the decline in both traditional and nontraditional export earnings, insufficient domestic savings and foreign investments, and the trade account deficits led to a shortage of foreign exchange for the state, thus deteriorating the balance of payments.

The government was in a dilemma. The IMF insisted that devaluation of the dollar and further public sector reductions were prerequisites for continued loans. This was a difficult political proposition, as the middle and lower classes were fast becoming alienated from the state and any further burdens on them would certainly undermine their confidence in the government. Inflation was up, as real wages plunged considerably. By early 1983, there was an 18 percent increase in the cost of living after single digit increases in 1981 and 1982. The majority classes were becoming restless.

Faced with budget deficits, and potential working-class antigovernment mobilization, Seaga made a swift political move against the business classes, transferring some private-sector resources to the state for its own use. At the same time that devaluation of the exchange rate was announced, Seaga increased taxation on the business classes (the classes widely perceived to be given preferential treatment by the government) to offset the budget deficits created by a high level of public spending. Caught in the grips of a depressed domestic market, high interest rates, tight monetary policies, and increasingly scarce foreign exchange, the business classes were faced with more than J$100 million in new taxes. The JLP government's credibility as a promoter of private investment was damaged because the private sector viewed the tax policies as a major disincentive to business investment. The business classes began to withdraw their support (which up to that point was presumed to be unequivocally for the government). Constrained by the state's need to perpetuate its own political base, the government was unable to shift substantial resources from the public to the private sector as was necessary for efficiency and economic growth, according to its liberal orthodox economic advisers.

Taking advantage of patriotic support for its role in the Grenada invasion, the government followed IMF guidelines, and in November 1983 imposed a 40 percent devaluation on the dollar, reducing the exchange rate from US$1=J$3.30 to US$1=J$5.50; this devaluation was extended and completed in December 1983. Contrary to the government's and the IMF's expectations, devaluation did not improve net export, given import inelasticity in the international markets for Jamaican exports. The fiscal deficit did not disappear because the state did not restructure the tax system to assure enough revenues to eliminate the deficit.

This large devaluation had a devastating and immediate effect on the cost of living. The Consumer Price Index increased by 31.4 percent in 1984, as subsidies were removed from basic foods and prices were deregulated. Electricity rates increased by 116 percent within a three-month period in 1984 because devaluation of the dollar led to increased costs of servicing the Jamaica Public Service's (JPS) capital expansion programs, which were financed by external loans. In some instances, electricity bills surpassed the costs of rental housing. The small business sector was also affected because credit was reduced and interest rates skyrocketed as the government made an effort to stimulate domestic savings. The housing construction industry, dominated by local capitalist interests, experienced a downturn in economic activity as the high cost of financing and mortgaging affected the consumer's ability to purchase. The result was a decline in the housing construction industry, with total housing completions in 1984 amounting to slightly more than 3,000 units compared to 6,200 in 1982 (Davies 1986b).

The combined impact of declined export earnings and import liberalization worsened the trade balance, so that by mid-1984 the deficit was more than half the export earnings, and in 1985 it was larger than export earnings. In 1986, the deficit was nearly two-thirds of the value of exports. The total value of exports in 1986 was 60 percent of the value in 1980 (Clive Thomas 1988:234). The external debt in 1986 had grown to US$3500 million, which was almost double the 1980 level. This debt as a percentage of GDP stood at 170 in 1986 as compared with 82 in 1980 (Clive Thomas 1988:234).

The impact of these statistics wreaked havoc on the lives of the Jamaican people. Stone's December 1983 poll showed that partisan support had been reduced to 38 percent for the JLP, and stood at 43 percent for the PNP with 19 percent uncommitted. Bitter resentment against the visible affluence of the small (largely) light-skinned and white rich Jamaican elite was expressed by the lower classes, who were being subjected to belt-tightening policies, high rentals, unemployment, and other economic pressures. There was a general perception that there was a reversal on the racial question as the administration catered to the nonblack minorities and white foreign interests with little sensitivity to black self-determination. Foreign and local minorities felt comfortable to once more express their prejudice against blacks without incurring penalties from the government (Figueroa 1988).

Seaga's governing style also served to antagonize the poor, as they cringed under their economic burdens. Manley's personalistic style (often characterized as "charismatic" or "messianic") appealed to the population's desire for patrons who would solve their problems. In contrast, Seaga's technocratic style, admired during the 1980 election campaign, now appeared to the majority classes to be cold and aloof. Public opinion shifted decisively to the PNP by early 1983, as the majority of the electorate began to perceive it as the party with the more concern for the poor. The PNP's credibility as an alternative was rapidly restored between October 1980 and late 1982, although the party had an extremely low profile in opposition (Stone 1982).

Seaga's single-minded focus on access to foreign capital and the interests of those providing it served to ostracize his administration from the local capitalists. The structure of Jamaica's political economy and the realities of statism in the postindependence era created a dependency of the domestic capitalists on the state, particularly for protection from international capital and for access to resources to maintain profitable enterprises. Thus, clientelistic relationships developed between politicians representing middle-class interests and the domestic capitalist elite. Some of the latter are highly attracted to nationalist policies and policies directed at state control of the economy. The PNP policies were considerably more attractive to capitalists in the manufacturing sector than those of the JLP. The state–private sector antagonisms of the Manley period resurfaced as manufacturing interests challenged the government's "open economy" policy. Manufacturers accustomed to a protected domestic market panicked in reaction to the challenge of having to face competition from imported goods. Merchants were in constant competition with each other for scarce U.S. dollars, which they often tried to export. Tensions increased between the private sector and the government as the latter imposed punitive laws against currency racketeering. Continued high interest rates in the United States reduced the expected inflow of foreign exchange in the form of hard currency investments.

Desperately seeking additional resources to appease its rioting mass clients in the urban areas, the government increased taxes in the 1984–1985 year to try to collect more than J$1 million. This tax burden was felt largely by the business community and middle-class consumers. The postelection spirit of cooperation that had emerged in public and private-sector relations evaporated, as by early 1983 Seaga has lost much of his 1980 multiple-class support (Stone 1983). Many private-sector persons lost confidence in Seaga and concluded that perhaps he was as incompetent as Manley at managing the economy. His image of being a financial wizard became a myth as the economy sank further and further into crisis. The Jamaica Manufacturers Association (JMA) and other private sector interest groups began to criticize the government and organize against it. Fears were being expressed that the JLP was catering too much to foreign investors.

Maintaining IMF stabilization policies dictated a series of policies with disastrous economic and political consequences. The need for foreign resources to meet its debt service payments and thus to maintain its credit worthiness (to continue borrowing) forced a government committed to state and party clientelism to cut public spending, tighten fiscal policies, and devalue the dollar. These policies conflicted with the interests of the majority classes who had come to rely on the public sector for patronage resources for employment. Simultaneously, the government sought to squeeze whatever resources it could from the domestic economy by rapidly raising taxes on the business classes. Major cuts in domestic current spending in the public sector, along with devaluation of the dollar and raising private sector taxes, exacerbated the financial crisis in the economy.

Reducing the Tole of the State in the Economy:
The Challenge of Clientelism

Under democratic socialism, state corporations became the dominant form of economic organization, far surpassing local private companies in terms of business turnover and capital invested (Stone 1986:88–96). The free-enterprise system was portrayed by the PNP government as one that allowed foreign and domestic capitalists enormous control of the economy. The objective of the Manley government was not only to create public enterprises to generate surplus capital, but also to satisfy its nationalistic desires for state control of the "commanding heights" of the economy. PNP developmental ideology prompted it to set up state enterprises charged with project generation and the provision of social services. By 1977, that administration had spent 22.1 percent of GDP on government expenditure, increased from 6.2 percent in 1955 (under the PNP) and 12.1 percent in 1970 (under the JLP). Public-sector workers and staff increased from 57,000 in 1968 to 107,000 in 1973 (Stone 1986:88–89).

With the collapse of the economy in 1980, multilateral financial aid donors urged free-market policies and privatization of public enterprises. Both the lending agencies and the JLP government believed that privatization would lead to profitability and operating efficiency of public enterprises. Indeed, privatization was an explicit condition for IMF loans to the government in 1987 (Manley 1987; Payne 1988b). The IMF held the view that the overextended public sector slowed down growth in the economy, accounting for the financial crises of the seventies. A significant portion of the state budget is used for patronage to supporters through access to jobs and corruption. Although the political issue of clientelism was not addressed directly, the free-market economic policies advocated by external lenders were intended both to affect the performance of the economy and to indirectly weaken the clientelist system. An important political argument for liberalization, deregulation, and reducing government subsidies is that those controls facilitate corruption and patronage among the population. However, in the postindependence period, both JLP and PNP governments have generated policies that committed the population to clientelism (see Chapter 4).

Despite the population's disenchantment with democratic socialism, the JLP government learned that policy prescriptions directed toward reduction in the size of the public sector involved serious political costs. Any significant changes in the role of state involvement in the economy threatened to undermine the compliance mechanism of the patron-clientelist relationships that characterized Jamaica's political economy. The range of corrective actions that the government could have implemented through privatizing the economy without threatening political stability was thus significantly curtailed.

Administrative Reform. Under pressure from foreign donors to reduce public expenditure, Seaga was compelled to make some changes. The JLP government reduced the number of civil servants from 108,000 in 1980 to 99,800 by October 1983. The official government explanation to the population was that adjustments had to be made to increase government efficiency and to balance the budget. The civil service is known to have a preponderance of PNP supporters, and the government's action caused further political divisions within the society, as civil servants supporting the PNP accused the government of playing politics.[4]

The government embarked on a program of budgetary reform that would not require shifting resources from the public sector. In the 1984/85 budget debate, Seaga revealed that power would become more centralized in his Ministry of Finance, and the responsibilities of the MPs were recast. MPs were perceived to have traditionally acted in advisory roles to ministries, which spent money on various projects in the constituencies. Seaga explained the new role of the MP:

A vote of $J30 million has been provided under a new programme, the Local Development Programme to provide an amount of $J500,000 to each MP which can be spent at his discretion.

The vote is not all new money. It absorbs a number of votes such as the Relief Employment Programme, Christmas Work, Indigent and Poor Houses, Welfare Assistance, etc. These votes are now incorporated into the Local Development Programme so that an M.P. can exercise his own discretion as to how he determines these funds should be employed.

The Local Development Programme will enable M.P.'s to assist their constituencies promptly and restore manhood to the largely emasculated positions of Members of Parliament who are excluded from Parish Councils and left out of Ministries. (*Budget Speech* 1984/1985)

The demand for reduction of public expenditure led the government to implement a policy that only led to further concentration of power in the elected official. Responsibility for fiscal affairs was placed in the hands of the MP and the Ministry of Finance. Through the Local Development Programme, the MP emerged as the central fulcrum of power. This favored a resurgence of clientelism as the MP's new role demanded that he strengthen his position among his constituents. Considerably more governmental resources were allocated to the MP than at any other time in the post-1945 period. It may seem strange to the outside observer that the government was now officially giving the MP power (which Chapter 3 demonstrated he always had) that he had enjoyed for over four decades.

This was government manipulation at its best, as the population did not oppose a policy from which they have reaped benefits in the past. The government used the channel that had been legitimized by the Jamaican people and the one to which they had become accustomed. Although the public may object to a reduction of public-services expenditures, there has been no documented opposition to the government's new proposal. With an abundance of new resources, the MP continued to succeed in establishing patron-client relations with his constituents. The government further strengthened the political environment, which necessitated the use of personalistic contacts with public and elected authorities. Interviews carried out by the author in 1986 reveal that the people still perceive the elected officials (the MP in particular) as the best and the only means to get needed public resources. There was no indication that the MP was reluctant to use personal influence to meet the needs of his constituents.[5]

Elected officials continued to fulfill reciprocity obligations to clients through exchange for material goods and services. This aspect of the JLP's administrative reform program failed to replace clientelism with an adequate new means for the distribution of resources within the Jamaican society.

Privatizing Public Enterprises. Jamaica was one of three developing nations (the others included Pakistan and Senegal) that was given a structural adjustment loan by the World Bank in 1981 with privatization as an explicit condition. The World Bank has argued that privatization is perhaps the best tool for encouraging managerial efficiency in developing nations (Hayter and Watson 1985). The World Bank, perhaps unlike the IMF, has been convinced that in some developing nations outright privatization may not be appropriate. As Table 6.5 indicates, the World Bank has a range of policies consisting of attempts to institute competition for and reforms within state enterprises and outright privatization.

With regard to public enterprises in Jamaica, the policy changes that the Bank asked for and actually achieved were limited to the termination of the powers of the External Marketing Organizations. A program of studies was undertaken to reduce the marketing functions of the EMOs. The intent was to ensure competition in external marketing. The EMOs were retained, however, and continued to have a number of nonmarketing functions such as fertilizer supplies, extension systems, and farmer credit.

The sugar and banana industries experienced a slump in the early 1980s (see Table 6.3), and the Seaga administration was able to use the economic downturn in both industries as an excuse to turn over portions of sugar cane and banana production to private industry. Tate and Lyle, United Brands, Booker McConnell, and Gulf & Western were invited to own, manage, or restructure the country's two main export industries. The sugar workers, the island's largest work force, opposed government plans to privatize the industry, particularly as this would mean a freeze on all wage increases and possible loss of jobs. The government paid little attention to the sugar worker protests and embarked on its plan to "increase the development of the agricultural sector."

In order to increase efficiency, the sugar cooperatives were dismantled and passed over to state management by the government-owned NSC. Furthermore, some of the NSC's factories were divested and its staff was reduced by 650 at the end of 1982, with further reductions targeted for the following year. NSC operations were decentralized, increasing accountability of factory managers. To further improve the financial viability of the sugar industry, government froze the factory gate price of sugar at the 1981 level, while increasing the local price by 30 percent. Finally, a subsidy to the local condensary was significantly reduced (Looney 1987).

Air Jamaica and the government-owned Jamaica Broadcasting Corporation (JBC) were targeted for reform and limited divestment. At the time of writing, those areas identified for divestment had still not been divested. In spite of 1980 pre-election rhetoric against the State Trading Corporation, the government changed its name but did not dismantle the corporation because it recognized its role as an efficient bulk buyer of basic food items that was able to provide lower prices to the consumer. In this case, it was practical to continue PNP policy instead of displaying ideological rigidity. The ailing and bankrupt government-owned urban bus company, the Jamaica Omnibus Services (ironically known in the Jamaican vernacular as "jolly bus") was dismantled, and small entrepreneurs operating minibuses profited from the transfer. They took over transportation services in the metropolitan area of Kingston and St. Andrew and in Spanish Town. Although these small minibuses had a relatively high casualty rate, due to the speed at which they were driven and their overcrowdedness, the consumers were willing to pay the increased fares as they were now able to get to their destinations on time. Hotels and other commercially viable enterprises were passed from government to private management rapidly.

Divestment was limited, despite Seaga's desire to move to a market economy. There appeared to have been more a commitment to public-sector reform than an attempt to sell many unprofitable government assets to wary local and foreign entrepreneurs. There could have been considerable political repercussions that would follow a program of extensive denationalization, particularly because the potential buyers would be wealthy racial minorities in Jamaica or white foreign interests. However, a limited program of privatization was undertaken as a necessary policy measure to secure the continued inflow of foreign assistance from the international lending agencies

TABLE 6.5 World Bank Structural Adjustment Lending: Policy Reforms Involving
State Enterprises as Conditions for Loans

Country/Number of Structural Adjustment Loan	Date	Details of Policy Reform Requested	Implementation
Outright Privatization			
Ivory Coast I	November 1981	Denationalize local rice milling	Yes
Togo I and II	June 1983– February 1985	Privatization of steel and other state enterprises	Yes
Kenya II	June 1982	National Crops Marketing Board to withdraw to role of buyer and seller of last resort	No
Partial privatization			
Thailand	February 1982	Develop a concrete program to implement policy that commercially oriented state enterprises (e.g., power, water, airlines) will be financially independent or liquidated by end of 1983	Very little
		Allow private slaughter houses to operate in competition with govern-ment	Yes
Panama	October 1983	Financial restructuring of all public sector corpor-ations; sale of one loss-making hotel; termination of subsidy to private cement company	No
Jamaica III	October 1984	External Marketing Organi-zations (for coffee, bananas, etc.) to divest themselves of marketing functions such as transport and extension	Yes

Source: World Bank, *President's Reports*; cited in Paul Mosley (1988).

and the United States. Privatization occurred in agriculture, municipal services, transportation, manufacturing, communications, and tourism.

From Import-Substitution to Export-Led Development: Domestic and External Responses

Export-led industrialization was a central part of the development strategy of the Seaga government. This represented a shift away from the import-substitution industrialization policies that were actively promoted in the post–World War II and postindependence periods. It has been argued that the import-substitution approach failed because it placed limits on the capacity of the Jamaican economy to generate growth, employment, and incomes in a self-sustained manner. Industrial production was mainly for the small national market, and local manufacturers were unable to compete in the international market when the domestic market became saturated (Long 1989). Export emphases geared to selling products to the large U.S. market were to be the new economic strategy, to be carefully planned with the U.S. government, U.S. corporations, and the local private sector.

"New" exports of manufactures (textiles, garments) of Jamaica grew more than tenfold between 1980 and 1984. In 1980, the value of export sales was J$1.7 million, increasing to J$8.3 million in 1981 and J$18.0 million in 1984 (Long 1989:123–124). At the same time, traditional manufactured exports were virtually stagnant between 1980 and 1983 (from US$14.1 million to US$14.8 million) and real growth of manufactures was minus 1.8 percent (*Economic and Social Survey* 1983). Diversification was the only plausible solution to the economic vulnerability that characterized Jamaica, a nation highly dependent on a few primary exports and its mineral sector for its foreign-exchange earnings. Developing nations are often vulnerable to uncontrollable fluctuations in world commodity prices; in the case of agricultural commodities, to unpredictable changes in weather conditions.

Export production was intended to encourage private enterprise through market forces that encouraged savings, investments, productivity, new technologies, and economic efficiency. As an initial step to encourage nontraditional export production, in March 1981 the government issued "no funds" licenses in large numbers for the import of raw materials, spare parts, and capital goods. This meant that licenses were issued to importers who did not need foreign exchange from the Bank of Jamaica to finance the imports for which the licenses were required. The entire import licensing system was radically overhauled and simplified, with the abolition of the trade administrator's department and its replacement by a trade board with private-sector representation.

The Caribbean Basin Initiative opened up for Jamaica duty-free access to the U.S. market for a wide range of exports. The CBI was intended to provide a strong incentive for the government's shift away from import-substitution toward export-led growth. From the very outset, the CBI did not appear as if it would have much of an impact on the Jamaican economy. First, U.S. military and national security interests played a key role. Socialist and Marxist-oriented regimes such as Nicaragua and Grenada were excluded from the benefits. One-fourth of the US$350 million allocated for the CBI was to be used to support one country, El Salvador, in its war against insurgents. Second, the CBI extended its duty-free benefits to only 7 percent of the region's exports. Prior to the CBI, 87 percent of Caribbean exports already entered the U.S. market duty free under existing trade preference agreements. The most important export items in the Caribbean—namely sugar, textiles, petroleum products, and footwear—were subject to import quotas and duties that were not lifted by the CBI. The reason was that special-interest lobbying by U.S.-based manufacturers led the U.S. Congress to retain import duties on textiles, petroleum products, footwear, handbags, luggage, work gloves, leather apparel, and tuna, thereby narrowing the line of industries that could benefit from duty-free entry (Berger 1984; Newfarmer 1985; Stone 1987).

The demand for foreign investment was very strong, as the government designed generous liberal and fiscal incentives to attract foreign companies. Although investment applications had to be monitored, screened, and filed for approval with the government-created JNIP, these were miniscule regulations designed to give the state control over the terms of access to domestic markets, cheap labor, and other factors of production. These limited control measures allowed the state political control, but perhaps deterred some foreign investors from coming to Jamaica.

Owing to the weakness of the Jamaican private sector, the government chose to embrace as many private foreign investors as possible with little restrictions. Incentive legislation virtually eliminated corporate taxes, income taxes, and custom duties for foreign corporations. Transnational corporations from the United States dominated the industrial sector (e.g., Proctor and Gamble, Bristol-Meyers, Richardson-Vicks, Johnson and Johnson, and Gillette) with a strong representation of European and Canadian firms (Berger Paints, Kiev Holdings, Henkel, and Bata Shoes). Realizing that they could undermine the local manufacturers, the government encouraged joint-ventures between local and foreign capital or participated in those vital sectors itself (Stone 1987). The government's liberal import policies forced thirty-three Jamaican garment and shoe factories to close by 1982, and many others were then operating at only 40 percent capacity. Local capital was increasingly weakened and undermined, as it could not compete with the new rapid inflow of foreign investors. The only potential countervailing force against the overwhelming foreign sector was the state sector as a local entrepreneur.

Despite the government's aggressive campaign to bring foreign investors to Jamaica, investments were not as forthcoming as the government had hoped. The government reported US$141 million in private investments in 1985, a far cry from what had been expected (Looney 1987). Many investors were still skeptical about the unstable economic and political situation, which really had not changed significantly by 1983. Few were interested in investing in nontraditional agricultural exports or in flowers for the U.S. market. Only Kaiser Aluminum made a commitment in starting Jamaica Floral Exports. After 1983, the Seaga government could not find new investors. Rather than large TNCs, it was able to attract only small corporations like Affordable Custom Dental Appliances, which used cheap Jamaican labor to manufacture dentures. The government failed to attract private bank loans that the country needed to build its foreign-exchange reserve.

In January 1983, in the midst of a balance-of-payments crisis, the government expanded its export promotion strategy to include an Export Development Fund (EDF) that assured the availability of foreign exchange to finance imported inputs used by exporters; created the Kingston Free Zone, a free trade environment for the functioning of enclave-type industries; implemented a phased elimination of the 364 quantitative restrictions (QRs) over a five-year period, to encourage domestic producers to become more efficient; and allowed exporters to third markets to retain 50 percent of their export proceeds (Looney 1987). During the previous year, the government had introduced the Jamaican Export Free Zone Act, which offered generous incentives, including tax exemption, 100 percent tax holidays, the elimination of import licensing and normal customs provisions, duty-free import of raw materials and capital goods, and repatriation of assets, etc.

These measures were expected to be a significant incentive to exporters. They were to enhance their competitiveness by improving production runs through unrestricted access to the foreign exchange required not only for export-related imports but also for the imported inputs needed for production for the domestic market. Furthermore, Jamaica's abundant supply of cheap unskilled and semiskilled labor appeared to have given momentum to the "new" export activities. Weekly wages for machine operators in export-oriented industries between 1982 and 1983 were equivalent to US$15 to US$25 (*Labor Viewpoint* 2, 4, 1984). Although these wages were an incentive to local and foreign investors, the trade unions (both BITU and NWU) vigorously protested against them. Given the superior political strength of the government in its alliance with foreign capital, it was able to continue its low-wage policies to make the way for increased penetration by foreign capital.

The government provided attractive investment opportunities to domestic entrepreneurs but they were unwilling to respond. They had become disillusioned after Seaga's second year in office. They viewed his structural adjustment policies as essential, but believed they were deceived as to the pace of this adjustment (Looney 1987). These entrepreneurs were particularly disappointed by the government's quick desire to allow foreign investors to encroach on the private sector, and soon became unhappy and skeptical about future commitments to what they saw as an increasingly foreign dominated economy. They broke with the government by 1985.

CONCLUSION: SEAGA'S FAILED POLICIES

The danger signals for the JLP were already evident in early 1983 when Jamaican pollster Carl Stone's polls showed that the Manley-led PNP had a decisive 10 percent lead over Seaga's JLP, with most of the 1980 defected PNP voters returning to the party (Stone Polls:1980–1983, in Stone 1989b:41). The JLP made a slight comeback after the October 1983 government-backed U.S. invasion of Grenada.[6] By mid-1984, the JLP had again slipped in the polls, and local pollsters predicted that the PNP would win the next elections. Many believed that had the JLP called the elections between January and October 1983, the PNP would have won, thus invalidating the two-term cycle theory of Jamaican politics.

Seaga's post-1983 administration lost its legitimacy in the eyes of the majority of the population. There was a general perception that Seaga deceived the PNP. Economic conditions, coupled with its political deception, served to deeply undermine the government, culminating in the January 1985 riots. There were riots all over the urban areas of Kingston and St. Andrew in response to a gasoline price hike from J$8.99 to J$10.90 per gallon. Seaga's response to the urban riots was limited to a nationally televised speech on the necessary hardships the population must endure during the period of "adjustment," and the negative affects that the riots would have on the tourist economy and foreign investments (Payne 1988a). By August 1985, Seaga was faced with a general strike (led by students, teachers, and police officers), the first in Jamaica's postindependence history.

By the end of 1985, the Jamaican economy had begun a downward spiral that alienated the upper, middle, and lower classes and resulted in the election of a new government in February 1989. An economy that had come to rely heavily on foreign finance and its bauxite earnings was hit by an international recession (which led to increases in interest rates and inflation), stagnation in the global bauxite/alumina industry, and marked deterioration in its terms of trade. The JLP regained some support after Hurricane Gilbert in September 1988, when support for the PNP declined. However, the PNP recovered quickly (Stone 1989b:106). Stone's polls between January 1988 and January 1989 (excluding the Gilbert poll) showed a 56.9 percent average strength for the PNP.

The government gained the support of uncommitted voters among the poor and unemployed, who quickly backed the former in an effort to secure some of the Gilbert allocations sent from overseas. The shift in political support was based on clientelist patronage. Stone predicted a PNP victory of

48 seats with 57 percent of the popular vote in the 1989 elections. His prediction was amply confirmed by the results: PNP, 44 seats and 57 percent of the vote; JLP, 16 seats and 43 percent of the vote (see *Jamaica Daily Gleaner*, February 13, 1989, p. 3). The JLP lost about 15 percent of its vote with respect to 1980, but its share of the vote remained high, reflecting the even support given to both parties. Despite its substantial loss of seats, from 51 seats in 1980 to 16 in 1989, the JLP continues to represent more than 40 percent of the electorate and thus remains a critical force in the political process.

Seaga's humiliating defeat baffled both local and international observers. How can the loss of JLP strongholds in the rural parishes be explained? What had happened since 1980 when more than 57 percent of the electorate rejected the failed policies of democratic socialism and placed its hopes in the JLP? What message was the Jamaican electorate sending with its voting behavior? Was it rejecting Seaga's free-market policies in favor of a return to Manley's democratic socialism?

Empirical studies conducted after the 1980 elections (Stone 1981a; Payne 1988a) show that support for the JLP outside of its traditional base (rural small farmer, marginal working class, trade unionist, and import–export–oriented capitalist) had been more of a case of voter protest against the PNP by its established supporters, and by the "swing vote" of the desperately poor uncommitted voters. Given the die-hard support given to the parties by its followers, it was unlikely that the JLP could have hoped to maintain those PNP defectors. Similarly, the unemployed "floating" voters (who are normally responsible for the swing vote), organized by party brokers at the grass-roots level, supported the JLP in exchange for resources. Their relationship was contingent on concrete results and was therefore potentially subject to fluctuation. The capitalist classes had shifted to the JLP as early as 1976, two years after the PNP's adoption of its democratic socialist ideology (Stone 1981b). They saw a vote for the JLP as a vote for a more competent, efficient group of state-controllers who would favor the private sector at the expense of public-sector interests. Moreover, Manley's friendship with Castro made them suspicious and uneasy. In 1989, this multiple-class coalition still wanted "deliverance" from oppression, and money to jingle in its pockets, as it did in 1980.

Why was the JLP unable to deliver and make the people's pockets jingle? Was the JLP rejected simply because the Jamaican electorate appears to be programmed to remove governments after two terms? To answer these questions, one must examine the political context in which Seaga's free-market policies were implemented.

Regardless of the strengths of the free-market policy approach, the JLP government's economic policies proved incompatible with the patronage relationships that characterized state-society relations in Jamaica. Collaboration with international capitalist interests became the government's top priority, to which the demands for improvement in the standard of living of the working classes and the poor were subordinated. This strategy served to dismantle the JLP's domestic multiple-class alliance.

As a dependent client of international capitalist agencies and the U.S. government, Seaga pursued the policies that were recommended by his patrons in exchange for their critical capital transfers. IMF guidelines for Jamaica's economic recovery included, first and foremost, drastic cuts in public-sector spending and a reallocation of public-sector resources to the export sector. In response to IMF policies in which he firmly believed, within his first two years in office Seaga made drastic cuts in public-sector spending, particularly through the elimination of critical social services as well as relief employment programs set up by the PNP.

By 1986, it had become apparent to the JLP government that its policies were not producing the desired results. Despite substantial foreign aid, economic growth had not been achieved. Wages fell, prices increased, the dollar was devalued several times, and the government ran up a huge foreign debt—all designed to stimulate the economy into export-led growth. But none of that happened. The GDP, measured in constant prices, was barely more in 1986 than in 1980. Between 1981 and 1987, the average annual growth rate was a mere 0.44 percent (*Economic and Social Survey* 1986:1, 9). By 1987, there was mass apathy as the lower classes buckled under the burdens of the faltering economy.

For Seaga, the reason for his failed policies was the shortfall in bauxite earnings, which led to a balance-of-payments crisis and an enormous debt rate. Had there been additional revenues from bauxite, he argued, structural adjustment would have worked. Like Manley, he blamed his electoral defeat on external actors, disregarding the connection between Jamaica's internal clientelistic political structure and the management of the economy.[7] Seaga's free-market policies placed him in a bind, as he was forced, through his commitment to structural adjustment policies, to eliminate the state monies required for clientelist patronage. Seaga was defeated not because he lacked international capital, but because his policies led to a breakdown of patronage relationships between the state, the private sector, and the middle and lower classes. Once the state lost its capacity for patronage, inevitably its dependent clients mobilized against it—"1980 revisited."

The leadership of both the JLP and the PNP have been unsuccessful in their attempts to alter the clientelistic character of the Jamaican polity. Under democratic socialism, the mass of PNP supporters were still attached to the party through patron-client ties rather than as a response to the PNP's ideological appeals. With its extensive clientelist structure, the PNP was therefore not a useful vehicle for real democratic reform. The transformational goals of the PNP were insufficient to alter the clientelistic features of the political system. Resources allocated to the government sectors continued to progressively increase under the 1980–1989 Seaga government. The JLP government with its free-market economic policies did not reflect any changes in the clientelistic control of the party system. Its policies reinforced the socioeconomic conditions, which made it imperative that it maintain clientelism and its supporting values in the Jamaican society.

NOTES

1. There has been much debate about state intervention versus the free market in development studies. This is a false dichotomy, as it is a question of whether the market system can be run efficiently and whether supply-side factors are right. There is no reason why the state should be inherently incapable of providing the requisites for an efficient market system. For a useful discussion of the issues central to this debate, see G. Dutto (1968); Gary L. Cowan (1983); Michael Lofchie (1985); and Haile-Mariam Yacob and Berhanu Mengistu (1988).

2. Kissinger's recommendations underscored President Reagan's security thesis: the crisis in the Caribbean originated in Communist subversion, and gradual reform in the area must be through selective economic aid. The Kissinger Commission recommended that Communism be contained by all necessary social and economic stability through investments and trade. If this was not done, it was argued, the U.S. national security could be jeopardized. See *The Report of the President's National Bipartisan Commission on Central America* (Kissinger Commission) (New York: Macmillan, 1984). The perspective expressed by the Kissinger Commission was common in the post–World War II period and is similar to the one articulated in George Quester's (1982) *American Foreign Policy: The Lost Consensus.*

3. Citizens of the Third World as well as African-Americans approached the author after the 1980 elections demanding to know how it could be possible for a country with a 90 percent black and brown population to elect a white Lebanese-Syrian prime minister. They not only implied that the prime minister's race should have disqualified him from holding such a post, but also that the black electorate ought to have had racial considerations in making its choice. African-American media such as *Jet* and *Ebony* constantly played up the fact that Seaga was a nonblack prime minister. (See the November 1980 issues of *Jet* and *Ebony* magazines.) The Jamaican capitalist class (of which Seaga is a representative) is largely of Jewish and Arab ethnic origin, dating back to merchant-class families of the late nineteenth and early twentieth centuries. See Stone (1987): 38–40.

4. Personal interview with fired civil servants who were PNP supporters, December 15, 1986, New York.

5. Personal interviews with forty JLP and PNP MPs in Kingston, St. Andrew, St. Catherine, St. James, Clarendon, St. Thomas, St. Mary, Manchester, Portland, Westmoreland, and St. Ann, July–December 1983.

6. For an analysis of Jamaican reactions to the U.S.-led Grenada invasion, see Carl Stone (1983).

7. Edward Seaga, "The Recession and Jamaica-Problems and Solutions," address by Prime Minister to the Inter-American Press Association Conference, Kingston, 1984, p. 6, cited in Payne (1988a:29).

7

The 1989 PNP Victory and the Future of the State-Centered Patronage System

THE RETURN OF THE PNP

The 1989 victory of the Manley-led PNP suggests a thesis of a "resurgence of clientelism" rather than a return to democratic socialism. The PNP victory reflected a vote for a "better clientelistic system." The JLP was unable to compete with the opposition PNP in providing clientelistic channels whereby access to state resources could be obtained with the proper connections. Unable to fulfill the expectations it created, the Seaga government was rejected by the Jamaican electorate, which returned to the traditional image of the state as patron providing benefits for its survival.

Although the PNP is still regarded as the ideologically liberal party in Jamaica today, it has abandoned its radical image of the 1970s. Manley understood that the PNP's democratic socialist policies created tremendous burdens on the Jamaican people as a result of local and international responses to its programs (Manley 1982, 1987). These factors, coupled with its realization that the Jamaican economy is chronically dependent on foreign capital, led the new PNP government to adopt a strategy of "moderation" and "pragmatism." It has broken ties with the WPJ, with whom it had a close alliance in the 1970s, and its own radical left wing has been expelled from its ranks. Leftists such as attorney-at-law Anthony Spaulding and Dr. D. K. Duncan have disappeared, with the party's realization that it was almost torn apart by ideological factionalism in the 1970s.

In the local and international media, PNP leader Manley has made general acknowledgments of the errors made by his government during the 1972–1980 period:

> While we did many good things in the 1970s, we made some mistakes. Chief among them was believing that governments can be a convenient shortcut to production. My experience tells me that is not so. . . . With a peaceful democracy firmly in place, Jamaica could look forward to an era of unprecedented growth; *one fuelled by the private sector as an engine of growth* [my emphasis] . . . I am happy to tell you that those of you

(who invest) in Jamaica are doing so in absolute safety, your right to foreign exchange and your rights to repatriation of profits indisputable. (*Jamaica Daily Gleaner*, April 10, 1989, p. 8)

What is clear from this statement is that the PNP's new strategy accords a leading role to the private sector in the economy—a shift from its policy of the 1970s, which placed the state at the center of the economy. The PNP has also expressed its continued commitment to education, health, transportation, housing, strengthening of regional institutions such as CARICOM, and a foreign policy of nonalignment.

Manley continues to denounce the policies of the Reagan administration (Manley 1987). He supported the Sandanistas in the 1990 Nicaraguan elections, and has maintained friendly relations with Cuba. However, his former Third World activism has been scaled down considerably. Manley refrains from the use of rhetoric that could be construed as "provocative" and from using the term "democratic socialism" on most occasions, although he expresses a firm commitment to egalitarianism. His credibility has been enhanced in Western circles by his cordial relations with the Bush administration. His new posture has been taken as a sign of repentance by some Western journalists and commentators (NBC's "Today Show," March 19, 1989).

After one and a half years in office, the PNP government, like its predecessor, is facing serious financial and economic problems. Social and political tensions have increased as austerity measures continue to weaken support for the government. Price hikes and drastic cuts in food subsidies were announced scarcely three months after the new government took office (*Jamaica Daily Gleaner*, May 1, 1989, p. 7). The government was expected to present a budget with new policy directions or tangible commitments to policy changes likely to benefit the people. Instead, the June 1989 budget increased taxes (more than J$200 million), cut critical areas of public expenditure, and offered no populist initiatives to confirm its image as a party that is people-oriented. The government was forced to operate within the narrow limits of the tight restrictions imposed by the World Bank and the IMF (*Jamaica Weekly Gleaner*, June 26, 1989, p. 4).

Despite Manley's cordial relationship with the Bush administration, in an unprecedented move Bush diverted Jamaican aid funds to Poland in March 1990. Significant amounts of aid destined for the Caribbean (for example, US$25 million earmarked for Manley's marijuana reduction program) were sent instead to Eastern Europe. Manley had hoped that he would have been rewarded for his efforts to dismantle the drug economy. After his meeting with Bush at the White House in May 1990, Manley was still unable to get a firm commitment of new aid, or to have a restoration of the aid diverted to Poland. As one commentator bluntly stated, "all Manley obtained was the familiar Bush Administration's expression of moral support for Washington's most valuable anglophone Caribbean ally, as Jamaica struggles with underdevelopment" (Brotherson 1990:2).

The failure of the Bush administration to provide expected financial assistance sent a clear signal that the Caribbean (in the absence of the Communist threat) has become an area of the lowest priority on the U.S. agenda. The United States has opted, instead, to develop influence in a rapidly changing Eastern Europe. In response, the Manley government has begun to expand its sources of aid. In March 1990, the Canadian government canceled Jamaica's debt of C$93.4 million in a package that wrote off the debts of Caribbean states totaling C$181 million. At the same time, the Japanese government also loaned Jamaica US$4.8 million for the restoration of coffee farms damaged by Hurricane Gilbert (Brotherson 1990:2).

Despite the PNP's lofty intentions, the question that remains is whether these policies will be enough. The central problems continue to be the system of international dependency and middle-class domination of the state via clientelism. Given the lack of political organization necessary to seriously confront the protracted problems of dependency and clientelism, there is little reason to expect dramatic changes under the 1989 PNP administration.

THE FUTURE OF THE
STATE-CENTERED PATRONAGE SYSTEM

Although developing nations have shown renewed interest in democracy, few scholars have attempted to make a theoretical contribution to an understanding of democratic processes in the Caribbean in the postindependence period (notable exceptions are Stone 1980, 1986; Hintzen 1989). The recent four-volume series by Diamond, Linz, and Lipset (1988) *Democracy in Developing Countries*, does not include a single contribution (footnote or otherwise) on the English-speaking Caribbean—the only area among developing nations with continuous democratic institutions in the postindependence period.

The recent flurry of books and articles on Jamaican political economy have been largely descriptive, chronological studies of political leaders Manley and Seaga and their failed policies (see Manley 1982, 1987; Stephens and Stephens 1987; Payne 1988a and 1988b). There have been few analyses on the nature of the Jamaican state, particularly its dual role in maintaining social cohesion through clientelist patronage and its symbiotic relationship with international capitalist actors that provide the resources for its domestic clientelist strategy (Edie 1984, 1986, 1989). Most other political studies on Jamaica (Stone's works are the single exception) do not address the theoretical linkage between the party system, the state, and external dependency and domestic clientelism. Clientelism is often referred to as a "tendency" that leads to an escalation in violence during election periods (e.g., Lacey 1977; M. Kaufman 1985; Stephens and Stephens 1987; Payne 1988). That is, of course, only a description of the phenomenon and not an explanation of it.

Clearly, my approach is not derived from the dependency school of political economy, except to the extent that I have considered the role of international structures of exchange relationships and the asymmetric power relations that sustain them. In looking at the Manley (1972–1980) and Seaga (1980–1989) periods, I have not only attempted to raise new points and contribute new insights, but also to advance a new mode of analysis. By way of concluding, I would like to make explicit the analytic framework I have employed.

Dual Clientelism and State Capacity

Why has the Jamaican state capacity for political effectiveness been so low? The PNP lost considerable support after 1976 and was unable to maintain social order. The JLP lost support after 1982. In both instances, state effectiveness was extremely low, particularly in terms of economic function. Why were the successive governments not able to effectively maintain political and economic control? My thesis is that the incapacities for maintaining a state-centered patronage system explain the demise of both parties.

State capacity derives from underlying elite support, structured mass support, and externally derived patronage resources. In the postindependence period, the state managed to enhance its capacity by locking the majority classes into the patronage system in an involuntary way. Flynn (1974) correctly asserts that clientelism is coercive because the clients do not often have the choice to make decisions made on preferred alternatives.

The state achieved a considerable degree of autonomy both from the masses of the lower classes and the poor, and from the upper classes. Clientelism insulated the state-controlling middle-class party leaders from the mass base of their multiple-class coalition, and a mix of collaboration, bargaining, and clientelism has enabled them to be relatively independent of the upper classes. External resources reduced the necessity of relying on the local capitalist class for domestic revenues, and thus increased the state's autonomy from the social base. The result of clientelistic control is that the state is dominated by the educated middle classes and has consistently pursued policies favoring their expansion. Economic policies of both JLP and PNP governments were centered on foreign borrowing, which served largely as revenue sources of patronage rather than as a basis for economic growth and transformation of the local economy. Even the 1980–1989 orthodox liberal capitalist JLP government, dominated by technocrats, was governed by policies of elite linkages and patronage considerations.

With the enormous allocations made to education in the

postindependence period, particularly during the 1962–1980 years, the educational system produced thousands of students who formed the recruitment base for the political and state bureaucratic elite systems. Those recruited into these systems have been socialized into Jamaican values, which accord the greatest prestige to those who are educated. They are not likely to challenge the prevailing clientelist norms and practices. The economic opportunities offered to the educated middle classes who join the political and administrative classes have created a fairly cohesive "state bourgeoisie" similar in many respects to the bureaucratic bourgeoisie, managerial bourgeoisie, or prebendal class said to dominate other developing nations.[1]

The dual clientelist character of the state thwarted all efforts toward economic growth via democratic socialism or orthodox free-market policies. Democratic political institutions and economic growth have not been interactive in Jamaica. There have been periods of economic decline (particularly during 1972–1980) and relatively strong political institutions. At the same time, the characteristics of clientelism and patronage prevented economic growth. Recent comprehensive studies on Jamaican and Caribbean politics, such as *Democratic Socialism in Jamaica* by E. H. Stephens and J. D. Stephens (1987), *Politics in Jamaica* by Anthony J. Payne (1988a), and *The Poor and the Powerless: Economic Policy and Change in the Caribbean* by noted Guyanese development economist Clive Y. Thomas (1988), omit this crucial political variable when they discussed failed economic politics in the postindependence period in Jamaica. "Correct" economic policies (be they democratic socialist or liberal capitalist) cannot be successfully implemented in an environment such as Jamaica's where clientelism is hostile to the sustenance of economic markets.

Although the middle class has achieved a relatively high degree of insulation from both the lower classes and the capitalist elite, control by powerful external capitalist actors has continued to limit its autonomy. Foreign capital has been incorporated into the political economy in a dominant position vis-à-vis the state and all other domestic groups. The state has neither been able to coopt nor neutralize foreign capitalist interests, but instead has been forced to accommodate them due to external dependency. The 1972–1980 Manley democratic socialist government attempted to achieve some degree of state autonomy in economic decisionmaking and foreign policy. Its welfarist policies and programs were halted prematurely as critical external resources were withdrawn. IMF-guided policies of the Seaga period did not increase investments, savings, growth, efficiency, and employment in the Jamaican economy, although they were rationalized in those terms (Looney 1987).

The economic policies of the 1989 PNP government have not emphasized state sector dominance, nor has the government pursued populist welfare policies with which it has become intimately linked. The lower classes began to lose hope within a year of the government's tenure in office.

What is unusual for Jamaican electoral politics is that although the PNP has lost support, the JLP's credibility has not been restored. Part of the reason for this is the leadership crisis faced by the JLP, precipitated by allegations of a conspiracy to oust party leader Seaga (*Jamaica Weekly Gleaner*, March 12, 1990):1. Another factor is lower- and middle-class disillusionment with JLP free market policies. Commenting on the postelection disillusionment, Stone reported that "voters are coming to the conclusion . . . that our politicians do not run things as they claim but things run them" (Stone 1989:27). Offering a gloomy prognosis, Stone reflected with candor, "frankly, a political vacuum has emerged in our body politic" (Stone 1989:27).

Democratic party politics has become undermined by the JLP and PNP governments' inability to make significant changes in the lives of the majority of the population. The external resource base (of party politics) is shrinking as the state is finding it increasingly difficult to secure the vast resources necessary to support its patronage system. With the recent changes in Eastern Europe and the relaxation of tensions between the United States and the Soviet Union, the Caribbean has not been given priority for U.S. aid funds by the Bush administration. The new PNP government has accepted IMF structural adjustment policies, which demand first and foremost a decrease in public-sector spending. As a result of internal policies and external factors, the state's resource base is shrinking.

If the scarcity of international resources should continue, the state will lose its legitimacy in the eyes of the population. If it is no longer able to obtain the vast resources necessary for an extensive system of patronage, it will lose the support of its lower- and middle-class clients. The state may then be forced to shift to a system of coercion and control to maintain its dominance. Faced with legitimacy crises in the decade of the seventies and eighties, the state's coercive resources increased under both the PNP and JLP administrations, with the police and military given enormous power to maintain order and "national security" (Muñiz 1988). The 1989 and 1990 U.S. Department of State Human Rights Reports cited police brutality as Jamaica's most persistent human-rights violation. The state in the English-speaking Caribbean is increasingly using coercion against lower-class dissent in the face of economic crisis (see Young and Phillips 1986).

The existing leadership crisis within the JLP increased the vulnerability of the two-party system at a time when U.S. aid funds have begun to be withdrawn. If factionalism within the JLP leads to disintegration of the party, then the Jamaican political system could easily shift to an authoritarian system of one-party dominance. The state would be relieved of the obligation to seek clientelist patronage by using coercion to protect itself against lower-class mobilization. This is the basis of the system of regimentation in other Caribbean states such as Guyana, where coercion has been the sole basis of regime power since 1977; in Grenada under the Gairy regime in the 1970s and under the New Jewel Movement between 1981 and 1983; and in Trinidad and Tobago between 1970 and 1973 (Hintzen 1989). Coercive control, like the mechanism of clientelism, would continue to assure middle-class dominance of the state.

THE JAMAICAN EXPERIENCE:
ANY LESSONS FOR OTHER DEVELOPING NATIONS?

In trying to understand the nature of the political process in postcolonial Jamaica, this study has focused on two major questions: (1) What is the relationship between international capital transfers and the state? (2) What is the mechanism of control that facilitates middle-class domination via democratic politics within Jamaica? Although this study has been restricted to Jamaica, the detailed exploration of the case has relevance to more general theoretical propositions about the nature of political development in dependent economies. I have explored the inextricable relationship between international capital and the clientelist state. The success of a development strategy based on external capital is limited by its dependence upon the availability or nonavailability of capital. It is also dependent on the ideological position of the government in power. The difficulties encountered by the 1976–1980 Manley PNP administration in its attempt to initiate change through a democratic socialist path underline some more general considerations about the options that faced dependent countries in the context of the bipolar West-East conflict.

Economic change in developing countries involves a struggle against the colonial legacy of psychological dependence. The prevailing view of the leaders in many developing countries that the population has a limited capacity to transform the environment is an impediment to progress. Despite historical developments of the colonial era, and an existing world order in which developing countries are in a subordinate position, possibilities for transformation do exist. Developing nations are not condemned forever to remain neocolonial appendages. The leaders in those societies must transform and develop the productive forces based on an *internal* strategy. The economic system must be able to function with a high degree of internal autonomy so that its survival will not be linked to actions taken in Washington, Moscow, or Paris. As Clive Thomas (1974) demonstrated, there must not be a divergence between what the population produces and what it consumes. There must be a dynamic convergence of resources and production, demands and needs. The absence of such a dynamic convergence contributes to the perpetuation of dependent economic structures.

A well-intentioned political directorate (in Jamaica, or any other developing nation) with a concern for the poor must weigh its options carefully. Jamaica can continue to bargain in the international economic system for changes in the structural bias against developing nations.

Economic planners must focus on ways to change the structural arrangements of property relations that has skewed income distribution against the black poor throughout the colonial period until today. The cooling of tensions between the two superpowers has provided an opening for the political directorate to mobilize its population for structural changes without getting caught up in the ideological language of the superpower conflict.

If the "Westminster model" is to survive in Jamaica, fundamental changes must be made in the distribution of wealth and property. An honest discussion of colonialism and the historical process that led to the systemic inequity in income and property relations must be raised. The clientelistic party system must be openly challenged. Both major parties must come to a consensus on the role of the state in the economy if Jamaica can expect to survive its present economic crisis.

The scarcity of resources for patronage may inevitably lead to the collapse of the clientelist system. According to the thesis developed in the study, once the patronage system becomes ineffective, democratic institutions could also crumble. The consequence of this may be a move toward authoritarianism, a common feature in neighboring Latin America. If the majority are no longer committed to electoral politics, and the patronage system is ineffective, then the state may be forced to use authoritarianism to maintain political order. Thus, there is an urgent need to search for creative economic solutions to Jamaica's problems if the democratic multiparty system is to persist.

NOTES

1. See Shivji (1975); Sklar (1979); Clapham (1982); Callaghy (1984); and C. Young (1984).

Bibliography

Alavi, Hamza. 1972. "The State in Post-Colonial Societies: Pakistan and Bangladesh." *New Left Review*. No. 74 (July/August).

Alm, James. 1988. "Noncompliance and Payroll Taxation in Jamaica." *The Journal of Developing Areas*. Vol. 22 (July):477–496.

Althoff, P., and S. Patterson. 1966. "Political Activists in a Rural Country." *Midwest Journal of Political Science*. Vol. 10, No. 1 (February):39–51.

Ambursley, F. 1981. "Populism in Jamaica." *New Left Review*. No. 128 (July/August):76–87.

———. 1983. "Jamaica: From Michael Manley to Edward Seaga." In F. Ambursley and Robin Cohen, *Crisis in the Caribbean*, 72–104. London: Heinemann.

Ambursley, F., and Robin Cohen. 1983. *Crisis in the Caribbean*. London: Heinemann.

Amin, S. 1976. *Unequal Development*. New York: Monthly Review Press.

Barry, Tom, Beth Wood, and Deb Preusch. 1984. *The Other Side of Paradise: Foreign Control in the Caribbean*. New York: Grove Press.

Bates, Robert. 1983. *Essays on the Political Economy of Rural Africa*. Berkeley: University of California Press.

Beckford, George. 1972. *Persistent Poverty: Underdevelopment in the Plantation Economies of the Third World*. New York: Oxford University Press.

———. 1980. "Socioeconomic Change and Political Continuity in the Anglophone Caribbean." *Studies in Comparative International Development*. Vol. 15, No. 1:3–14.

Beckford, George, and Michael Witter. 1980. *Small Garden, Bitter Weed: Struggle and Change in Jamaica*. St. James, Jamaica: Maroon Publishing House.

Bell, Wendell. 1965. *Jamaican Leaders*. Berkeley: University of California Press.

———. 1967. *The Democratic Revolution in the West Indies*. Cambridge, Mass.: Schenkman.

———. 1979. "Attitudes Toward Social Equality in Independent Jamaica: Twelve Years After Nationhood." *Comparative Political Studies*. Vol. 11, No. 4 (January):499–531.

Berger, P. 1984. "Can the Caribbean Learn From East Asia?" *Caribbean Review* (Spring):9.

Best, Lloyd. 1967. "Independent Thought and Caribbean Freedom." *New World Quarterly*. Vol. 3, No. 4:1–5.

———. 1968. "A Model of a Pure Plantation Economy." *Social and Economic Studies*. Vol. 17, No. 3 (September):283–326.

Best, Lloyd, and Kari Levitt. 1974. *Studies in Caribbean Economy*, Vol. 1. Kingston: ISER.

Bienen, Henry. 1970. "Political Parties and Political Machines in Africa." In M. Lofchie, ed., *The State of the Nations: Constraints on Development in Independent Africa*, 195–213. Berkeley and Los Angeles: University of California Press.

Blömstrom, Magnus, and Bjorn Hettne. 1984. *Development Theory in Transition*. London: Zed Books.

Bradley, C. Paul. 1960. "Mass Parties in Jamaica: Structure and Organization." *Social and Economic Studies*. Vol. 9, No. 4 (December):375–416.

Brathwaite, L. 1953. "Social Stratification in the Caribbean," *Social and Economic Studies*. Vol. 2, No. 2, 3 (October):5–175.

Brewster, Havelock. 1973. "Economic Dependence: A Quantitative Interpretation," *Social and Economic Studies*, Vol. 22, No. 1.

Broom, Leonard. 1954. "The Social Differentiation of Jamaica." *American Sociological Review*. Vol. 19, No. 2 (April):115–129.

Brotherson, F. 1989. "The Foreign Policy of Guyana, 1970–1985." *Journal of Inter-American Studies and World Affairs*. Vol. 31, No. 3 (Fall):9–35.

———. 1990. "Manley Gets Nothing From Bush." *Caribbean Contact*. (May/June):2.

Brown, Adlith. 1982. "Issues of Adjustment and Liberalization in Jamaica: Some Comments." *Social and Economic Studies*. Vol. 31, No. 4 (December):192–200.

Brown, Aggrey. 1979. *Color, Class and Politics in Jamaica*. New Brunswick, N.J.: Transaction Books.

Budget Debate. 1986/87. Jamaica Parliament. Kingston: Jamaica Information Service.

Budget Speech. 1984/85. Jamaica Parliament. Kingston: Jamaica Information Service.

Burn, W. L. 1956. *Emancipation and Apprenticeship in the British West Indies*. London: Johnathan Cape.

Callaghy, T. 1984. *The State-Society Struggle: Zaire in Comparative Perspective*. New York: Columbia University Press.

Campbell, Horace. 1980. "Rastafari: Culture of Resistance." *Race and Class*. Vol. 22, No. 1:1–22.

Cardoso, F. 1972. "Dependency and Development in Latin America." *New Left Review*. No. 74:83–95.

———. 1973. "The Contradictions of Associated Development." Reprinted in Cardoso, F., *Current Themes on Latin American Development: A Critique*. New York: Monthly Review Press.

———. 1977. "The Consumption of Dependency Theory in the United States." *Latin American Research Review*. Vol. 12, No. 3:7–25.

Carnegie, James. 1973. *Some Aspects of Jamaica's Politics, 1918–38*. Kingston: Institute of Jamaica.

Carty, R. K. 1981. *Party and the Parish Pump: Electoral Politics in Ireland*. Atlantic Highlands, N.J.: Humanities Press.

Chilcote, Ronald H. 1974. "Dependency: A Critical Synthesis of the Literature." *Latin American Perspectives*. Vol. 1, No. 1 (Spring):4–29.

Clapham, Christopher, ed. 1982. *Private Patronage and Public Power: Political Clientelism in the Modern State*. New York: St. Martin's Press.

———. 1985. *Third World Politics*. England: Croom Helm Ltd.

Cook, Paul, and Colin Kirkpatrick. 1988. *Privatization in Less Developed Countries*. Sussex: Wheatsheaf Books.

Cowan, Gary L. 1983. *Divestment and Privatization: Case Studies of Five Countries.* Washington, D.C.: AID.

Cumper, G. 1960. *The Economy of the West Indies.* Kingston: ISER.

Curtin, Phillip. 1955. *Two Jamaicas: The Role of Ideas in a Tropical Colony: 1830–1865.* Cambridge, Mass.: Harvard University Press.

Cuthbert, Marlene, and Vernon Sparkes. 1978. "Coverage of Jamaica in the U.S. and Canadian Press." *Social and Economic Studies.* Vol. 27, No. 2 (June):204–220.

Dale, Edmund. 1977. "Spotlight on the Caribbean: A Microcosm of the Third World." *Regional Geographical Studies,* No. 2. New Haven, Conn.: Yale University Press.

Davies, Omar. 1984. "Economic Transformations in Jamaica." *Studies in Comparative International Development.* Vol. 19, No. 3: 40–59.

————, ed. 1986a. *The State in Caribbean Society.* Kingston: University of the West Indies.

————. 1986b. "An Analysis of the Management of the Jamaican Economy: 1972–1985." *Social and Economic Studies.* Vol. 35, No. 1 (March):73–110.

Davis, Merle. 1942. *The Church in the New Jamaica.* London: International Missionary Council.

Davis, N. 1988. "Debt Conversion: The Jamaican Experience." *Social and Economic Studies.* Vol. 37, No. 4:151–170.

Dawes, Hugh N. 1982. *Public Finance and Economic Development in Jamaica.* New York: University Press of America.

Demas, William. 1965. *The Economics of Development in Small Countries with Special Reference to the Caribbean.* Montreal: McGill University Press.

————. 1978. "The Caribbean and the New International Economic Order." *Journal of Inter-American Studies and World Affairs.* Vol. 20, No. 3 (August):229–264.

Denoon, David B. 1979. *The New International Economic Order: The U.S. Response.* New York: New York University Press.

Department of Statistics, *Statistical Digest and Annual Reports* (1951, 1962, 1971, 1976) Kingston: National Planning Agency.

de Smith, S. A. 1961. "Westminster's Export Models." *Journal of Commonwealth Political Studies.* Vol. 1, No. 2 (November):2–16.

Despres, Leo. 1964. *Cultural Pluralism and Nationalist Politics in British Guiana.* Chicago: Rand McNally.

Diamant, A. 1962. "The Bureaucratic Model: Max Weber Rejected, Rediscovered, Reformed." In Ferrel Heady and Sybil L. Stoices, eds., *Ann Arbor Papers in Comparative Public Administration.* Ann Arbor: Institute of Public Administration, University of Michigan.

Diamond, Larry, Juan J. Linz, and Seymour M. Lipset, eds. 1988. *Democracy in Developing Countries,* Vols. 1–4. Boulder, Colo.: Lynne Rienner Publishers.

Dos Santos, T. 1970. "The Structure of Dependence." *American Economic Review,* Vol. 60, No. 2 (May):231–236.

Duncan, W. Raymond. 1978. "Caribbean Leftism." *Problems of Communism.* (May–June):35.

Dunning, J. H. 1970. *Studies in International Investment.* London: Allen and Unwin.

Dutto, G. 1968. *Financial Performance of Government-owned Corporations in Less Developed Countries.* Washington, D.C.:IMF.

Easton, David. 1965. *A Systems Analysis of Political Life.* New York: John Wiley and Sons.

Eaton, George. 1975. *Alexander Bustamante and the New Jamaica*. Kingston: Kingston Publishing.

Economic and Social Survey. (various years). Kingston: National Planning Agency.

Edie, Carlene J. 1984. "Jamaican Political Processes: A System in Search of a Paradigm." *Journal of Development Studies*. Vol. 20, No. 4 (July):248–270.

———. 1986. "Domestic Politics and External Relations in Jamaica under Michael Manley, 1972–80." *Studies in Comparative International Development*. Vol. 21, No. 1 (Spring):71–94.

———. 1989. "From Manley to Seaga: The Persistence of Clientelism in Jamaica." *Social and Economic Studies*. Vol. 38, No. 1 (March):1–36.

Edmondson, L. 1983. "Jamaica." In Jack W. Hopkins, ed., *Latin America and Caribbean Contemporary Record, Vol. 1, 1981–82*. New York and London: Holmes and Meier, pp. 587–597.

Eisenstadt, S. N. 1963. "Bureaucracy and Political Development." In Joseph La Palombara, ed., *Bureaucracy and Political Development*, 96–118. Princeton, N.J.: Princeton University Press.

Eisenstadt, S. N., and Lemarchand, René, ed. 1981. *Political Clientelism, Patronage and Development*. Beverly Hills, Calif.: Sage Publications.

Eisner, Gisela. 1961. *Jamaica, 1830–1930: A Study in Economic Growth*. Manchester: Manchester University Press.

EPICA Task Force. 1979. *Jamaica: Caribbean Challenge*. Washington, D.C.: A People's Primer.

Erisman, H. Michael, and John D. Martz, eds. 1982. *Colossus Challenged: The Struggle for Caribbean Influence*. Westview Special Studies on Latin America and the Caribbean. Boulder, Colo.: Westview Press.

Evans, Peter. 1979. *Dependent Development*. Princeton, N.J. Princeton University Press.

Figueroa, Mark. 1988. "The Formation and Framework of Middle Strata National Leadership in Jamaica: The Crisis of the Seventies and Beyond." *Caribbean Studies*. Vol. 21. No. 1–2 (June):44–66.

Flynn, Peter. 1974. "Class, Clientelism and Coercion: Some Mechanisms of Internal Dependency and Control." *The Journal of Commonwealth and Comparative Politics*. Vol. 12, No. 2:133–156.

Foner, Nancy. 1973. *Status and Power in Rural Jamaica: A Study in Educational and Political Change*. New York and London: Teachers College Press.

Fortune, Mark. 1989. "Courting Capitalism, Manley Takes Over in Jamaica." *Black Enterprise* (May):38.

Frank, André Gunder. 1967. *Capitalism and Underdevelopment in Latin America*. New York Monthly Review Press.

Gafar, John S. 1988. "The Anatomy of Unemployment in a Third World Country–Jamaica". *Caribbean Studies*. Vol. 21, No. 3–4 (July–December):71–90.

Gerth, H. H., and C. Wright Mills. 1958. *From Max Weber*. New York: Oxford University Press.

Girvan, Norman. 1970. "Multinational Corporations and Dependent Underdevelopment in Mineral-Export Economies." *Social and Economic Studies*. Vol. 19, No. 4.

———. 1971a. *Foreign Capital and Economic Underdevelopment in Jamaica*. Kingston: ISER.

———. 1971b. "Why We Need to Nationalize Bauxite and How." In Norman Girvan and Owen Jefferson, eds., *Readings in the Political Economy of the Caribbean*. Kingston: ISER.

———. 1973. "The Development of Dependency Economics in the Caribbean and

Latin America: Review and Comparison." *Social and Economic Studies.* Vol. 22, No. 1 (March):1–33.

———. 1978. *Corporate Imperialism: Conflict and Expropriation.* New York: Monthly Review Press.

Girvan, Norman, and Richard Bernal. 1982. "The IMF and the Foreclosure of Development Options: The Case of Jamaica." *Monthly Review.* Vol. 33 (February):34–48.

Girvan, Norman, and O. Jefferson, eds. 1971. *Readings in the Political Economy of the Caribbean,* Vol. 2. Kingston: ISER.

Girvan, Norman, Richard Bernal, and Wesley Hughes. 1980. "The IMF and the Third World: The Case of Jamaica, 1974–80." *Development Dialogue.* No. 2:113–144.

Gonsalves, Ralph. 1977. "The Trade Union Movement in Jamaica: Its Growth and Resultant Problems." In Carl Stone and A. Brown, eds., *Essays on Power and Change in Jamaica.* Kingston: Jamaica Publishing, pp. 89–105.

Gosnell, Harold F. 1937. *Machine Politics, Chicago Model.* Chicago and London: The University of Chicago Press.

Greene, J. E. 1974. *Race and Politics in Guyana.* Kingston: ISER.

Haley, P. E., and L. W. Snider. 1979. *Lebanon in Crisis.* New York: Syracuse University Press.

Hall, A. 1975. "Concepts and Terms: Patron-Client Relations." *Journal of Peasant Studies.* No. 1:506–509.

Hall, Douglas. 1959. *Free Jamaica: An Economic History, 1938–65.* New Haven, Conn.: Yale University Press.

———. 1968. "The Colonial Legacy in Jamaica." *New World Quarterly.* No. 3:6–15.

Harris, Donald J. 1977. "Notes on the Question of a National Minimum Wage for Jamaica." In Carl Stone and A. Brown, eds., *Essays on Power and Change in Jamaica,* 106–115. Kingston: Kingston Publishing.

Hart, Richard. 1972. "Jamaica and Self-Determination." *Race.* Vol. 13, No. 3:271–296.

Hayter, T., and C. Watson. 1985. *AID: Rhetoric and Reality.* London: Pluto Press.

Henriques, F. 1953. *Family and Colour in Jamaica.* London: MacGibbon & Kee.

Henry, Paget, and Carl Stone, eds. 1983. *The Newer Caribbean: Decolonization, Democracy and Development.* Inter-American Politics Series, Vol. 4. Philadelphia: ISHI Publications.

Hicks, J. R., and U. K. Hicks. 1956. *Report on Finance and Taxation in Jamaica.* Kingston: Government Printing Office.

Hill, R. 1983. "Leonard P. Howell and Millenarian Visions in Early Rastafari." *Jamaica Journal* No. 16:24–39.

Hillman, Richard S. 1979. "Legitimacy and Change in Jamaica." *Journal of Developing Areas.* Vol. 13, No. 4.

Hintzen, Percy. 1989. *The Costs of Regime Survival: Racial Mobilization, Elite Domination, and Control of the State in Guyana and Trinidad.* Cambridge: Cambridge University Press.

———. 1990. "Democracy and Middle Class Domination in the West Indies." Paper presented at the 15th Annual Meeting of the Caribbean Studies Association, May 22–26, Port of Spain, Trinidad and Tobago, West Indies.

Huggins, H. D. 1965. *Aluminium in Changing Societies.* London and Kingston: Andre Deutsch.

Huntington, Samuel. 1968. *Political Order in Changing Societies.* New Haven, Conn.: Yale University Press.

Hyden, Goran. 1980. *Beyond Ujamaa in Tanzania: Underdevelopment and an Uncaptured Peasantry.* Berkeley: University of California Press.

Jackson, R. H., and C. G. Rosberg. 1982. "Why Africa's Weak States Persist: The Empirical and the Juridicial in Statehood." *World Politics.* Vol. 35, No. 1 (October):1–24.

Jefferson, Owen. 1971. "Some Aspects of the Post-war Economic Development of Jamaica." In Norman Girvan and O. Jefferson, eds., *Readings in the Political Economy of the Caribbean,* 109–120. Kingston: New World Group.

———. 1972. *The Post-War Economic Development of Jamaica.* Kingston: ISER.

Jessop, Bob. 1977. "Recent Theories of the Capitalist State." *Cambridge Journal of Economics,* Vol. 1, No. 1:353–373.

Johnson, Harry. 1971. *Trade Strategy for Rich and Poor Nations.* Toronto: University of Toronto Press.

Johnson, Howard. 1984. "The Anglo-American Caribbean Commission and the Extension of American Influence in the British Caribbean, 1942–1945." *Journal of Commonwealth and Comparative Politics.* Vol. 22, No. 2 (July):180–203.

Jones, Edwin. 1974. "Administrative Institution Building in Jamaica." *Social and Economic Studies.* Vol. 23, No. 2 (June):264–291.

———. 1975. "Tendencies and Change in Caribbean Administrative Systems." *Social and Economic Studies.* Vol. 24, No. 2 (June):239–256.

Jones, Edwin, and G. E. Mills. 1976. "Institutional Innovation and Change in the Commonwealth Caribbean." *Social and Economic Studies.* Vol. 25, No. 4 (December):323–346.

Kaplan, Irvin, Howard I. Blutstein, Kathryn T. Johnston, and David S. McMorris. 1976. *Area Handbook for Jamaica.* Washington, D.C.: American University Foreign Affairs Studies.

Kaufman, M. 1985. *Jamaica Under Manley.* London: Zed Books.

Kaufman, Robert R. 1974. "The Patron-Client Concept and Macro-Politics." *Comparative Studies in Society and History.* Vol. 16 (June):284–308.

Keith, Sherry, and Robert Girling. 1978. "Bauxite Dependency: Roots of Crisis," and "Jamaica vs. the Transnationals: Battle Over Bauxite." *NACLA.* Vol. 1, No. 3 (May–June):3–26.

Kirton, Claremont. 1977. "A Preliminary Analysis of Imperialist Penetration and Control via the Foreign Debt: A Study of Jamaica." In Carl Stone and A. Brown, eds., *Essays on Power and Change in Jamaica,* 72–88. Kingston: Jamaica Publishing.

Klein, H. 1969. *Parties and Political Change in Bolivia, 1880–1952.* Cambridge: Cambridge University Press.

Kuper, Adam. 1976. *Changing Jamaica.* London: Routledge and Kegan Paul.

Kuper, Leo. 1969. "Plural Societies: Perspectives and Problems." In Leo Kuper and M. G. Smith, eds., *Pluralism in Africa,* 7–26. Los Angeles: University of California Press.

———. 1971. "Political Change in Plural Societies: Problems in Racial Pluralism." *International Social Sciences Journal.* Vol. 33, No. 4:594–608.

Kuper, Leo, and M. G. Smith. eds. *Pluralism in Africa.* Los Angeles: University of California Press.

Lacey, Terry. 1977. *Politics and Violence in Jamaica.* Manchester: Manchester University Press.

Landé, C. J. 1973. "Networks and Groups in Southeast Asia." *American Political Science Review.* Vol. 67 (March):103–111.

Langton, Kenneth P. 1966. "Political Partisanship and Political Socialization in

Jamaica." *British Journal of Sociology*. Vol. 17, No. 4 (December):419–429.

Lee, Errol. 1978. "The Trade Union Movement." Kingston: Trade Union Institute, University of the West Indies.

Lee, J. M. 1967. *Colonial Government and Good Government*. Oxford: Clarendon Press.

Legg, K., and René Lemarchand. 1972. "Political Clientelism and Development." *Comparative Politics*. Vol. 4, No. 2:149–178.

Legum, Colin. 1962. *Pan-Africanism: A Short Political Guide*. New York: Praeger Publishers.

Lemarchand, René. 1972. "Political Clientelism and Ethnicity in Tropical Africa." *American Political Science Review*. Vol. 66, No. 1:68–90.

Lewin, Arthur. 1982. "The Fall of Michael Manley." *Monthly Review*. Vol. 33, No. 9 (February):49–60.

Lewis, Gordon K. 1968. *The Growth of the British West Indies*. New York: Monthly Review Press.

Lewis, R., and T. Munroe. eds., 1967. *Readings in the Political Economy of the Caribbean*, Vol. 1. Kingston: University of the West Indies.

Lewis, W. Arthur. 1955. *Theory of Economic Growth*. London: Allen and Unwin.

Leys, Colin. 1965. "What is the Problem about Corruption?" *Journal of Modern African Studies*. Vol. 3, No. 2:215–230.

———. 1974. *Underdevelopment in Kenya: The Political Economy of Neo-Colonialism*. Berkeley and Los Angeles: University of California Press.

———. 1976. "The Overdeveloped Post-Colonial State: A Re-Evaluation." *Review of African Political Economy*. No. 5 (January–April):41–55.

Lindsay, Louis. 1975. *The Myth of Independence: Middle Class Politics and Non-Mobilization in Jamaica*. Kingston: ISER.

Lipjhart, A. 1968. *The Politics of Accommodation*. Los Angeles: University of California Press.

———. 1977. *Democracy in Plural Societies*. New Haven and London: Yale University Press.

Lipset, Seymour M., and Stein Rokhan, eds. 1967. *Party Systems and Voter Alignments: Cross National Perspectives*. New York: The Free Press.

Lofchie, Michael. 1985. "Africa's Agrarian Malaise." In G. M. Carter and D. O'Meara, eds., *African Independence: The First Twenty-Five Years*. Bloomington: Indiana University Press.

Long, Frank. 1989. "Manufacturing Exports in the Caribbean and the New International Division of Labour." *Social and Economic Studies*. Vol. 38. No. 4 (March):115–131.

Looney, Robert E. 1987. *The Jamaican Economy in the 1980s: Economic Decline and Structural Adjustment*. Boulder, Colo.: Westview Press.

Lowenthal, David, ed. 1961. *The West Indies Federation: Perspectives on a New Nation*. New York: Columbia University Press Research Series, No. 23.

Maingot, Anthony P. 1979. "The Difficult Path to Socialism in the English-speaking Caribbean." In Richard P. Fagan. ed., *Capitalism and the State in U.S.–Latin American Relations*. Stanford, Calif.: Stanford University Press.

Mandle, J. 1972. "The Plantation Economy: An Essay in Definition." *Science and Society*. Vol. 36 (Spring):49–62.

Mandlebaum, S. 1965. *Boss Tweed's New York*. New York: Wiley.

Manley, Michael. 1973. "The Private Sector and the Profit Motive." Address to the Underwriters Society of Jamaica. Cited in *Jamaica Sunday Gleaner*. June 3, p. 3.

———. 1974a. *The Politics of Change*. London: Andre Deutsch.

————. 1974b. Address to the 27th Session of the UN General Assembly. Plenary Meeting 2049, May 10.

————. 1975. *A Voice at the Workplace*. London: Andre Deutsch.

————. 1980. "Third World Under Challenge: The Politics of Affirmation." *Third World Quarterly*. Vol. 2, No. 1 (January):28–43.

————. 1982. *Jamaica: Struggle in the Periphery*. London: Third World Media.

————. 1987. *Up the Down Escalator: Development and the International Economy—A Jamaican Case*. Washington, D.C.: Howard University Press.

Marshall, W. K. 1968. "Notes on Peasant Development in the West Indies Since 1838." *Social and Economic Studies*. Vol. 17. No. 3 (September):252–263.

Marvick, D., and C. Nixon. 1961. "Recruitment Contrasts in Rural Campaign Groups." In D. Marvick, ed., *Political Decision Makers*, 203–213. New York: The Free Press.

Melson, R., and H. Wolpe, eds. 1971. *Nigeria: Modernization and the Politics of Communalism*. East Lansing: Michigan State University Press.

Michels, Robert. 1959. *Political Parties*. New York: Dover Publications.

Migdal, Joel S. 1988. *Strong Societies and Weak States*. Princeton, N.J.: Princeton University Press.

Mills, G. E. 1970. "Public Administration in the Commonwealth Caribbean: Conflicts and Challenges." *Social and Economic Studies*. Vol. 19, No. 1 (March):1–35.

————. 1971. "Central-Local Government Relations in the Commonwealth Caribbean." *Proceedings of the UN-ECLA Regional Seminar on Local Government*. Georgetown, Guyana: Government Printer.

————. 1973. "The Environment of Commonwealth Caribbean Bureaucracies." *International Review of Administrative Science*. Vol. 39, No. 1:14–24.

————. 1974. "Public Policy and Private Enterprise in the Commonwealth Caribbean." *Social and Economic Studies*. Vol. 23, No. 2 (June):210–262.

Mills, G. E., and Paul Robertson. 1974. "The Attitudes and Behavior of the Senior Civil Service in Jamaica." *Social and Economic Studies*. Vol. 23, No. 4:341–366.

Morales, Cecilio. 1979. "Seaga's Sleight of Hand Trips Up Jack Anderson." *Covert Action*. No. 7 (December 1979–January 1980):8–9.

Moran, T. 1973. "Transnational Strategies and Defense by Multinational Corporations: Spreading the Risk and Raising the Cost for Nationalization in Natural Resources." *International Organization*. Vol. 27, No. 2 (Spring):273–287.

Mordecai, John. 1968. *The West Indies: The Federal Negotiations*. London: Allen & Unwin.

Moskos, Charles. 1965. *The Sociology of Political Independence*. Mass.: Schenkman.

Mosley, Paul. 1988. "Privatization, Policy-Based Lending and World Bank Behaviour." In Paul Cook and Colin Kirkpatrick, *Privatization in Less Developed Countries*. Sussex: Wheatsheaf Books.

Muñiz, Humberto Garcia. 1988. "Defense Policy and Planning in the Caribbean: An Assessment of the Case of Jamaica on Its 25th Independence Anniversary." *Caribbean Studies*. Vol. 21. No. 1–2 (June):67–123.

Munn, Keble A. 1973. *Green Paper in Agricultural Development Strategy* (November 21). Kingston: Gordon House.

————. 1974. *Second Green Papers in Agricultural Development Policy* (March 27). Kingston: Gordon House.

Munroe, Trevor. 1972. *The Politics of Constitutional Decolonization: Jamaica, 1944–62*. Kingston: ISER.

————. 1975. *The Marxist Left in Jamaica*. Kingston: ISER.

————. 1987. "Contemporary Marxist Movements: Assessing WPJ Prospects in Jamaica." *Social and Economic Studies*. Vol. 36, No. 3 (September):1–35.

Murray, David. 1965. *The West Indies and the Development of Colonial Government*. Oxford: Clarendon Press.

Murray, R. 1971. "The Internationalization of Capital and the Nation State." *New Left Review*. No. 67 (May–June):84–109.

Nettleford, Rex. 1968. *Manley and the New Jamaica: Selected Speeches and Writings, 1938–68*. London: Longmans Caribbean.

————. 1979. *Caribbean Cultural Identity: The Case of Jamaica*. Los Angeles: CAAS Publications.

Newfarmer, Richard. 1985. "Economic Policy Toward the Caribbean Basin: The Balance Sheet." *Journal of Inter-American Studies and World Affairs*. (February):63–90.

Nkrumah, K. 1961. *I Speak of Freedom*. London: Heinemann.

Noguera, Pedro A. 1990. "The Basis of Regime Support in Grenada from 1951–1988: A Study of Political Attitudes and Behavior in a Peripheral Society." Ph.D. dissertation, University of California at Berkeley, Berkeley, California.

Nunes, F. E. 1974. "The Declining Status of the Jamaican Civil Service." *Social and Economic Studies*. Vol. 23, No. 2 (June):344–357.

————. 1976a. "Weber and the Third World: Ideal Types and Environment." *Social and Economic Studies*. Vol. 25, No. 2 (June):134–152.

————. 1976b. "The Nonsense of Neutrality." *Social and Economic Studies*. Vol. 25, No. 4 (December):347–366.

Ordre-Browne, G. St. 1939. *Labor Conditions in the West Indies*. London: Her Majesty's Stationery Office, CMD 6070.

Pantojas, Emilio. 1988. "The CBI and Economic Restructuring in the Caribbean and Central America." *Caribbean Studies*. Vol. 20, No. 3–4:46–58.

Parry, J. H., Phillip Sherlock, and Anthony Maingot. 1987. *A Short History of the West Indies*, 4th ed. New York: St. Martin's Press.

Payer, Cheryl. 1974. *The Debt Trap: The International Monetary Fund and the Third World*. New York: Monthly Review Press.

Payne, Anthony. 1976. "From Michael with Love: The Nature of Socialism in Jamaica." *Journal of Commonwealth and Comparative Politics*. Vol. 14, No. 1:82–100.

————. 1981. "Seaga's Jamaica after One Year." *World Today*. Vol. 37, No. 11:434–440.

————. 1988a. *Politics in Jamaica*. London and New York: C. Hurst and St. Martin's Press.

————. 1988b. "Orthodox Liberal Development in Jamaica." *Third World Quarterly*. Vol. 10, No. 3 (July):1217–1238.

Perkins, Dexter. 1966. *The U.S. and the Caribbean*, Rev. Ed. Cambridge, Mass.: Harvard University Press.

Petras, James, and Robert Laporte. 1972. "Can We Do Business with Radical Nationalists? Chile: No." *Foreign Policy*. No. 7 (Summer):132–158.

Phelps, O. 1960. "The Rise of the Labor Movement in Jamaica." *Social and Economic Studies*. Vol. 9 (December):417–468.

Phillips, Peter. 1977a. "Jamaican Elites: 1938 to Present." In Carl Stone and A. Brown, eds., Essays on Power and Change in Jamaica, 1–14. Kingston: Jamaica Publishing.

————. 1977b. "The Business Sector and Jamaican Foreign Relations: A Study of National Capitalist Orientations to Third World Relations." *Social and Economic Studies*. Vol. 26, No. 2 (June):146–168.

Pizzorno, A. 1974. "I Ceti Medi Nei Meccanismi del Consenso." In F. L. Cavazza and S. Graubard, eds., *Il Caso Italiano*, Vol. 2, 315–338. Milan: Garzanti.

PNP. 1974. *PNP Manifesto: Democratic Socialism, the Jamaican Model.* Kingston: Peoples National Party.

———. 1979. *Principles and Objectives of the Peoples National Party.* Kingston: Peoples National Party.

Post, Ken. 1968. "The Politics of Protest in Jamaica in 1938: Some Problems of Analyses and Conceptualization." *Social and Economic Studies.* Vol. 18, No. 5:374–390.

———. 1979. *Arise Ye Starvelings: The 1938 Jamaican Labor Rebellion and its Aftermath.* Boston and Uppsala: Nijhoff Publications.

Powell, John D. 1970. "Peasant Society and Clientelist Politics." *American Political Science Review.* Vol. 64, No. 2:411–425.

Premdas, Ralph. 1972. *Party Politics and Racial Division in Guyana*, Vol. 4 (Study 4), 1972–1973. Denver: Center on International Race Relations, Studies in Race and Nation.

Presthus, R. 1961. "Weberian v. Welfare Bureaucracy in Traditional Society." *Administrative Science Quarterly.* Vol. 6, No. 1 (June):1–24.

Proctor, Jesse. 1956. "Britain's Pro-Federation Policy in the Caribbean: An Inquiry into Motivation." *Canadian Journal of Economics and Political Science*, Vol. 12, No. 3 (August).

Punnett, R. M. 1968. *British Government and Politics.* New York: Norton.

Quester, George. 1982. *American Foreign Policy: The Lost Consensus.* New York: Praeger.

Radovanovic, L. 1961. *From Bandung to Belgrade.* Yugoslavia: Yugoslavia Information Service.

Ragatz, Joseph. 1971. *The Fall of the Planter Class in the British Caribbean.* New York: Octagon Books.

Randall, V., and R. Theobald. 1985. *Political Change and Underdevelopment.* Durham, N.C.: Duke University Press.

Redwood, P. 1972. *Statistical Survey of Government Land Settlement in Jamaica, B.W.I., 1929–1949.* Kingston: ISER.

Reid, Stanley. 1977. "An Introductory Approach to the Concentration of Power in the Jamaican Corporate Economy and Notes on its Origin." In Carl Stone and A. Brown, eds., *Essays on Power and Change in Jamaica*, 15–44. Kingston: Jamaica Publishing.

Reno, Phillip. 1970. "Aluminium Profits and Caribbean People." In Robert I. Rhodes, ed., 1970, *Imperialism and Underdevelopment: A Reader*, 79–88. New York: Monthly Review Press.

Report of the Director of Elections: General Elections 1980. 1980. Kingston: Government Printer.

Report of the Committee on the Reform of Local Government in Jamaica. 1974. Kingston: Government Printer.

Robertson, Paul. 1972. "Party Organization in Jamaica." *Social and Economic Studies.* Vol. 21, No. 1 (March):30–43.

Robotham, Don. 1977. "Agrarian Relations in Jamaica." In Carl Stone and A. Brown, eds., *Essays on Power and Change in Jamaica*, 45–57. Kingston: Jamaica Publishing.

Robotham, Don, and Trevor Munroe. 1977. *Struggles of the Jamaican People.* Kingston: Worker's Liberation League.

Rodney, Walter. 1967. *The Groundings with My Brothers.* London: MacGibbon and Kee.

———. 1972. *How Europe Underdeveloped Africa.* London: Bogle L'Ouverture.

———. 1975. *The Groundings with My Brothers*. London: Bogle L'Ouverture.

Rousslang, David, and John Lindsey. 1984. "The Benefits to Caribbean Basin Countries from the U.S. CBI Tariff Eliminations." *Journal of Policy Modelling*. (November):513–530.

Rubin, Vera. 1960. "Social and Cultural Pluralism in the Caribbean." In *Annals of the New York Academy of Sciences*, 780–785.

Ryan, Selwyn. 1972. *Race and Nationalism in Trinidad and Tobago*. Port of Spain: PNM Publishing Company.

Saul, J. 1979. *The State and Revolution in Eastern Africa*. London: Heinemann.

Scott, James C. 1966. "Machine Politics in Southeast Asia." *American Political Science Review*. Vol. 66, No. 1:1–25.

———. 1969. "Corruption, Machine Politics and Political Change." *American Political Science Review*. Vol. 63, No. 4:1142–1158.

———. 1972a. "Patron-Client Politics and Political Change in Southeast Asia." *American Political Science Review*. Vol. 66, No. 1:91–113.

———. 1972b. *Comparative Political Corruption*. Englewood Cliffs, New Jersey: Prentice Hall, Inc.

Seaga, Edward. 1982. "Government Policy and the Jamaican Economic Turnaround." *Atlantic Economic Journal*. (September):1–7.

Senior, Olive. 1972. *The Message is Change*. Kingston: Kingston Publishing.

Sewell, William. 1861. *The Ordeal of Free Labor in the British West Indies*. London: Sampson Low & Sons Company.

Sherlock, Phillip. 1980. *Norman Manley*. London: MacMillan.

Shifflett, Crandall A. 1982. Patronage and Poverty in the Tobacco South: Louisa County, Virgina, 1860–1900. Knoxville: University of Tennessee Press.

Shivji, Issa. 1976. Class Struggles in Tanzania. New York and London: Monthly Review Press.

Simey, T. S. 1946. Welfare and Planning in the West Indies. Oxford: Clarendon Press.

Simpson, George. 1955. "A Study of Race and Conflict." *Social Forces*. Vol. 32, No. 2:107–110.

Singham, A. W. 1967. "The Political Socialization of Marginal Groups." *International Journal of Comparative Sociology*. Vol. 8, No. 2:182–198.

———. 1968. *The Hero and the Crowd in a Colonial Polity*. New Haven, Conn.: Yale University Press.

———. 1973. "Cultural Domination and Political Subordination: Notes Towards a Theory of the Caribbean Political System." *Comparative Studies in Society and History*. Vol. 15, No. 3 (June):258–288.

Sklar, R. L. 1976. "Postimperialism: A Class Analysis of Multinational Corporate Expansion." *Comparative Politics*. Vol. 9 (1976):75–92.

———. 1979. "The Nature of Class Domination in Africa." *Journal of Modern African Studies*. Vol. 17, No. 4 (December):531–552.

Skocpol, Theda. 1979. *States and Social Revolution*. Cambridge: Cambridge University Press.

Smith, M. G. 1961. "The Plural Framework of Jamaican Society." *British Journal of Sociology*. Vol. 13, No. 3:249–262.

———. 1965. *The Plural Society in the British West Indies*. Los Angeles: University of California Press.

Smith, M. G., R. Augier, and R. Nettleford. 1960. *The Rastafarian Movement in Kingston*. Kingston: ISER.

Smith, T. 1979. "The Underdevelopment of Development Literature: The Case of Dependency Theory." *World Politics*. Vol. 32, No. 2:247–288.

Stavenhagen, R. 1974. "The Future of Latin America: Between Underdevelopment and Revolution." *Latin American Perspectives*. Vol. 1, No. 1 (Spring):124–128.

Stephens, Evelyn, and John Stephens. 1983. "Democratic Socialism and the Capitalist Class in Dependent Capitalism: An Analysis of the Relation between Jamaican Business and the PNP Government." Paper delivered at the Ninth Meeting of the Caribbean Studies Association, May 25–28. Santo Domingo, Dominican Republic.

―――. 1985. "Bauxite and Democratic Socialism in Jamaica." In Peter Evans et al., eds., *States Versus Markets in the World System*. Beverly Hills: Sage Publications.

―――. 1987. *Democratic Socialism in Jamaica*. Princeton, N.J.: Princeton University Press.

Stone, Carl. 1973. *Class, Race and Political Behaviour in Jamaica*. Kingston: ISER.

―――. 1974a. *Electoral Behavior and Public Opinion in Jamaica*. Kingston: ISER.

―――. 1974b. "Political Aspects of Post-War Agricultural Policies in Jamaica (1945–70)." *Social and Economic Studies*. Vol. 23, No. 2 (June):145–173.

―――. 1976. "Class and the Institutionalization of Two-Party Politics in Jamaica." *Journal of Commonwealth and Comparative Politics*. Vol. 14, No. 2:177–196.

―――. 1977a. "Tenant Farming Under State Capitalism." In Carl Stone and A. Brown, eds., *Essays on Power and Change in Jamaica*, 117–125. Kingston: Jamaica Publishing.

―――. 1977b. "Worker Participation in Industry—A Survey of Workers Opinions." In Carl Stone and A. Brown, eds., *Essays on Power and Change in Jamaica*, 182–202. Kingston: Jamaica Publishing.

―――. 1978. "Decolonization and the Caribbean State System—The Case of Jamaica." In Carl Stone and A. Brown, eds., *Essays on Power and Change in Jamaica*, 3–41. Kingston: Jamaica Publishing.

―――. 1980. *Democracy and Clientelism in Jamaica*. New Brunswick, N.J.: Transaction Books.

―――. 1981a. "Jamaica's 1980 Elections." *Caribbean Review*. Vol. 10, No. 2 (Spring):5–7.

―――. 1981b. "Democracy and Socialism in Jamaica." *Journal of Commonwealth and Comparative Politics*. Vol. 19, No. 2 (July):115–133.

―――. 1982a. *The Political Opinions of the Jamaican People, 1976–81*. Kingston: Blackett Publishers.

―――. 1982b. "Seaga is in Trouble: Polling the Jamaican Polity in Midterm." *Caribbean Review*. Vol. 11, No. 4 (Fall):4–7, 28–29.

―――. 1983. "The Jamaican Reactions: Grenada and the Political Stalemate." *Caribbean Review*. Vol. 12, No. 4 (Fall):31–32, 60–63.

―――. 1984. "Jamaica: From Manley to Seaga." In Donald E. Schulz and Douglas A. Graham, eds., *Revolution and Counter-Revolution in Central America and the Caribbean*, 385–419. Boulder, Colo.: Westview Press.

―――. 1985. "Jamaica in Crisis: From Socialist to Capitalist Management." *International Journal* (Spring):288–289.

―――. 1986. *Power in the Caribbean Basin: A Comparative Study of Political Economy*. Philadelphia: ISHI Publications.

―――. 1987. *Class, State and Democracy in Jamaica*. New York: Praeger.

―――. 1989a. "Budget Politics." *Jamaica Weekly Gleaner*. June 26, p. 27.

―――. 1989b. *Politics Versus Economics: The 1989 Elections in Jamaica*. Kingston: Heinemann Publishers (Caribbean) Ltd.

Stone, Carl, and A. Brown, eds. 1977. *Essays on Power and Change in Jamaica.* Kingston: Jamaica Publishing.

————. eds. 1981. *Perspectives on Jamaica in the Seventies.* Kingston: Jamaica Publishing House.

Sudana, Trevor. 1983. "Class, Race and the State in Trinidad and Tobago." *Latin American Perspectives.* Vol. 10 No. 4 (Fall):75–96.

Sunkel, Osvaldo. 1983. "Transnational Capitalism and National Disintegration in Latin America." *Social and Economic Studies.* Vol. 22:132–176.

Thomas, Caroline. 1987. "Jamaica and the Search for Security in the 1970s." In *In Search of Security: The Third World in International Relations.* Boulder, Colo.: Lynne Rienner Publishers.

Thomas, Clive Y. 1974. *Dependence and Transformation: The Economics of the Transition to Socialism.* New York: Monthly Review Press.

————. 1988. *The Poor and the Powerless: Economic Policy and Change in the Caribbean.* New York: Monthly Review Press.

Von Freyhold, Michaela. 1977. "The Post-Colonial State and its Tanzanian Version." *Review of African Political Economy.* Vol. 8 (January–April):75–89.

Weber, M. 1964. *From Max Weber: Essays in Sociology,* Translated and edited by H. H. Gerth and C. Wright Mills. New York: Oxford University Press.

Weiner, Myron. 1962. *The Politics of Scarcity.* Chicago: University of Chicago Press.

Weingrod, A. 1968. "Patrons, Patronage and Political Parties." *Comparative Studies in Society and History.* Vol. 10 (July):377–400.

West India Royal Commission Report. 1945. Her Majesty's Stationary Office. CMD 6607. London.

Williams, Eric. 1944. *Capitalism and Slavery.* Chapel Hill: University of North Carolina Press.

Wilmot, S. 1984. "Jewish Politicians and Black Voters in Free Jamaica." *Social History Project Newsletter.* No. 9 (June). Published by the University of the West Indies, Mona, Kingston.

Yacob, Haile-Mariam, and Berhanu Mengistu. 1988. "Public Enterprises and the Privatisation Thesis in the Third World." *Third World Quarterly.* Vol. 10. No. 4 (October): 1565–1587.

Young, Alma and Dion Phillips, eds. 1986. *Militarization in the Non-Hispanic Caribbean.* Boulder, Colo.: Lynne Rienner Publishers.

Young, C. 1984. "Zaire: Is There a State?" *Canadian Journal of African Studies.* Vol. 18.

Young, Ruth C. 1976. "The Structural Context of Caribbean Agriculture: A Comparative Study." *Journal of Developing Areas.* Vol. 10 (July):425–444.

DOCUMENTS

Annual Reports. Department of Statistics (various years).

Budget Speeches 1972, 1977, 1983, 1985, 1989. Jamaica Parliament.

Economic and Social Survey. National Planning Agency. (various years).

General Elections, 1972, 1976, 1980, 1981, 1983. Director of Elections.

Jamaica—ALCOA Agreement. 1976.

Jamaica Bauxite Institute.

Jamaica Hansard.

Kingston Export Free Zone. 1985.

U.S. Overseas Loans and Grants. Aid. 1983.

NEWSPAPERS AND MAGAZINES

Caribbean Contact
Caribbean Insight
Financial Times of London
Los Angeles Times
Miami Herald
Newsweek
New York Times
Jamaica Daily Gleaner
Jamaica Weekly Gleaner (North American Edition)
Jamaica Daily News
Time
Wall Street Journal
Weekend Star
West Indies and Caribbean Yearbook

Index